The Business Guide to Sustainability

Jim —

What a delight to work w/ you & your students! I'm so excited to see what comes of this collaboration.

Best wishes!

—Doug

ABOUT THE AUTHORS

Darcy Hitchcock and Marsha Willard founded AXIS Performance Advisors in 1990. In the early years, they developed a reputation for helping organizations implement cutting-edge management techniques, including high-performance work teams. They were proud of their win–win approach. Employees were happier because they had more control; management was happier because they got better performance; customers were happier because they got better quality and service. They published a number of popular management books including *Why Teams Can Fail and What to Do About It.*

In 1996, however, they noticed the term 'sustainability' showing up in management literature. In the process of investigating what this entailed, they realized that in some cases, by showing their clients how to be more productive, they'd also showed them how to deplete the world's resources better, faster and cheaper. This was not the legacy they had in mind! This epiphany set them on a journey to discover how they could correct this oversight.

Initially, they wondered if there was anything they could do. They weren't trained as biologists or chemical engineers. However, they discovered that many of the problems organizations had were not so much technical as relating to organizational development. So, after learning all they could about the topic, they developed a thriving practice around helping organizations implement sustainable business practices.

Since then they have developed a reputation for being able to make the abstract concept of sustainability easy for lay people to understand and act upon. They broke the process of implementing sustainability into bite-sized pieces and analysed each step in a set of how-to booklets, the Sustainability Series™.

Marsha and Darcy are active members in the Oregon Natural Step Network, coaching members and teaching classes. They designed and taught the Implementing Sustainability Certificate Program through Portland State University. They also teach at the University of Oregon and Oregon State University.

For several years, Darcy acted as an advisor to the Oregon Sustainability Board; Marsha was senior examiner for the Oregon Performance Excellence Award. They are both affiliated with the Zero Waste Alliance and run the SustainABLE Frontiers study tour programme for Sustainable Northwest. They also manage several free e-lists related to sustainability (articles and book reviews). To learn more, visit their website at www.axisperformance.com.

The Business Guide to Sustainability

Practical Strategies and Tools for Organizations

Darcy Hitchcock and Marsha Willard

London • Sterling, VA

First published by Earthscan in the UK and USA in 2006
Reprinted 2007

ISBN-13: 978-1-84407-320-7
ISBN-10: 1-84407-320-3

Typeset by Domex e-Data Pvt. Ltd, India
Printed and bound in the UK by Bath Press
Cover design by Yvonne Booth

For a full list of publications please contact:

Earthscan
8–12 Camden High Street
London, NW1 0JH, UK
Tel: +44 (0)20 7387 8558
Fax: +44 (0)20 7387 8998
Email: earthinfo@earthscan.co.uk
Web: **www.earthscan.co.uk**

22883 Quicksilver Drive, Sterling, VA 20166-2012, USA

Earthscan is an imprint of James and James (Science Publishers) Ltd and publishes in association
with the International Institute for Environment and Development

A catalogue record for this book is available from the British Library

Library of Congress Cataloging-in-Publication Data

Hitchcock, Darcy E.
The business guide to sustainability / by Darcy Hitchcock and Marsha Willard.
P. cm.
ISBN-13:   978-1-84407-320-7 (pbk.)
ISBN-10:   1-84407-320-3 (pbk.)
1. Management – Environmental aspects. 2. Sustainable development.
3. Environmentalism. I. Willard, Marsha L. II. Title. HD30.255.H58 2006 658.4'083–dc22,
2006001863.

The paper used for the text pages of this book is FSC certified.
FSC (the Forest Stewardship Council) is an international
network to promote responsible management of the world's
forests.

Mixed Sources
Product group from well-managed
forests and other controlled sources
www.fsc.org Cert no. SGS-COC-2121
© 1996 Forest Stewardship Council

Contents

List of Figures and Tables xi
Acknowledgements xiii
Abbreviations xv
Introduction xix
    How this book is structured xx
    How to get the most out of this book xx
    How to use the self-assessments xxi
    Disclaimer to the sustainability experts xxiv

PART 1 – FOUNDATION CONCEPTS

1   **Sustainability as a Strategic Issue** **3**
    Benefits of pursuing sustainability 3
    Threats if you don't pursue sustainability 5
    Risks in pursuing sustainability 7
    What is sustainability? 8
    Why is sustainability a strategic issue? 11
    Factors that define sustainability 16
    How do you know whether your organization is sustainable? ... 18
    Conclusion 20

2   **Change Agent/Sustainability Coordinator: How to Keep a Sustainability Effort on Track** **23**
    What you should know about sustainability 23
    Strategies you can use 26
        Change agents with no formal authority 26
            Begin within your span of control 26
            Sow seeds 26
            Discussion groups 27
            Green teams 27
        Sustainability coordinators with formal authority ... 28
            Steering committees 28
            Task forces and project teams 28

Individuals   29
Award programmes and certification systems   29
Sustainability management systems   29
Conclusion   30
SCORE the sustainability coordinator   31

PART 2 – SUSTAINABILITY BY INDUSTRY SECTOR

3   Sustainability in Services and General Office Practices   37
What you should know about sustainability   37
Strategies you can use   40
Clean up your own operations   40
Facilities   40
Technology   41
Paper products   42
Break room   43
Take responsibility for your ripples   44
Evaluate strategic threats   46
Explore emerging opportunities   46
Conclusion   48
SCORE services and office practices   48

4   Sustainability in Manufacturing and Product Design   53
What you should know about sustainability   53
Strategies you can use   56
Product design   57
Design for environment   57
Life cycle assessment and life cycle costing   59
Grey lists, black lists and supply chain management   61
Green chemistry   62
Converting products to services   63
Biomimicry   64
Operations   65
Energy and greenhouse gases   65
Collaborate with the supply chain   67
Product certification   68
Zero waste   70
Extended producer responsibility, product stewardship
and product take-back   71
Conclusion   74
SCORE Manufacturing   74

5 Sustainability in Government Agencies 79
What you should know about sustainability 79
Strategies you can use 83
Spend tax revenue wisely, maximizing the benefit to society 83
Conserving energy 83
Take advantage of wasted resources 84
Streamline red tape 85
Employ green building practices 85
Find new funding sources 86
See the municipality as a whole system 86
Provide infrastructure and security 87
Ensure security 87
Design efficient, vibrant urban spaces 88
Design effective public transportation 89
Protect the commons 90
Engineer market-based incentives 92
Reclaim public goods and charge the full cost 94
Create preserves 94
Adopt the precautionary principle 95
Implement regulations 96
Create a level playing field 96
Privatize the resource within the right boundaries 96
Get the numbers right 97
Eliminate perverse subsidies 98
Protect and help people who need it 100
Perform triage 101
Combat hunger 101
Provide housing 102
Guide us toward a better future 102
Model and encourage new behaviour 103
Use purchasing as a way to drive markets 103
Develop social capital 104
Provide incentives and grants for needed research 105
Create audacious goals and policies 106
Sponsor award programmes 107
Make information visible 107
Integrate sustainability into education 108
Equalize opportunities 109
Use public pension funds as a signal to business 111
Conclusion 111
SCORE Government 111

PART 3 – SUSTAINABILITY BY ORGANIZATIONAL FUNCTION

6   **Senior Management: How to Lead the Sustainability Effort**   119
    What you should know about sustainability   119
    Strategies you can use   122
        Assess threats, opportunities and constraints   123
            Strategic planning   124
            Scenario planning   124
            Stakeholder management   125
            Backcasting   125
        Choose terms and frameworks   126
            Alternative terms   127
            Frameworks   128
        Devise an implementation strategy and enlist support   129
            Pick the best entry point   130
            Set up the best structure   131
            Demonstrate support   132
        Align business systems   133
        Provide for transparency and stakeholder involvement   134
            Sustainability reports   135
            Partner NGOs   135
            Stakeholder engagement activities   137
            Stakeholder audits   137
        Conclusion   137
        SCORE Senior management   138

7   **Facilities: How to Save Energy and Water, Improve Productivity
    and Reduce Waste**   141
    What you should know about sustainability   141
    Strategies you can use   142
        Construct/remodel a high-performance building   142
            Daylighting   143
            Site selection   144
            Material selection   145
            Mechanical systems   145
            Construction waste   146
        Operate the building efficiently   147
            Commissioning   147
            Energy management   147
        Manage waste   148
        Provide green cleaning and landscaping services   149
        Manage transportation issues   150

Conclusion 151
SCORE Facilities 151

**8 Human Resources: How to Support the Change Process and
Bolster Employee Commitment** 155
What you should know about sustainability 156
Strategies you can use 157
Introduce the concept to top executives 157
Consult on the implementation 159
Align human resource systems 160
Model appropriate behaviours 164
Measure the benefits 164
SCORE Human resources 165

9 Purchasing: How to Determine What to Buy and How to Work with Suppliers 169
What you should know about sustainability 169
Strategies you can use 171
Purchasing practices 171
Adopt sustainable or environmentally preferable purchasing (EPP) policies 171
Embed EPP or sustainable choices into online systems 172
Embed sustainability language into RFPs and contracts 172
Use service contracts to align the interests of your vendors with your own 173
Implement a supply chain environmental management system 174
Buy green power 176
Create incentives and checklists for making more sustainable choices 176
Work with disadvantaged businesses and people as an economic
development strategy 177
Life cycle assessment and life cycle costing 178
Purchasing projects 179
Conduct a waste or purchasing audit 179
Create a reliable market for a targeted product 181
Research sustainable alternatives for a specific function or product 182
Partner an NGO 185
Conclusion 185
SCORE Purchasing 186

**10 Environmental Affairs: How to Support the Move Beyond
Compliance and Eco-efficiencies to Sustainability** 189
What you should know about sustainability 189
Strategies you can use 191
Environmental management systems 191
Chemical management systems 192

Chemical substitution   193
Green chemistry   194
Conclusion   195
SCORE Environmental affairs   195

11 Marketing/Public Relations: Whether and How to Promote Your Sustainability
   Efforts   199
What you should know about sustainability   201
Strategies you can use   206
   Community-based social marketing   206
   Cause-related marketing   207
   Labelling, certification and standards   208
   Stakeholder involvement   208
   Sustainability reporting   209
   Market transformation   209
Conclusion   210
SCORE Marketing and public relations   211

12 Accounting and Finance: How to Account for Environmental and Social Impacts 213
What you should know about sustainability   213
Strategies you can use   218
   Develop a metrics framework and report on results   218
      The Natural Step   219
      Triple bottom line/Three Es   219
      Sustainability or environmental management system   220
      Organization's vision or values   221
   Determine what is 'better'   223
      Activity-based costing (ABC)   223
      Life cycle costing (LCC)   224
      Life cycle assessment (LCA)   224
   Decision tools to balance trade-offs   226
      Brainstorm how to add more value   226
      Weighted criteria charts   227
      Compare a sustainability rating with cost   227
Conclusion   229
SCORE Finance and accounting   229

Appendix A – Sustainability frameworks and tools   231
Appendix B – Certification schemes   237
Notes   239
Index   245

Figures and Tables

FIGURES

1.1	Steps to sustainability	12
1.2	How do you know whether your organization is sustainable?	19
5.1	Value, ownership and product life cycle	100
6.1	Collins team structure	132
11.1	Concern versus influence	209
12.1	SD Solutions results	228
A.1	Hierarchy of sustainability frameworks	231

TABLES

I.1	Which chapters should you read?	xxii
1.1	Examples of organizations pursuing sustainability	10
5.1	Liveability for Portland, Oregon versus Atlanta, Georgia	90
5.2	Perverse subsidies	99
9.1	Options for working with suppliers	174
9.2	Environmental score sheet	177
9.3	Sustainable products checklist	183
12.1	Metrics based on The Natural Step system conditions	220
12.2	Metrics based on the triple bottom line	221
12.3	Metrics based on mission and values	221
12.4	Comparison of ABC, LCC and LCA	223
12.5	Weighted criteria chart	227

Acknowledgements

This book would not have been possible without the courageous and innovative early adopters who have shown us all how sustainability can be applied in real life. We would also like to acknowledge all those who helped us write this book by reading sample chapters, verifying case examples and refining the SCORE self-assessment.

Allison Hensey, Oregon Watershed Enhancement Board
Amanda Tucker, BSI Global
Anne Landfield, First Environment
Betsy Power, Highwater Research
Carsten Henningsen, Progressive Investment Management
Cheryl Welch, Tualatin Valley Water District
CJ Hardy, Oregon Dept of Corrections
Damon Fordham, Oregon Department of Transportation
Dan Atkins, SB Practices
Dan Zalkow, Portland State University
Dave Tooze, Portland Office of Sustainable Development
Don Harker, Communities by Choice
Dorothy Atwood, Zero Waste Alliance
Duke Castle, The Castle Group
Elaine Jane Cole, Pacific University
Josh Skov, Good Company
Julie O'Shea, Farmers Irrigation District
Kate Nash, Kate Nash Workplace Consulting
Kim Hughes, Zero Waste Alliance
Larry Chalfan, Zero Waste Alliance
Lori Stole, Zero Waste Alliance
Mark Hamilton, Ecos Consulting
Mary Cook Swanson, Clackamas County, Oregon
Mary Steckel, City of Corvallis, Oregon
Michele Crim, Portland Office of Sustainable Development
Mike Hill, WestWyck

Nik Blosser, Celilo Group
Pamela Brody-Heine, Zero Waste Alliance
Paul Steuke, Fort Lewis Army Base
Rick Schulberg, International Sustainable Development Foundation
Rick Woodward, Coastwide Laboratories
Scott Harris, JR Simplot
Scott Young, Oregon Dept of Corrections
Sheryl Bunn, Community Environmental Services
Steve Kokes, Coates Kokes
Susan Anderson, Portland Office of Sustainable Development
Tim O'Riordan, University Of East Anglia
Wayne Rifer, Zero Waste Alliance

We would also like to dedicate this book to Amy Joslin, sustainability coordinator for Multnomah County, who was taken far too young. We will miss her.

Abbreviations

ABC	activity-based costing
AC	air conditioning
BEES	Building for Environmental and Economic Sustainability
BREEAM	BRE Environmental Assessment Method
CalPERS	California Public Employees' Pension System
CAFE	Corporate Average Fuel Efficiency; a measure of fuel efficiency of automobiles
CARS	Chemical Assessment and Ranking System
CERES	Coalition for Environmentally Responsible Economies (www.ceres.org)
CEO	chief executive officer
CFCs	chlorofluorocarbons; a class of chemicals that deplete the ozone layer
CO_2	carbon dioxide
CPR	cardio-pulmonary resuscitation
CSR	corporate social responsibility
DfE	design for environment
EH&S	environment, health and safety
EMS	environmental management system
EPA	Environmental Protection Agency (US)
EPP	environmentally preferable purchasing
EPR	extended producer responsibility (or extended product responsibility)
FEE	Fédération des Experts Comptables Européens (European Federation of Accountants)
FROG	First Raise Our Growth; a scenario
FSC	Forest Stewardship Council
GDP	gross domestic product; a measure of economic activity
GMO	genetically modified organism
GNP	gross national product; a measure of economic activity (was replaced by GDP in 1991)
GRI	Global Reporting Initiative

HCFC	hydrochlorofluorocarbon; less damaging to the ozone layer than CFCs
HVAC	heating, ventilating, air conditioning system
ICLEI	International Council for Local Environmental Initiatives; a trade association for local governments. ICLEI no longer uses the longer name and instead refers to itself as ICLEI, Local Governments for Sustainability (www.iclei.org).
ISO	International Organization for Standardization
JAG	Job Alike Group
LCA	life cycle assessment
LCC	life cycle costing
LEED	leadership in energy and environmental design; a rating system for buildings
LEED EB	LEED for existing buildings
LLC	Limited Liability Corporation
LOHAS	lifestyles of health and sustainability; a segment of the population
MIT	Massachusetts Institute of Technology
MSDS	material safety data sheet; a document explaining safe use and accident response for products containing chemicals with potential human health impacts
NAFTA	North American Free Trade Agreement
NGO	non-governmental organization
O&M	operations and maintenance budget
OHSAS 18000	Occupational Health and Safety international standards (see www.ohsas-18001-occupational-health-and-safety.com/)
OMSI	Oregon Museum of Science and Industry
OPEC	Organization of the Petroleum Exporting Countries
PBTs	persistent bioaccumulative toxins
POPs	persistent organic pollutants (often used interchangeably with PBTs)
PVC	polyvinyl chloride; a form of plastic
REACH Directive	Registration, Evaluation and Authorisation of Chemicals Directive
RESOP	related enterprise share ownership plan
RFP	request for proposal
RoHS Directive	Restriction of the Use of Certain Hazardous Substances in Electrical and Electronic Equipment Regulations 2005
ROI	return on investment
SA 8000	Social Accountability 8000; a scoring system for social responsibility
SCEM system	supply chain environmental management system

SCORE	Sustainability Competency & Opportunity Rating & Evaluation assessment (available from AXIS Performance Advisors and the Zero Waste Alliance)
SF_6	sulphur hexafluoride; a greenhouse gas
SMS	sustainability management system; an environmental management system with sustainability embedded
SWOT	strengths, weaknesses, opportunities and threats; a common strategic planning tool
UGCA	Unified Green Cleaning Alliance
UK	United Kingdom
UN	United Nations
US or USA	United States of America
VOC	volatile organic compounds; chemicals that tend to evaporate or off-gas
WEEE Directive	Waste Electrical and Electronic Equipment Directive

Introduction

Sustainability can be a confounding topic and not everyone has the passion to wade into all the literature to learn about it. Yet virtually everyone is willing to take steps towards sustainability if someone would just explain, in clear and understandable language, what can be done. The explosive growth in the US green building industry, for example, was fuelled largely by the LEED (Leadership in Energy and Environmental Design) system of checklists that made it easy for architects, developers and facilities managers to make more sustainable choices. This book does for every organization what LEED did for the building industry: it translates the abstract concepts of sustainability into tangible actions.

This book explains what organizations (businesses, governmental agencies and non-profit organizations) can do to move towards sustainability. It can be used by people new to sustainability to learn about the field. It can also be helpful for those who have been pursuing sustainability for some time but who have reached a plateau, wondering what else they can do.

This book is different from the many other excellent sustainability books that have been written, for the following reasons:

- First, we don't just talk about the problems; we give tangible examples of what organizations can and have done.
- Second, we don't advocate any one framework; instead we help you determine which frameworks might be most useful to you and list resources so that you can learn more.
- Third, we embed self-assessments in each chapter so that you can track your progress.
- Last, and perhaps most important, we have organized the book in the way organizations are structured; this allows each reader to focus on the content that will be most relevant and provides a way of assigning organizational accountability to elements of sustainability.

Our emphasis throughout is to make sustainability understandable to the layperson. For the sustainability movement to continue, we can't rely on the 'early adopters' and the zealous minority; we must find a way to make sustainable practices easy for everyone to do. Fortunately, once people understand sustainability, they are often surprised to find how many untapped sustainable practices make good bottom-line business sense now. If all organizations take a small first step forward, we can make a huge difference. And once people begin down the path of sustainability, they usually keep going. The health of our economy, our communities and our environment all hinge on our ability to make sustainable practices mainstream. This book can help make that happen.

HOW THIS BOOK IS STRUCTURED

Following an overview chapter on sustainability, Chapters 2 to 12 are organized by major sectors (services, manufacturing and government) and common organizational functions or departments (top management, human resources, purchasing, etc.). Each of these chapters contains three sections:

1   What you should know about sustainability – This section explains, from the point of view of the sector or function, why sustainability is important and how it affects you. You'll understand how sustainability relates to your role in the organization.
2   Strategies you can use – As with any new field, terms, frameworks and buzzwords are proliferating. Here you are provided with a honed list of ones that will be most useful to you. Think of this section as a customized encyclopaedia of methods and tools used by people pursuing sustainability, complete with case examples. We also give relevant resources, listed roughly in order of usefulness, to help you learn more. This section will help you identify concrete actions you can take.
3   Self-assessment – Each chapter ends with a SCORE (Sustainability Competency & Opportunity Rating & Evaluation) self-assessment that can help you identify your strengths and areas for improvement. These self-assessments were developed in collaboration with the International Sustainable Development Foundation and the Zero Waste Alliance. They can be combined to provide you with an overall picture of your organization's sustainability performance. Each practice listed in the assessment benchmarks three levels of performance so that you can identify the low-hanging fruit to do early but also see what will be necessary in the long term to become fully sustainable. Instructions on how to use the assessments and how to interpret your score are given with the first SCORE assessment (pages 31–33).

HOW TO GET THE MOST OUT OF THIS BOOK

Certainly, this book can be read cover to cover to get an overview of the issues and strategies associated with sustainability, but for some that might feel like a drink from a fire hose. People new to sustainability might find it most useful to read the 'What you should know about sustainability' sections, then pick one issue and explore the handful of tools we provide in the 'Strategies you can use' section. People well versed in sustainability may want to go directly to the SCORE self-assessments to identify areas for improvement and then seek out the appropriate strategies.

Based on your current understanding of sustainability, the position you hold and the sector in which you work, certain chapters will be more relevant than others. Chapter 1, on sustainability as a strategic issue, will be helpful for anyone not already familiar with sustainability concepts. Since every organization has a service and office component, we recommend that all readers, regardless of their industrial sector, read Chapter 3 (on services). People in government or manufacturing will also want to read their respective sector chapters. Then read the chapter or chapters related to functions you perform. Obviously there are many more position titles than the ones represented in this book, so choose chapters most relevant to the work you do. For example, an office manager may maintain the office, purchase supplies and manage the safety programme.

Table I.1 represents our advice for what to read. A ● indicates the primary chapter related to the position. A ○ indicates other chapters that would be helpful.

Think of this as a sustainability idea book. Read a chapter, find something worth pursuing, implement that idea, and then return to the book to uncover another opportunity.

HOW TO USE THE SELF-ASSESSMENTS

The SCORE (Sustainability Competency & Opportunity Rating & Evaluation) self-assessments at the end of the chapters can be used in a variety of ways. If you are a lone voice for sustainability in your organization, the assessment related to your function and sector should give you actions you can take within your existing span of control. If your organization is already well versed in sustainability and has been actively working towards it, these assessments can help you identify missing elements in your sustainability strategy. For people new to sustainability, these assessments can help clarify what sustainability means in their context.

- Service organizations (for example, banks, restaurants, hotels, architects and most non-profits) will want to take the service sector assessment and then all the relevant functional ones (senior management, human resources, etc.).
- Manufacturing businesses will want to take both service and manufacturing sector assessments as well as all the functional ones.
- Governmental organizations (meaning policy-setting and enforcing agencies or departments at all levels of government, as opposed to public services such as utilities

Table I.1 *Which chapters should you read?*

Position	1 Sustainability as Strategic Issue	2 Change Agent	3–5 Chapters by sector	CHAPTER 6 Senior Management	7 Facilities	8 Human Resource	9 Purchasing	10 Environmental Affairs	11 Marketing/ PR	12 Finance/ Accounting
Executive/ Board member	●	O	● Services (and other sector if appropriate)	●	O	O	O	O	O	O
Office manager	O		● Services		O if you own your building, can influence lease, or are remodelling		O			
Plant manager	O		● Manufacturing		O		O	O		
Product/ industrial designer, engineer	O		● Manufacturing		O		O	O		
Facilities manager, architect, developer	O		● Appropriate sector		●		O	O		
Human resources manager	●	O	● Services (and other sector if appropriate)			●	O			O

Position									
Purchasing manager or people responsible for purchasing supplies	○			○	○	●		● Appropriate sector	○
Environmental, health/safety, or pollution prevention professionals	●	○	○	○	●	○	● Appropriate sector	○	○
Marketing, sales or public relations	●		○				● Appropriate sector	●	○
Finance/ stockholder relations/ accountants	●		○	○	○	○	● Appropriate sector	○	●
Sustainability coordinator	●	●	○	○	○	○	● Services (and other sector if appropriate)	○	○
Business school student	○	○	○	○	○	○	● Services (and other sector if appropriate)	○	●
Economist	●						● All sectors, esp. government		○
Organizational or sustainability consultant	●	●	○	○	○	○	● Appropriate sector(s)	○	○

● Of primary importance to position   ○ Useful but not essential to position or public transport authorities) will want to take the service and government sector assessments and then all relevant functional ones.

If you compile the results from all the assessments, you can get a large-scale view of how far you have come and how much further you need to go.

Electronic files of the SCORE assessment and support services are available from the Zero Waste Alliance (www.zerowaste.org/score/) for people who want to administer it in their own organization. You can download promotional material from the website, which can help you to explain the assessment to others. For a small fee, the Zero Waste Alliance can benchmark your assessment results against other similar organizations and send you a customized report with recommendations. If you plan to use the SCORE assessments on clients, please contact the Zero Waste Alliance about their certification and licensing process so that you can learn the subtleties of the tool, get listed as a certified SCORE consultant, and receive updates as the tool evolves.

These assessments are not intended to replace various scoring systems that are being developed around the world to evaluate organizational sustainability performance (for example, the Global Reporting Initiative, British Standard 8900 and AccountAbility 1000). Nor do they collectively define ultimate sustainability, as that is a global phenomenon, not one that can be achieved by any single organization. Rather, they are intended as a tool to help organizations make decisions and move towards sustainability.

To keep our assessments simple and short, they often focus on process (have you done an energy audit in the last five years?) more than results (how much energy you saved). The scoring is tied to the degree to which you have institutionalized practices internally but also the degree to which you are influencing others. We want to thank the smart people at the International Sustainable Development Foundation and the Zero Waste Alliance for their input into the design of this tool.

DISCLAIMER TO THE SUSTAINABILITY EXPERTS

The field of sustainability is exploding and exciting practices are bubbling up all over the world. It was not possible to include every example, every country, every framework or every method. We've tried instead to choose examples that illustrate our points and give preference to ones that could easily be researched further (ie those that have been described in print or have web resources). So we apologize in advance to all the sustainability experts who may read this book and find their pet projects omitted. We welcome your feedback and suggestions in case we print an updated edition. And we thank you all for your commitment, creativity and willingness to collaborate. Together we are crafting a better future for us all.

Part 1

Foundation Concepts

1

Sustainability as a Strategic Issue

It is hard to manage an organization in today's turbulent world. Practically every day, we learn of a new technology, social dilemma or environmental problem. Businesses worry about the proliferation of new regulations and the effects of globalization. Governments struggle to maintain services while addressing the needs of an increasingly diverse and growing population amid an anti-tax culture. Unless you want to be buffeted by each change, you need a framework for making sense of what is happening in the world so that you can foresee changes and take action before they happen.

Sustainability is such a framework. It doesn't encompass everything you'll need to track to be successful and it's not a crystal ball. However, sustainability does help you see relationships between issues and more accurately forecast what may occur in the future. It examines our world as a whole system, revealing threats and opportunities. It forces you to see relationships between social, economic and environmental trends. This improved foresight can prevent unfortunate surprises and uncover previously unrecognized opportunities. If you understand sustainability, you can be a step ahead of the companies or communities with which you compete.

Sustainability challenges us to make decisions that simultaneously improve the economy, the community and the environment. That challenge may seem far outside the scope of your responsibility. Why would an organization take time to examine its impacts on these large and 'squishy' issues? Think of sustainability as a wide-angle lens. It helps you to see beyond your normal field of vision to take in potential threats and opportunities that you might have missed before.

Benefits of pursuing sustainability

Here are some of the benefits you should expect, based on the experience of other businesses and communities that have embraced sustainability.

Reduce energy, waste and costs. Some organizations have achieved the goal of zero waste to landfill. These organizations are able to eliminate haulage costs and also get paid for the 'residual products' (formerly known as waste). The Collins Company, a manufacturer of wood products in the US, found a way to put waste back into the product, not only saving money but also reducing the need for resins and improving the quality of the plywood. A prison in Oregon has reduced its natural gas bills by about 65 per cent by preheating water with solar (thermal) energy before putting it in the boilers.

Differentiate yourself. Companies and communities are always looking for ways to differentiate themselves from their competitors. Sustainability, at least until it becomes standard practice, can provide a way of making your organization stand out. For example, Scandic Hotels in Sweden was losing market share until they adopted sustainability as a focus. Sustainability gave them a story to tell. Guests don't just find a place to sleep; they become part of an exciting trend.

Sidestep future regulations. Regulations are constantly changing. For those who want to get ahead of the curve, sustainability provides a useful framework for understanding the 'endgame'. Due to new regulations, a Swiss textile manufacturer was going to have to treat their trimmings as hazardous waste. They switched to benign chemicals and now their product is biodegradable; so their 'waste' is now turned into a new product instead of being thrown away.

Create innovative new products or processes. By helping you to see the world's present and future challenges, sustainability can help you develop new products or processes that can be part of the solution. By focusing its funding on sustainability projects, ShoreBank Pacific, a small financial institution in Ilwaco, Washington, has attracted deposits from across the nation. Toyota developed its hybrid technology and is now selling it to other manufacturers. An entire cluster of renewable energy companies is being formed in Bend, Oregon, providing good jobs and a bright future in this remote area.

Open new markets. Most companies focus on serving those in industrialized nations, less than one-sixth of the world's population. Believe it or not, you can make a handy profit serving even the most destitute 3 billion people, *if* you have a product they want at a price they can afford. Amul, a dairy cooperative in India, discovered they could sell ice cream to the poor in India if they could get the cost down to around a rupee a scoop. Since most of the cost is in refrigeration, they developed a much cheaper way to keep the product cold. This new process opens up a gigantic marketplace and has uncovered a radically cheaper refrigeration process that could be used in other venues, providing them with a competitive advantage.[1]

Attract and retain the best employees. Many of today's employees want to work for companies that share their values. Sustainability can help infuse even mundane jobs with meaning. Hot Lips Pizza, a small restaurant chain in Portland, Oregon, found that pursuing sustainability helped them attract a much higher quality employee because the mission made the work seem more meaningful. Sustainability can unleash a sense of passion not possible with most other organizational change efforts. Even burger-flippers at Swedish McDonald's can feel as if they are changing the world by serving organic dairy products and beef. Sustainability, because it includes both environmental and socio-economic issues, is broad enough to encompass most people's concerns, whether they are the future of the rainforest or the future of schools. When employees feel as if their work is a means to solving major societal issues of concern to them, you tap into a powerful source of commitment and loyalty.

Improve your image with shareholders and the public. Sustainability can put organizations on the leading edge of an exciting and socially responsible trend. This can help the largest corporations, who are often targeted by non-governmental organizations (NGOs), build goodwill with the public. But it can also help tiny organizations get recognition. Gerding/Edlen, a developer in the northwest US, has received national recognition in trade journals and on a Public Broadcasting TV show. 'We couldn't have bought this type of PR,' the owners say.

Reduce legal risk and insurance costs. In order to manage risk, organizations must keep an eye on social and environmental practices. Sustainability can help organizations radically reduce those risks and the overhead costs that go with them. OKI Semiconductor discovered that, by eliminating certain toxic chemicals, their insurance company could offer them a lower rate. Swiss Re, one of the world's largest reinsurers, now is threatening to deny coverage to organizations that do not have a plan in place to reduce greenhouse gas emissions, recognizing that they will bear the brunt of the risk associated with climate change.

Provide a higher quality of life. Sustainability helps communities make decisions that maximize the quality of life through 'smart growth' design principles. Curitiba, Brazil, for example, combined insights in urban planning, transportation and social programmes to provide a much better quality of life for all their citizens, rich and poor. Their public transportation system is so convenient and well used that it requires no government subsidy. The whole city is designed for people, not cars, reducing air pollution while enhancing the quality of life.

Threats if you don't pursue sustainability

In addition to the benefits of pursuing sustainability, there are also threats you can avoid. Organizations that choose to ignore this worldwide trend may put themselves at unnecessary risk. In 2005 alone we can list a host of different disasters that might have been forecasted by an understanding of sustainability. Climatologists predict that climate change will bring bigger, more violent storms, of which the floods in Europe and hurricane Katrina may have been examples. Chemical companies may not have had to fight the Registration, Evaluation and Authorisation of Chemicals (REACH) Directive in Europe so strongly had they foreseen the need to clamp down on pollutants. The jump in oil prices has been predicted by Hubbert's Curve for decades, although the precise date for peaking oil supplies is still in dispute. The massive benzene spill in China could have been averted if the country had not pursued economic growth at the expense of the environment and if less toxic alternatives were in use. Even the Paris riots, a purely socio-economic issue, were foreseen by, among others, Thomas Friedman, the *New York Times* foreign correspondent who identified the European unwitting complicity in Arab terrorism in his book *Longitudes and Attitudes: Exploring the World After September 11*. Note that in all these cases it was not possible to predict the exact timing of the disaster or the location, but understanding sustainability made it possible to envision the probability that such a disaster could occur. Looking forward, effects of climate change (environmental and social), persistent toxins and emerging pollutants, invasive species, peaking fossil fuel supplies and water availability are at the top of our list of concerns. Prudent leaders factor these risks into their plans.

The threats to you may not be as dramatic as the ones described above. Here are some of the more everyday problems that sustainability can help you avoid.

Liability for pollutants. Even though smokestack emissions and waste-pipe discharges have long been the targets of environmental regulations, organizations are still often caught off guard every time a new substance is added to the list of regulated substances. Smart companies anticipate these hits by taking a proactive look at the raw materials they use in their processes. If it goes into your product, likely as not at least some of it will end up in your waste stream. Increasing attention to waste lead, for example, caught most of the members of the metal casting industry unprepared. One small metal caster in Oregon, Barr Casting, anticipated the problem and developed a casting process that didn't use lead. When the owner of a now-defunct competitor discovered what Barr had done, he moaned, 'Why didn't *my* engineer tell me about this?'

Liability is also beginning to extend beyond the factory gates. More and more industries are surprised at how far their liability for toxins and other damaging substances extends. The current trend toward product stewardship or producer responsibility increasingly holds manufacturers responsible for the impacts of their products for their entire life cycle. Electronics companies, for example, are scrambling to design end-of-life options for their products in anticipation of state and national regulations that are likely to prohibit the disposal of computers, televisions and cell phones.

Supply problems with raw materials and energy. Sustainability helps you to foresee potential future supply and demand problems. Wouldn't you like to know in advance if a material or resource is likely to become much more expensive or unavailable? When the energy crisis of the 1990s hit the US Pacific northwest, it resulted in closing down the area's entire aluminium industry, which had become dependent upon cheap hydropower. In the half-century they had been around, many other industries had undergone major transformations in process efficiencies, but the aluminium industry was still melting rocks with electricity. Had they been better able to foresee the future of energy, they might still be operating.

Attacks on your image. Sustainability helps you to understand the expectations of all your stakeholders. It can take years to recover from one well-publicized mistake or omission. Nike, for example, discovered the hard way that the public holds them responsible for the actions of their contract manufacturers. Nike is still trying to recover from bad publicity about sweatshop operations, years after the story broke.

Legal risks. Many companies have been held responsible for actions that were legal at the time but later determined to be harmful. General Electric is fighting litigation intended to make them pay to clean up toxic chemicals they dumped into the Hudson River. So staying within the bounds of current legal practice is no protection. Sustainability can help you assess your environmental legal risk, taking into account issues beyond compliance with current environmental regulations.

Bad-mouthing of your product. As others become more aware of sustainability, certain materials tend to get labelled as 'good' or 'bad'. Polyvinyl chloride (PVC) manufacturers have been on the defensive since Greenpeace labelled it as the worst plastic. A number of manufacturers, Nike included, have committed to phasing out PVC from their products. Sustainability can help you uncover your product's weaknesses so that you can overcome them before Greenpeace shows up on your doorstep or the media runs a story.

Being closed out of certain markets. Sustainability is driving the marketplace in many countries. The European Union, which is banning certain toxic chemicals, turned away an entire shipment of Sony Playstations because of too much cadmium in one of the parts. Agricultural sustainability certification schemes are popping up, closing the market to farmers who aren't yet certified.

Risks in pursuing sustainability

To be fair, there are risks in pursuing sustainability as well, but they are more easily managed than the risks in not pursuing it.

Greenwashing. Organizations that publicly tout their sustainability efforts without much action to back them up can be accused of 'greenwashing'. The larger and more visible the organization, the bigger target they make. You can manage to prevent greenwashing by starting quietly and humbly and by engaging stakeholders in your transformation.

Cannibalizing your own business. Whenever you engage in research and development, there is a risk that you will make obsolete the core product or service you offer. Certain transportation companies, for example, are now consulting with their clients on how *not* to transport materials as much. However, if you don't do it, it is likely that someone else will. Better to be part of the future than completely left behind.

Raising unrealistic expectations. Sustainability unleashes a sense of purpose, passion and urgency. So no matter how much you do, you will always be able to find someone – an employee, customer, NGO or shareholder – who thinks you should do more. Some organizations that have pursued sustainability have found that they lost a few good employees who felt the company wasn't moving fast enough. You may be able to handle or minimize this risk by managing expectations and involving stakeholders in the effort. Any attrition you experience may be offset by the ability to attract and retain others. You can view these unrealistic expectations as a nuisance to be managed or you can view them as a vaccination against complacency.

What is sustainability?

Let us now examine sustainability in more detail so that you can understand how to translate this abstract concept into meaningful action. Sustainability or sustainable development has been described in many ways: 'Meeting our needs while not compromising the ability of future generations to meet theirs' (Bruntland Commission), 'Living well within the limits of nature' (Mathis Wackernagel, author of *Sharing Nature's Interest*) or simply 'Not cheating on our children' (former UK Environment Minister John Gummer).

Regardless of the definition, those working in the field of sustainability generally all envision sustainability as having three realms: economic, social and environmental. Businesses have long referred to this as the 'triple bottom line'. Instead of trading these realms off against one another (jobs *or* the environment; economic growth *or* environmental health; development *or* habitat), sustainability aims to optimize all three.

In the long term, you can't have one without the others. China, for example, has been reporting 9 per cent economic growth or more over the past decade but is beginning to recognize that the environmental costs of that growth (eg flooding, pollution, health problems and resource depletion) wipe out most of those gains. Pan Yue, deputy director of China's State Environmental Protection Administration, figures that environmental injury costs China 8 to15 per cent of its annual gross domestic product.

These three realms are intimately intertwined. Without a healthy economy, unemployment is high, leading to a host of social problems; and without a healthy economy, governments don't have the revenues to handle these increased social ills. Without a healthy environment, we deplete the resources upon which our economy depends and contribute to human illness. Without a vibrant community, we don't have the employees to work in businesses, and people in crisis don't have the luxury of being concerned about environmental degradation.

When we don't understand these interdependencies, we often make poor decisions. We tend to focus on one realm over the others. As the Clinton/Gore presidential campaign put it, 'It's the economy, stupid.' This may be true for voters and in the minds of many. However, the economy is not independent of the health of the environment and community. Holding the other realms hostage to one ultimately backfires. For example, a few years ago, the US Congress decided not to raise the Corporate Average Fuel Efficiency (CAFE) standards for automobiles. They didn't want to hurt the economy, and the automobile industry represents a significant portion of US gross domestic product. However, by not improving these standards, the US is more dependent on foreign oil, and now, during the Iraq War, economic health is being syphoned off to OPEC countries at the pump. Furthermore, US cities have higher air pollution levels, which is putting more people in hospital with lung disorders. Pollution can trigger asthma, which, according to the Agency for Healthcare Research and Quality, cost the US economy $13 billion in 1998, driving up businesses' healthcare expenses. The additional emissions also contribute to climate change, a debt the world is already beginning to pay through increased property damage, crop failures and coastal erosion. Is the economy *really* better off as a result of Congress's decision? Maybe, maybe not.

Notice that sustainability is different from the environmental movement in that it recognizes the need for a healthy economy. Nature does have certain limits that we must learn to live within or suffer the consequences. But Alan AtKisson, author of *Believing Cassandra*, makes a distinction between 'growth' (being bigger, having increased material throughput, having an increasingly negative impact on nature) with 'development' (moving forward, getting better, without having bigger impacts). As AtKisson puts it, 'Growth must cease. If human beings do not stop their growth willingly, Nature will stop it forcefully. Paradoxically, however, for Growth to cease, Development must accelerate.'[2] We need to speed up the rate at which new, cleaner technologies are implemented. We need a healthy economy to have the money to invest in these innovations. Once people reach a reasonable quality of life, they begin to demand a healthier environment. We just need to devise ways where their increasing affluence no longer exacerbates the pressure on the environment. We need to get better, not bigger.

Sustainability is also no longer a fringe issue. Consider the fact that the fastest growing segment of the energy sector is wind power; in the travel industry, it's eco-tourism; in the investment community, it's socially responsible investments; in agriculture, it's organic farming. These trends all point in the same direction, towards sustainability. True, these segments may still make up a small fraction of their respective sectors, but assuming their exponential growth continues, they'll soon become major contenders.

Table 1.1 gives an idea of how many major organizations and communities are actively pursuing sustainability in one form or another.

Table 1.1 *Examples of organizations pursuing sustainability*

Energy	Manufacturing	Food	Services	Government		Colleges and Universities
				USA	Rest of the World	
BP	Coca Cola	Bon Appétit	Aspen Skiing Company	Chicago, Illinois	Australia	Cornell
Conoco	Dell	Chiquita	Bank of America	Madison, Wisconsin	Bogota, Colombia	Darden, University of Virginia
Philips	DuPont	Fetzer Winery	Calvert (mutual funds)	National Aeronautics and Space Administration (NASA)	China	George Washington
Florida Power and Light	Electrolux (largest white goods manufacturer in the world)	Frito Lay	Goldman Sachs	San Francisco, California	Curitiba, Brazil	Harvard
Royal Dutch Shell	Epson	Heinz	Kaiser Permanente	Santa Monica, California	European Union	Imperial College London
	Ford	Unilever	Munich Re (the largest reinsurance company in the world)	State of Arizona	UK	Iowa State
	General Electric		Price-waterhouse-Coopers	State of Massachusetts	Japan	Lowell Center for Sustainable Production, University of Massachusetts
	General Motors		Starbucks	State of Minnesota	Kerala, India	Massachusetts Institute of Technology
	Herman Miller		Swiss Re (the second largest reinsurance company in the world)	State of New Jersey	New Zealand	Michigan
	Hewlett-Packard		Wal-Mart	State of North Carolina	Sweden	Oregon State University
	IKEA				Whistler, British Columbia, Canada	Portland State University
	Intel					Stanford
	Interface (largest manufacturer of commercial carpet tiles)					University of British Columbia
	Johnson Controls					

Table 1.1 *Examples of organizations pursuing sustainability* (cont'd)

Energy	Manufacturing	Food	Services	Government		Colleges and Universities
				USA	Rest of the World	
	Mattel Nike Philips RR Donnelley & Sons (largest printer in North America) Toyota Volkswagen			State of Oregon State of Washington US Department of Defense US Environmental Protection Agency		University of California (Berkeley, San Diego, Santa Barbara) University of East Anglia (UK) University of Victoria Yale York University, Canada

Hopefully you can see that it's not just the usual idealistic suspects like Ben & Jerry's, Seventh Generation and Patagonia that are interested in sustainability. And while none of these organizations is fully sustainable as yet (no organization to the best of our knowledge is), what is important is that sustainability is on their radar: they are developing strategies to respond to its threats and opportunities. Some are doing a better job than others, of course. But they all recognize sustainability as a significant strategic issue.

The organizations listed above are just the tip of the iceberg. In fact, according to a 2002 PricewaterhouseCoopers study, 75 per cent of US companies surveyed are adopting some sustainability practices, 73 per cent plan to issue a sustainability report and 89 per cent expect sustainability to be more important after five years. To be fair, surveys like this tend to overstate the level of support, but even if the numbers were halved, this would be a significant business trend.

Why is sustainability a strategic issue?

If you hadn't heard much about sustainability until now, you may be wondering why it is drawing so much attention among such heavy-hitters. Why is sustainability suddenly on the radar screen? There are a host of reasons.

Sustainability is a natural extension of other organizational changes. Over the last century, society has increasingly raised its expectations of business. In the early 1900s, codes of ethics and government policies began to discourage monopolies, misleading product claims and underhand business dealings. Then through to the 1970s employee rights showed up on the radar with the rise of organized labour and quality of worklife programmes, all intended to combat unfair and inhumane labour practices. With the quality movement in the late 1970s and early 1980s, organizations adopted a focus on the needs of customers to stay competitive. In 1984, an accidental chemical release at a Union Carbide plant in Bhopal killed thousands in the community; then the Exxon Valdez ran aground in Alaska in 1989. Suddenly environmental practices were added to the list of expectations. More recently, the internet has increased corporate transparency with such sites as WalMartWatch.com and the WhirledBank.org often raising corporate social responsibility issues like international labour practices. And just in the last two to three years, shareholders have started using their proxies in an unprecedented way to oust corporate leaders and redirect policies when they feel corporations are not living up to their expectations on ethical, social and environmental issues.

As you can see, the expectations of business have grown step by step, adding new stakeholders along the way (see Figure 1.1).

Today society wants it all. According to the Millennium Poll conducted in 1999, surveying 25,000 people in 23 countries on six continents, the majority of people expect companies to go far beyond just making a profit, obeying laws, paying taxes and providing jobs. Instead, they expect corporations to 'exceed all laws, setting a higher ethical standard, and helping build a better society for all'.[3] Employee health and safety, fair treatment of employees, elimination of corruption, protecting the environment and ending child labour practices are high on the priority list. All these issues fall under the economic–social–environmental framework of sustainability.

Stepping up to increasing societal expectations

Figure 1.1 *Steps to sustainability*

In a sense, sustainability is nothing new – it is simply providing some structure to a set of emerging societal expectations.

Natural resources are now a limiting factor. At the beginning of the industrial revolution we had a seemingly endless supply of natural resources and a dearth of skilled labour to work in our factories. Now the situation is reversed. The global population is over 6 billion, with many people under- or unemployed. According to the best estimates of the UN, we should expect our population to increase by another 3 billion by 2050. At the same time, many of our natural resources are dwindling. According to the UN Food and Agriculture Organization, the world lost 94 million hectares of forestland in the 1990s alone – that's about 64,000 acres a day. Eleven of the 15 major fishing grounds in the world are already at or exceeding the maximum sustainable yield and some are in complete collapse. Soil erosion, desertification, urban sprawl, salinization and aquifer depletion are compromising our crop yields.

Management involves attending to bottlenecks and limits. If natural resources, not people, are our biggest constraint, then our policies and management practices should switch from ones that reward getting more from fewer people (eg lay-offs and depreciation schedules) to ones that reward getting more from less material (eg resource efficiencies including the use of energy, water, wood products, agricultural and marine resources, and mined minerals and metals). In the last century, we used technology and innovation to achieve a tremendous increase in human productivity. Now we need to apply that same know-how to resource productivity. Unlike previous corporate social responsibility programmes, sustainability acknowledges the finite limits of nature and the need to neutralize our wastes and emissions, to produce renewable resources and to maintain other critical ecosystem services.

Environmental issues are becoming global. Years ago, most environmental problems were relatively isolated: a tanker runs aground, a train filled with chemicals derails, a plant explodes, a company mishandles hazardous waste. But now, the biggest environmental problems are global – global warming, acid rain, the ozone hole, species extinctions, the destruction of rainforest, the dying of coral reefs – and it's not clear who to turn to in order to correct them. The impacts of these problems affect people everywhere. You can't just move on to the next frontier, the next fishing ground, the next forest. There is nowhere else to go. Since the publication of Rachel Carson's *Silent Spring* in 1962 and the first Earth Day in 1970, the public has become far more aware and concerned about these issues.

Health concerns are rising. Studies conducted around the globe have revealed that humans everywhere are carrying a number of synthetic chemicals in their blood and even breast milk: wood preservatives, industrial solvents, pesticides, fire retardants and so on. Some of these are known carcinogens; some, called endocrine disruptors or 'gender benders', mimic hormones and can cause birth defects as well as reproductive abnormalities that don't become apparent until our offspring reach childbearing age. Certain natural and synthetic substances accumulate in body tissue and their concentrations increase as they move up the food chain. For example, the US Food and Drug Administration recently issued warnings about mercury levels in certain types of fish. (Coal-fired power plants are a significant source of mercury and China is bringing more online at a break-neck pace.) This is not just a matter of fouling your own nest. The west coast of the US regularly gets pulses of air pollution from China. Many indigenous people in remote arctic regions have in their bodies high levels of pesticides used near the equator; they are being advised not to breastfeed their babies. The effects of pollution circulate around the globe.

Social, environmental and economic factors are entangling, creating instability. Environmental concerns such as the loss of natural resources, coupled with social issues like the explosive growth of population in developing countries, are combining in a bubbling cauldron. In some areas, we see a backlash against globalization and Westernization (what some now call 'Westoxification'). The rise in terrorism can be seen in this light. Thomas Friedman, a Pulitzer Prize-winning foreign affairs columnist for *The New York Times*, who has long studied the Arab world, states:

> If we've learned one thing since 9/11, it's that terrorism is not produced by the poverty of money. It's produced by the poverty of dignity. It is about young middle-class Arabs and Muslims feeling trapped in countries with too few good jobs and too few opportunities to realize their potential or shape their own future – and blaming America for it.[4]

The US Central Intelligence Agency has been warning that environmental degradation will increasingly become a source of political instability. They cite fresh water and climate change as particularly critical issues.[5] Political instability leads to economic collapse, which in turn leads to human misery. Once again, the environment, social and economic elements are intertwined. Sustainability can help you foresee how these global issues might play out and what you should do now in response.

Energy supplies are a significant threat. One arena where these factors are converging is that of energy supply. Based on the best estimates, worldwide production of oil is going to peak sometime between now and 2010. The disruption caused in the US when domestic production peaked in the 1970s – people lining up around the block to get petrol, subsequent recession – may serve as a warning here. Natural gas sources are being depleted much faster than originally thought, so fuel-switching isn't much of an option. Renewables tend not to provide the same net energy so experts are saying that the world will need to learn to live on less energy, just as its population is expected to increase by 50 per cent and China's demand is growing. The implications for the world economy, international conflict, the environment and social disruption are deeply disturbing.[6]

These problems are uncovering new opportunities. Yet all is not gloom and doom. Yes, there are serious problems, but these also represent interesting opportunities. Many of the practices we will need to correct these challenges are already in existence. Organic agriculture can build instead of deplete soil. Smart growth practices show cities how to plan urban environments that reduce the need for automobiles and also improve liveability and the health of their inhabitants. Marine sanctuaries have been found an effective way to rebuild fish stocks. Timber companies have developed a set of sustainable forest practices. Promising new products and processes include hydrogen fuel cells and nanotechnologies.

In many cases, we know what we need to do. Through some combination of resource conservation and new technologies, we might be able to have a soft landing. But the longer we wait, the more constrained our options. The only question is whether you have a handle on the issues relevant to your organization, can envision a better future and can muster the leadership to take the next steps. You can either start experimenting with these more sustainable methods or get left behind.

Sustainability tends to produce multiple, unintended benefits. Many sustainability actions yield unanticipated benefits. When architects design a green building to maximize natural light, the occupant saves on energy bills; companies operating in premises so designed also enjoy reduced absenteeism, improved productivity and increased employee satisfaction. In retail environments, 'daylighting' as it is called has been shown to increase sales dramatically; in schools, it improves learning; in nursing homes, it helps the elderly sleep well at night.

When C&A Floorcoverings set out to find a way to recycle old carpet into new carpet, they developed a product that performed better and cost less to produce. When Portland State University decided to emphasize sustainability in their urban planning programme, they experienced a significant increase in enrolments. When the City of Santa Monica wanted to reduce their use of pesticides and rodenticides, their integrated pest management system also improved the energy efficiency of their buildings since they sealed the holes where the creature were getting in. When DesignTex wanted to find a way to eliminate hazardous waste from the production and dying of their upholstery fabric, they ended up creating a new fabric that performed better, produced a new product from the fabric selvages and won international recognition for their efforts.[7]

When Hot Lips Pizza, a three-restaurant enterprise in Portland, Oregon, chose to pursue sustainability because of the owner's personal values, they began to attract a much higher quality employee. Aspen Skiing Company credits retrofitting the lighting in their parking garage (done to save money) with improved security. DuPont has reduced their greenhouse gases by 65 per cent since 1990, far beyond the Kyoto Protocol, saving hundreds of millions of dollars in the process. Michael Northrop of the Climate Group says of organizations that try to reduce their climate impact, 'It's impossible to find a company that has acted and has not found benefits.'[8]

One of the common unintended side effects of pursuing sustainability is employee commitment. Making any organizational change is bound to bring out the nay-sayers, but most organizations have found sustainability unleashes a wave of excitement, creativity and loyalty not associated with many other change efforts. As Ken Hopper, general manager for one of the Scandic Hotels in northern Europe, says:

> *I've been involved in Scandic for ten years. We've had all kinds of different campaigns or processes. Nothing has ever been close to creating as much excitement as this environmental campaign. It was just huge. You did not have anyone who didn't feel something. It was incredible that people got so involved in this that they are willing to make some sacrifices and put in some energy and effort to get involved. It brought people together in a way we've never ever been able to bring our staff together before, and we haven't since. Nothing we've done has mobilized a force that's created such unison.*[9]

For all these reasons, sustainability is now clearly a strategic issue. It helps organizations make sense of current trends, examine their threats and opportunities, and see relationships between them. From a practical, day-to-day perspective, sustainability helps you spark innovative ideas. As long as you put those ideas through normal business filters to determine whether they make sense as things to do now, you can't go wrong. If you don't begin the learning curve, you are at risk of being left behind.

Factors that define sustainability

Earlier we explained that sustainability involves optimizing the economy, environment and social elements. Since the economy and society are human constructs, what is considered sustainable is to some degree governed by culture. Nature, on the other hand, provides some non-negotiable requirements. Let's examine what we know about the needs of each.

Factors of a healthy economy. From Adam Smith's time on, we have developed a set of factors that contribute to a healthy economy, which usually include:

* multiple buyers and sellers;
* timely, accurate information;
* accounting standards and enforcement;
* absence of governmental corruption;
* markets for financing development (stock markets, bond markets, banks);
* agreed-upon method or currency of exchange; and
* absence of deflation or high inflation.

Factors for a healthy society. This element is heavily dependent upon culture. Someone from a tribal culture might answer the question differently than someone from the Western world, and both might have different emphases from those of a Muslim. However, Chilean economist Manfred Max-Neef distilled basic human needs down to nine universal, non-substitutable ones:[10]

1 subsistence;
2 protection/security;
3 affection;
4 understanding;
5 participation;
6 leisure;
7 creation;
8 identity/meaning; and
9 freedom.

In the Western world at least, our communities also rest upon such factors as:

- a strong education system;
- a robust middle class;
- the absence of a huge gap between the richest and poorest (a large gap often leads to revolutions);
- access to health care;
- security and the absence of crime; and
- equal rights and the absence of discrimination.

Factors for a healthy environment. One of the easiest ways to understand sustainability, especially the requirements of nature, is to use The Natural Step framework. Developed through the normal scientific peer-review process, this framework lays out four principles for a sustainable world. The first three factors relate to the physical environment; the fourth is a social one. We'll paraphrase the three environmental principles here, with a little explanation.

Nature must not be subjected to increasing concentrations from substances from the Earth's crust. There are three main raw materials we extract from deep inside the Earth: fossil fuels, metals and minerals. It took billions of years for nature to sequester these elements, many of which are toxic to most life on Earth. If we remove these materials and spread them around in nature at a rate faster than they can be redeposited, they will build up in the environment, eventually causing problems. For example, since the industrial revolution, we have increased carbon dioxide in the atmosphere by over 30 per cent. We are finding high levels of mercury and other metals in fish.

Similarly, we must not allow man-made substances to build up in nature. Humans make over 100,000 synthetic chemicals, molecules nature never made. Some of these are persistent (they don't break down easily) and accumulate in body tissue, the pesticide DDT being one example. Some of these compounds mimic hormones, frequently causing birth defects, cancer or neurological problems. Scientists and health departments are finding these synthetic substances (as well as some elements from the Earth's crust) in our bodies, in our blood and in the breast milk we feed our babies.

Third, we must not continue to destroy the productive capacity of nature to provide the services upon which we depend. Forests provide more than just wood products – they provide habitat for endangered species, clean our water and air, and protect soils. Barrier reefs provide habitat for the vast majority of marine life. Over-harvesting, development and genetic manipulation all contribute to this problem.

These three lists of factors may not be complete but they are certainly a place to begin. You can compare your practices to these factors to identify your largest impacts. You can adjust your practices to be less dependent upon materials that are clearly going to become more scarce, expensive or regulated.

How do you know whether your organization is sustainable?

A single organization can't be responsible for making all of society sustainable, but each can examine its inputs, outputs, processes and effects on the larger system in which it operates. We often use the 'bubble diagram' (Figure 1.2) to help organizations develop a clear vision of what it would look like to be sustainable.

To use this tool, follow this process. Inside the process box, list your primary processes. Then in each circle, list your most prominent examples (eg what forms of energy you purchase, materials you purchase the most, etc.) and describe the sustainable state. Then outside the circles, coming off as spokes, list ideas for projects to reduce your major impacts.

Let's use a simple example. Imagine you run a pizza restaurant. Your operation would be sustainable (or close to it) when:

- **Materials:** All your produce, pizza boxes, cleaning products, etc. came from sustainable/green/socially responsible sources. (You could buy organic tomatoes from farmers who provide good working conditions and wages for their migrant workers. Your pizza boxes could be made from 100 per cent recycled paper or pulp from certified forests. Cleaning products would be environmentally benign.)
- **Energy:** All your energy for cooking, transportation and space heat came from renewable sources. (You could buy 'green power' from your utility and your delivery vehicles could run on biodiesel.)

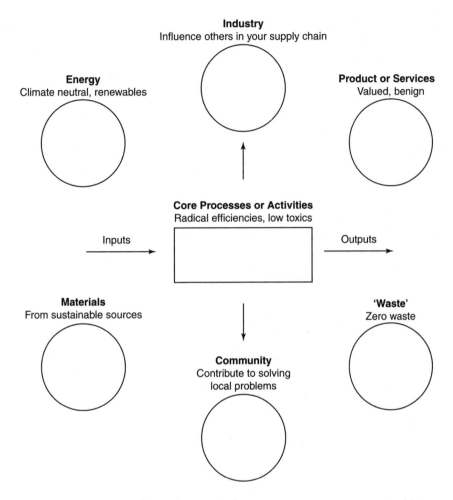

Figure 1.2 *How do you know whether your organization is sustainable?*

- **Process:** Your cooking and other processes are as efficient as possible. (You could use non-disposable tableware and capture the waste heat from your ovens.)
- **Product design:** Your main product is biodegradable, even edible, so it is quite benign as long as it is organic.
- **Waste:** All your waste products can either be reused, recycled, or composted. (You could choose biodegradable serving items, eliminating plastic drink covers or polystyrene cups.)
- **Industry influence:** You apply your leadership and buying power to drive the rest of the industry toward sustainability. (To have an adequate and affordable supply of organic produce, you might help set up a cooperative.)

- **Community contribution:** You have a programme to help solve a pressing social problem that relates in some way to your business. (You might work on migrant labour issues and/or hunger, for example.)

Notice that all of these actions are do-able now. Granted, making a semiconductor plant sustainable would be more complicated than a pizza restaurant, but the bubble diagram can help you see opportunities to move in the right direction. Create one for your own organization to understand what you can do now and what you can work towards in the long term to become sustainable.

Conclusion

In this chapter, we have tried to show that sustainability is a field that is growing and strategic. It helps you foresee the future and often produces many unintended benefits. Many of the possible sustainability-inspired actions make economic sense now. Some technologies still have a way to go, but you need to know *now* where the world is heading so that you can invest in platforms for the future instead of dead ends.

Choose the sustainable course and you will often reap benefits that others may not. Businesses may gain a competitive advantage over others in their industry. Governments may be able to free up precious funds to do more mission-related work and build trust with taxpayers.

The rest of this book will describe tangible actions that will help you, your organization, your community and the environment. It can seem daunting at first, but we promise the journey will be both intriguing and satisfying.

RESOURCES

Articles and Reports

Packard, Kimberly O'Neill and Forest Reinhardt (2000) 'What Every Executive Needs to Know about Global Warming', *Harvard Business Review*, July–August, p128. Explains how one of the biggest environmental issues of our time may affect business.

Hart, Stuart and Mark Milstein (1999) 'Global Sustainability and Creative Destruction of Industries', *MIT Sloan Management Review*, Fall, pp23–33. Distinguishes green from sustainable products and explains how to market to three different segments: consumer economy (1 billion people), emerging markets (2 billion people) and survival economy (3 billion people).

Senge, Peter and Goran Carstedt (2001) 'Innovating Our Way to the Next Industrial Revolution' *MIT Sloan Management Review*, Winter, Reprint #4222. Provides a good strategic overview for those who don't have time to read a book; some great examples.

The Millennium Ecosystems Assessment was performed at the request of the United Nations and employed thousands of the world's leading scientists, www.millenniumassessment.org/.

The Living Planet Index, published by the World Wildlife Fund, provides useful data about the state of the world, www.panda.org/livingplanet/.

Books

AtKisson, Alan (1999) *Believing Cassandra: An Optimist Looks at a Pessimist's World*. White River Junction, VT: Chelsea Green Publishing. A good overview of sustainability without a lot of the gloom and doom found in other books.

Brown, Lester (2001) *Eco-Economy: Building an Economy for the Earth*. WW Norton Company. A good overview of both the scientific basis for concern and emerging solutions and tools.

Hammond, Allen (1998) *Which World: Scenarios for the 21st Century*. Washington DC: Island Press. Lays out three possible future worlds: market world, fortress world and sustainable world.

Hawken, Paul, Amory Lovins and L. Hunter Lovins (1999) *Natural Capitalism*. Little Brown and Co. Describes good examples of sustainability-related technologies and practices in both business and government.

Huntington, Samuel P. (1996) *The Clash of Civilizations and the Remaking of World Order*. Simon & Schuster. Provides a compelling theory for understanding social and political changes in our world.

Jacobs, Jane (2000) *The Nature of Economies*. NY: The Modern Library. Explains how nature and economies work in the same fashion, helping to explain why globalization doesn't always result in a better lifestyle.

McDonough, William and Michael Braungart (2002) *Cradle to Cradle: Remaking the Way We Make Things*. NY: North Point Press. Inspiring reading for those who design or manufacture products.

Natrass, Brian and Mary Altomare (2002) *Dancing with the Tiger: Learning Sustainability Step by Natural Step*. Gabriola Island, BC: New Society Publishers. Provides an overview of the popular Natural Step framework with case studies from North America.

Wackernagel, Mathis and William Rees (1996) *Our Ecological Footprint: Reducing Human Impact on the Earth*. BC, Canada: New Society Publishers. An easy-to-read explanation of the environmental side of sustainability.

2

Change Agent/Sustainability Coordinator:
How to Keep a Sustainability Effort on Track

Many of the organizations best known for their commitment to sustainability are those with passionate and outspoken leaders at their helms. Ray Anderson of Interface, for example, tours the world telling his dramatic story of getting a 'spear through his heart' after reading Hawkens' *The Ecology of Commerce* and realizing the damage his company was doing to the Earth. Leaders are certainly in a prime position to drive change through their organizations; however, for most organizations change can sprout and grow in any number of places.

Regardless of where you are in the organizational structure, you can make a difference. Someone put *The Ecology of Commerce* on Ray Anderson's desk; the change did not start with him. People tend to point to the moment when their leader gets the 'spear through the heart' as the moment sustainability began in their organization, but that undervalues the critical actions of those within the organization who often bring sustainability to the leader's attention.

Within every organization that pursues sustainability, there is always someone who gets the effort going, usually a person with an unflagging passion for the topic. These change agents often begin without the overt approval of their organization. Over time they develop a compelling business case and enrol others. Eventually they may be given official responsibility for leading the effort.

For sustainability to be successful, it eventually must infiltrate all aspects of the organization. Until that happens it is usually necessary to have an individual or team whose job it is to shepherd the effort. When an individual holds this role, he or she is often called sustainability coordinator. This may be a full-time or part-time responsibility. This chapter is directed to those individuals who, with or without formal authority, move sustainability forward in an organization.

WHAT YOU SHOULD KNOW ABOUT SUSTAINABILITY

Sustainability change agents have come from virtually all parts of organizations. Sometimes, they emerge from environmental departments, but just as often they come from other fields. For example, the sustainability coordinator at Tualatin Valley Water District in Oregon is also their financial analyst, a particularly nice blend of skills that gives her credibility in the boardroom. So if you have the passion, there is a good chance you can make a role for yourself in sustainability.

Change agents face a number of challenges, however, no matter where they reside in an organization. Here is some advice for each of the most common hurdles.

Influencing without authority. Usually the sustainability coordinator acts in an advisory role and does not have line authority over all the people in the organization. From this position, they must cajole, influence, convince and assist. Expect the typical resistance and excuses: we're too busy, this effort is only a nice-to-have, our customers aren't asking for it, etc. Develop friends in high places and pick your battles. Build on successes and look for opportune moments to raise certain issues.

Getting the ear and respect of management. If your organization has not already adopted sustainability as a strategic focus, you will have to earn the respect of management. First, decide whether it's time to try to get management's attention. You may want to work on some small projects that fly under the radar until you can show dramatic business benefits. Then, begin introducing the concept to management. Often, new ideas are rejected, so begin sowing seeds. Pass on articles from respected business journals and expose your executives to peers in other organizations who have adopted sustainability. Avoid impassioned arguments and do not expect a quick conversion. Suggest that sustainability be one of many emerging trends that should be considered in strategic planning. Think strategically. How does sustainability inform your organization's strategy? Are there threats or opportunities? Talk in business terms.

Avoiding burn-out. All organizations are so far from a sustainable state that it's easy to become overwhelmed. You can't work on everything at once, so devise a method for setting priorities. What's really important? What would make the most impact? What is this the right time for? What has a high likelihood of success? What could provide a platform for other efforts?

Enrolling others. People are often so busy that when you approach them with one more thing to think about, you're more likely to see exasperation rather than excitement. Develop contacts with people and get to know their problems and challenges. For example, cleaning staff might complain about how certain cleaning products irritate their skin and eyes. That's your opening to propose more sustainable options. Do some of the homework for people and talk in terms that they use. Ask them to test the new product on a trial basis to see if it performs at least as well as the old one. Realize, too, that some people will be ready to listen and others not. Focus on those who are ready to hear the message or who have a reason to collaborate.

There are likely to be some in your organization who are outright resistant to your ideas or the notion of sustainability. Be strategic about how you approach and involve these people. If these people have influence – either because they are formal or informal leaders or their support is necessary to implement your ideas – consider involving them in your efforts. Invite them to participate on planning teams or convince them to come to presentations on sustainability. It can be very useful to have sceptics involved in planning because they may represent the position or attitudes of others and you will want to learn about and account for their concerns or doubts. If you are successful at winning over a sceptic in the process, you will probably build credibility with others. If these people are not influential, you might consider working around them for the time being and directing your energy towards those who can further your cause. You may find that engaging the critical few is more productive than trying to win the masses.

Once, while visiting a forest products company famous for their sustainability practices, we asked how many people in the plant really lived and breathed sustainability, who thought about it on a regular basis. After much hemming and hawing, the sustainability coordinator estimated 'only' 15 per cent. He found this figure discouraging but we think about it differently. This shows that you can make great headway with a minority of the population on board. It's unrealistic to think that you can capture the

---

RESOURCES

Gladwell, Malcolm (2000) *The Tipping Point.* Boston: Little, Brown and Co.

Moore, Geofrey A. (1999) *Crossing the Chasm: Marketing and Selling High-Tech Products to Mainstream Customers.* NY: HarperBusiness. Both *The Tipping Point* and this book describe important concepts about how changes happen in a population. The latter focuses on high-tech products, but the concepts are equally relevant to other industries.

Rogers, Everett M. (2003) *Diffusion of Innovations* (Fifth Edition). NY: Free Press. This book and its concepts provide the theoretical base for many other more recent change management books. The model provides useful concepts for thinking about whom to approach and how to influence them.

Wheatley, Margaret (2005) *Finding our Way: Leadership for an Uncertain Time.* San Francisco: Berrett-Koehler. This book dispels many of the myths about how change happens in organizations and suggests a more organic approach.

Maurer, Rick (1996) *Beyond the Wall of Resistance: Unconventional Strategies that Build Support for Change.* Austin, TX: Bard Books. Provides useful guidance for dealing with the inevitable resistance change agents face.

Robert, Karl-Henrik, et al (2004) *Strategic Leadership Towards Sustainability* (Second Edition). Karlskrona, Sweden: Blekinge Institute of Technology. The textbook for a masters-level programme on sustainability in Sweden.

passion of every employee. So find those who will be intrigued and use your collective influence to make improvements.

STRATEGIES YOU CAN USE

We have divided our schedule of tools into two sections, based on the level of authority the change agent has. The first section looks at tools appropriate for change agents who have no formal authority, the second for sustainability coordinators who have official authority (even if this is only a part-time responsibility).

Change agents with no formal authority

Change agents with no formal authority must carefully work to build support for sustainability over time. The following methods may be useful and tend to build on one another.

Begin within your span of control

Implement sustainable practices to the degree you can within your own span of control. Practically anyone can find more sustainable options for what they are doing. A cleaner might investigate green cleaning products; a secretary might source paper with more recycled content. You might need to do some research outside work if you don't have the flexibility to do so during work time. Focus your efforts on changes that make good bottom-line business sense, that save time or save money. Choose projects that have a high probability of success. Then communicate your results. Let management know how you improved productivity. They'll want to know how you could do it again.

Sow seeds

You need to begin to develop your advocates, others who will support the idea of sustainability inside the organization. To find those individuals, you can begin to sow seeds:

- Talk to people about what you've learned about sustainability and watch their reaction.
- Share interesting articles, attaching a note asking for their reaction.
- Invite people to attend presentations on sustainability topics with you.

As you sow these seeds, you'll find that the idea of sustainability will grow on some people. You may be able to find a related passion, something your contacts care about that you can reframe under the umbrella of sustainability. Invite their ideas. Together, explore where the opportunities might lie in the organization. Who do they know who also might be interested?

Discussion groups

Many organizations will allow employees to have informal discussion groups during lunch. Organizations such as the Northwest Earth Institute in the US Pacific northwest and the Global Action Plan have self-facilitated classes that can be done in this setting. Topics such as voluntary simplicity or deep ecology often develop a sense of urgency and empowerment. Or you might form a book group and read works related to sustainability. These venues can leave participants eager to change their behaviour at home and at work.

RESOURCES

The Northwest Earth Institute has a number of discussion courses that can be used in organizations or in your community,www.nwei.org.
  The Global Action Plan, www.globalactionplan.org, www.globalactionplan.org/uk.
  The following books might also provide good material for discussions:

- *Believing Cassandra* by Alan AtKisson is a good overview of sustainability with a positive spin.
- *Cradle to Cradle* by Bill McDonough provides positive examples of what can be done.
- *The Party's Over: Oil, War and the Fate of Industrial Societies* by Richard Heinberg explores the implications of peaking oil supplies.
- *The Millennium Eco-Assessment* was commissioned by the United Nations and involved thousands of leading scientists around the world. It and a shorter summary report lay out the global challenges we must overcome.
- *Biomimicry* by Janine Benyus explores how nature can be an inspiration to redesign our products, our agricultural system and our communities.

Green teams

Discussion groups often evolve into voluntary green teams, groups of people who meet usually during non-work time to explore how to educate others and improve the sustainability performance of their organizations. They may host speaker series during lunch or research opportunities to eliminate waste and conserve energy. These green teams often have no formal authority in their organizations but they can catalyse more formal initiatives. Make participation fun for those who attend but also work on projects that matter. Make sure that at least some of your efforts save or make the organization money.

Realize too that these green teams often peter out, so position them so that they will evolve into something more formal. See the examples of structures in the section below.

Sustainability coordinators with formal authority

Sustainability coordinators who are sanctioned by management have more clout. They can set up structures and processes to affect the entire organization. The following methods may be helpful in this situation.

Steering committees

A steering committee differs from a green team in that it is not voluntary and membership is designed. These committees are temporary, parallel organizational structures to facilitate the implementation of sustainability in the organization. Often organizations begin with a diagonal slice, taking people from all parts of the organization. This can be a good place to begin. However, these often evolve to be much smaller teams with carefully selected members. For example, at a Simplot plant in Idaho, the steering committee evolved from an unwieldy one with over 20 members to one with a handful of well-positioned individuals including two of their five senior managers, a member of the laboratory (a research function), a purchasing agent, an environmental representative and representatives from maintenance and planning. They also have seats for rank and file employees who rotate on and off the team. Together, when they decide to move in a direction, they have the clout to make it happen.

Task forces and project teams

Steering committees often spawn task forces or project teams to work on individual projects. For example, one team may conduct a greenhouse gas audit while another plans a remodel. It is often helpful to hire a professional facilitator to lead these efforts so that you have someone knowledgeable about the process leading the effort.

At the very least, assure that these teams get off on the right foot. Be thorough as you set up these groups, carefully considering mission, membership and methods, to minimize confusion, scope-creep and burn-out. We recommend a 'launching' process that addresses each of these critical components:

- **Why?** Be sure you can articulate the business need for the project. Link the outcomes you expect the team to achieve to strategic issues of the organization. The more important this effort seems to the participants, the more energy and commitment you will likely garner.
- **Who?** Be strategic in your choice of people. It's good to have volunteers because you are assured of their interests, but also consider enlisting people with relevant expertise,

leadership or influence and include representatives of those whose jobs or processes will be affected (eg the facilities managers for projects related to your building).

- **What?** Express the aims of these teams in terms of measurable outcomes including deadlines for deliverables. This will help them manage expectations as well as the scope of the project. If possible, frame their task as a simple question. Make clear what they can decide and what they can only recommend.
- **When and where?** It will be easier to enlist people if you can estimate the time commitment you are asking for: how often and for how long they will be expected to meet. Contribute to their success by assuring they have adequate time for the project and the necessary resources – meeting space, access to data, permission from their managers, etc.
- **How?** Ideally these groups will be run by skilled facilitators. It is also helpful to establish effective meeting roles and processes, and ground rules. Discuss any assumptions about assessments, tools, research, budgets and other resources they may use.

Individuals

Sometimes a team is not needed at all. If you approach the right people and embed sustainable practices into the organizational systems, you can often have a larger impact. For example, if you can convince the purchasing manager to implement environmentally preferable purchasing policies and to embed those preferences into the online purchasing system, the other employees don't have to think about sustainability in this context. They are simply presented with sustainable options. Where you can, make the more sustainable options the easy choice or the only choice.

Award programmes and certification systems

Many organizations have found that pursuing sustainability award programmes or certification systems has provided a powerful framework and incentive for progress. Many regions have environmental or sustainability award programmes that provide a structure, standards and, if you qualify, public recognition. You may also pursue certain certification schemes, for example LEED for a building remodel, ISO 14000 for an environmental management system or product-specific certifications like the Marine Stewardship Council certification for fish or the Forest Stewardship Council certification for forest products. See Appendix B for a list of common certification programmes.

Sustainability management systems

So that your first sustainability projects don't end up being your last, you need to develop a management system to support sustainability. These are often modelled on quality management systems (ISO 9000) and environmental management systems (ISO 14000). They include:

- a policy statement that describes intent and commitment;
- methods for setting priorities, metrics and targets;
- processes for starting, monitoring and completing projects;
- processes to review both the results of the projects and also to audit and improve the sustainability management system itself; and
- methods for institutionalizing the insights gained from projects into other systems such as work procedures, corrective action plans and training.

See more information about SMSs in the Environmental Affairs chapter.

RESOURCES

'Developing Effective Systems for Managing Sustainability' and 'Embedding Sustainability into your EMS' are two booklets in the Sustainability Series™ that provide an overview in lay terms, avoiding the language of ISO 14001, www.axisperformance.com/sust_series.html.
    ISO 14001 is a globally accepted set of standards for and certification of environmental management systems.

Conclusion

As the famous anthropologist Margaret Mead once said, 'Never doubt that a small band of caring and committed people can change the world. Indeed it is the only thing that ever has.' You can make a difference. It is not easy being a lone voice in an organization, so build your cadre of supporters. Look for win–win opportunities that help the organization as well as delivering social and environmental benefits. Build your credibility in the organization by choosing projects with a high probability of success. Once you've gained the respect of others and they have seen the positive results, it will be easier to take bigger leaps. So many people have found that once they understand sustainability, there is no going back to blissful ignorance. So as you introduce more and more people to the concepts, you may not be able to see all the ripples, but you can be sure that they are there. Try to be patient. It took a long time for humans to get to this unsustainable state and it will take time to shift our society and economy. You are part of a worldwide effort at an exciting turning point in human history.

SCORE THE SUSTAINABILITY COORDINATOR

INSTRUCTIONS

Scan the following checklist to see how many of these practices you have implemented in the past five years. Where you have performed one of the practices, use the scale to determine the number of points you can earn. We have described typical benchmarks for the pilot stage, the initiative phase and the fully integrated systemic phase. You can assign a rating between 1 and 3, or between 3 and 9, if you feel that best represents your current state. If a practice does not apply in your situation, enter NA. If a practice applies but you can't qualify for the pilot level, enter zero.

When you have completed the assessment, add up and average your scores. Then look for opportunities to expand practices you have already started or try ones you haven't yet implemented.

Sustainability Coordinator/Director of Sustainability				
Practice	Pilot *1 point*	Initiative *3 points*	Systemic *9 points*	Points
Sustainability management system: Have in place a process to routinely set priorities for sustainability improvements, monitor the results and institutionalize best practices. (See related practices under Sr Mgmt and Env Affairs.)	Implement a parallel structure and process to identify and make sustainability improvements (eg a steering committee).	Implement an environmental management system (EMS) equivalent to ISO 14001.	Implement an ISO-compliant EMS with sustainability policies, criteria and targets embedded.	
Vision: Have a clear vision for how sustainability relates to your organization's mission. (See related practices under Sr Mgmt.)	Develop a business case for pursuing sustainability; obtain executive support for pursuing sustainability initiatives.	Have conducted a process to develop a clear long-term vision of sustainability and interim goals. Get support of leadership to communicate these audacious long-term goals.	Help the organization develop a long-term vision of your organization's role in a fully sustainable society. Question basic assumptions of your mission or business model and engage in long-term efforts to transform your organization and sector.	

Sustainability Coordinator/Director of Sustainability				
Practice	Pilot *1 point*	Initiative *3 points*	Systemic *9 points*	Points
Implementation plan: Develop a realistic plan for implementing sustainability in the organization.	Develop and implement a plan for a pilot-level initiative.	Develop and implement a plan to spread sustainable thinking and actions across the organization.	Develop and implement a plan to embed sustainability into the fabric of the organization and into other strategic relationships.	
Performance metrics: Develop and track a set of sustainability metrics. (See related practices under Sr Mgmt and Finance/Accounting.)	Develop and track metrics to show return on investment and other benefits of sustainability projects.	Develop a holistic set of sustainability performance metrics to track the performance of the organization.	Develop metrics and methods for tracking sustainability performance of strategic partners (eg major suppliers) and major externalities associated with the operation.	
Reporting: Regularly report on the results of sustainability efforts. (See related practices under Sr Mgmt and Finance/Accounting.)	Report to management at least annually about the benefits and costs of sustainability projects.	Report to management on progress toward sustainability performance metrics. Develop and publish an internal sustainability report.	Report to management and other stakeholders on sustainability performance via a publicly available sustainability report that shows trend data on all major impacts.	
Role shift: Evolve the role of sustainability coordinator over time so that responsibility for sustainability is spread throughout the organization.	Lead the sustainability effort.	Show senior management how to lead the sustainability effort.	Educate others outside your organization about how to lead the sustainability effort (eg through public speaking, writing, supplier site visits).	
			Total Score	
			Average	

Interpreting your score:

If your average score is	Then you are
Less than 1	Lagging: You are beginning to fall behind others who are implementing sustainable practices and should look for ways to catch up. You may need to develop a more compelling business case for pursuing sustainability. We recommend beginning with projects that make good business sense from a traditional perspective.
1–3	Learning: You have made good progress but have a lot more that you can do. Look for ways to build on your existing successes or choose projects that are timely for other reasons.
Over 3	Leading: You are out in front, blazing the trail for others. Keep innovating and share your lessons learned through speaking and writing.

Part 2

Sustainability by Industry Sector

3

Sustainability in Services and General Office Practices

Service organizations often struggle to understand how they can participate in the sustainability movement. Since they have no smokestacks coming out of their offices and they dutifully recycle their paper, they question their impact. While it's true that the direct impacts of their own operations will be miniscule in comparison to manufacturing, they need to appreciate the impacts they indirectly cause or influence through the delivery of their services and the patterns of customer behaviour they create.

WHAT YOU SHOULD KNOW ABOUT SUSTAINABILITY

Every service organization occupies a facility, uses various forms of transportation and consumes paper, which in and of themselves suggest improvement opportunities. However, many service organizations also have a production component: accountants produce reports; hotels and hospitals wash laundry; restaurants cook food; graphic artists print posters; ski resorts make snow; non-profit organizations host fund-raisers; rental car companies maintain their fleets; museums construct exhibits; and retail stores sell goods. Service organizations have products too, and sustainability opportunities can be found in all these areas.

Even if your internal practices are as sustainable as possible, it's important to consider three other areas:

1 the ripple effect of the service you offer;
2 strategic threats (to your customers, image or business model); and
3 emerging opportunities to make a positive contribution.

The ripple effect. Often, the biggest impact of a service organization is not what it does itself but how it affects the behaviour and choices of its customers. When architects design a building and specify materials, their impacts go far beyond their blueprints! Their decisions determine the fate of the energy use of the building, the health of forests used for 2×4s, the air quality the building inhabitants will breathe and water quality in surrounding streams. When bankers decide to fund a home or business, their impacts far exceed the paper the loan is printed upon. Their decisions may affect the quality of life in the community, traffic congestion, opportunities for minorities and insurance costs shared by many. When a large superstore of a major chain locates on the edge of town and provides acres of free parking, it affects driving patterns, air quality, greenhouse gas emissions and the vitality of the town centre.

Strategic threats. The second area services should consider is the impact of sustainability on matters key to their business: their customers, their images and also the foundation factors for their businesses. The insurance industry, for example, is extremely concerned about how climate change may affect its customers. Property insurers worry that global warming will bring larger and more devastating storms, causing more property damage. Life insurers are worried about the spread of diseases that used to be restricted to equatorial zones. Swiss Re, the largest reinsurance company in the US and second largest in the world, expects climate change to be the next hotbed of litigation, following asbestos and tobacco. They are taking action to protect themselves and their customers before the lawsuits begin.

In some cases, sustainability-related trends may threaten the foundation of your business. Aspen and many other ski resorts are concerned that global warming might eliminate snow from their mountain tops or at least dramatically shorten the season. Sometimes the threat may be indirect. For example, many small-town barber's shops, garages and restaurants have been ruined when logging or fishing was curtailed in their communities. Sustainability helps you to foresee these potential threats and plan for them.

Service providers should also consider the impact of sustainability on their image. In Sweden, McDonald's was embarrassed by public demonstrations over their packaging. They changed to compostable wrappers and containers and also took a look at other parts of their operation. They conducted a waste audit and realized that about 35 per cent of their refuse by weight was liquid (left-over drinks and ice) so they installed a sink next to the rubbish bin with a sign asking customers to empty their cups before throwing them out. They used the savings there to fund more efforts, such as buying organic dairy products and beef. Instead of a plastic toy, their Happy Meals come with a bag of compost and a seed, closing the loop on their organic waste stream. Leadership at McDonald's asked the question, 'Where would we concentrate our sustainability efforts if we took responsibility for changing the whole system?' and realized that their biggest opportunities were in agriculture, building practices, packaging and energy. McDonald's found that working on sustainability improved their image dramatically. Burger King tried to mimic their actions but never got the same image benefits. Being first has its advantages.

Similarly, Home Depot, the world's largest retailer of timber, was targeted by the Rainforest Action Network for selling products from old-growth forests. After some embarrassing publicity stunts, including a protester broadcasting their message over the store's public address system, Home Depot management finally got the message: it's not OK to sell wood products from old-growth forests, ecologically sensitive 'hot spots' or illegal logging operations. Since then they have been quietly researching where all their wood – from 2 × 4s to hammer handles – comes from, replacing products made from questionable sources and giving preference to Forest Stewardship Council (FSC)-certified wood.

Emerging opportunities. Rather than wait to be attacked, why not find ways to make positive contributions to society and build goodwill? For example, Prison Pet Partnership Program designed their service for maximum benefit. They get dogs from animal shelters and give them to women prisoners who then learn how to train them to be service dogs for disabled people, fetching items for someone in a wheelchair or warning an epileptic of an impending seizure. Had they designed their service any other way, Prison Pet Partnership Program would have produced fewer benefits. By design, they make valuable use of a wasted resource (unwanted dogs), create training and meaningful work for an at-risk population, provide assistance to an underserved population and protect the community with lower recidivism rates of inmates in their programme.

You don't have to be a non-profit organization to have a mission to contribute to society. Starbucks, while sometimes vilified for their proliferation of stores, is trying to create a reliable market for fair-trade, shade-grown coffee. Through Conservation International, they provide premium price, long-term contracts with responsible growers who can prove they are living up to Starbucks' sourcing guidelines. Their guidelines include environmental requirements (eg shade-grown, bird-friendly practices), social elements (eg fair labour practices) and economic expectations (eg transparency and fair pay). Starbucks are doing what they can to transform the industry while only controlling about 1 per cent of the entire coffee market:

> *Last year (2003), 13.5 million pounds of Starbucks coffee beans were sourced through the Guidelines, which is way ahead of the initial forecast of 3.5 million and has encouraged Starbucks to more than double its forecast for the coming year. Sue Mecklenburg says the company has been surprised by its success. 'We were trying to do something extremely innovative and challenging, with big risks. We were trying to change our supply chain and did not realize the impact that we could have as a pretty small player in the coffee world.'*[1]

Sometimes, these efforts can yield new revenue streams. At least one office products retail chain has found that their electronics take-back programme is an effective revenue generator, especially for their commercial customers.

STRATEGIES YOU CAN USE

So what can you do? We've organized strategies into four broad categories:

1   Clean up your own operations.
2   Manage your ripple effect.
3   Evaluate strategic threats.
4   Explore emerging opportunities.

Clean up your own operations

Typically, the impact of your own operations will be a fraction of the impacts you have outside your organization. For example, the amount of energy and materials used by an architectural firm is dwarfed by the energy and materials used in the buildings they design. However, there are two good reasons to focus first on improving your own operations:

- This is often the best way to help your employees understand what sustainability is; and
- It ensures you are 'walking the talk', not asking others to do things you aren't willing to do yourself.

There may be some actions that will save you money, but many of these actions are more important for their symbolic and educational value than for their financial value.

Facilities

Energy efficiency is the first place to look for measures that will save costs. Unfortunately, some businesses lease office space and so may not have separate electric meters. That means the savings may go first to the landlord and trickle down into the rent indirectly, if at all. If you own and operate your building, conducting an energy audit can yield significant opportunities to save money. If you lease, try to get your landlord to improve the sustainability of the building. See the chapter on facilities for more information.

Here are a few stories to help inspire your own ideas:

- A large US laboratory discovered that many of their computers and monitors were left on even when not in use, often over night. According to their information technology professionals, in their situation, it was not wise to have everyone turn off their computers, but the monitors were fair game. So they printed small reminder labels and asked people to turn off their monitors when not in use. They estimate they saved $150,000 per year in energy costs. Granted, they have a large facility with a lot of computers, but this isn't small change.

- Ashforth Pacific, a west-coast property management and construction firm in the US, implemented a 'cookies-for-trash-cans' project in which employees got cookies in exchange for agreeing to give up their individual rubbish bins and throwing all of their refuse away in a central bin. This simple project was easy for employees to participate in and saved the company 9000 plastic bin liners a year.[2]
- Progressive Investment Management focuses on socially responsible investing. When they hired a gardener to maintain their landscaping, they of course chose one known for organic methods. They were dismayed, in the spring, with their windows wide open, to find the gardener using a loud leaf-blower, belching gas fumes into their offices. They ended up agreeing to pay a little more to have the person rake instead.
- TriMet, the transit authority for Portland, Oregon, during one month of high electricity use at its rail facility posted the electricity bill in the elevator, without entreaties or comment. When employees saw how much they spent on energy, they modified their behaviour. Their electricity bill dropped by 20 per cent the next month!
- Washington Park Zoo in Oregon allows their employees to bring to work items that are difficult to recycle at home: compact fluorescent bulbs, batteries, etc. Since these items are added to the Zoo's considerable pile from their own operations, the quantities are adequate to get them easily recycled.

Technology

Related to energy use is the choice of office equipment. In the US, computers, copiers, faxes, etc. represent the third largest electrical use (after lighting and heating/cooling) in commercial buildings. Since heating, ventilation and air conditioning (HVAC) systems are used mostly for air conditioning, the impact of this equipment is multiplied because of the heat they contribute to buildings.

Mark Hamilton of Triple Point Energy Services makes the following recommendations:

- When upgrading, consider efficiency specifications as part of the purchasing policy. Does it make more sense to have a bunch of small printers or a few large multi-function machines? When does it make sense to replace cathode ray tubes with liquid crystal displays (which are much more efficient)? What is the life of the office equipment and how should that be considered in terms of the environmental footprint of the organization? Look for more energy-efficient components, in particular power supplies. Set defaults for duplex printing, sleep modes and automatic shut-down to reduce resource consumption.

- Examine your practices around end of life. Do you purchase equipment from manufacturers that take back their products, or, if you are a manufacturer, do you have a product stewardship strategy? Do you choose suppliers that have converted their products into services? If you donate usable equipment to non-profit organizations or schools, are you just passing on responsibility for end-of-life issues? Are all your components recycled or disposed of properly?

RESOURCES

The US Environmental Protection Agency has created environmentally preferable guidelines for computers. Go to www.epa.gov/oppt/epp/electronics.htm.

For power supplies, see www.80plus.org and www.efficientpowersupplies.org.

Video: 'Exporting Harm'. This 23-minute film documents the real consequences of exporting e-waste to developing countries for 'recycling'. Produced by the Basel Action Network (BAN) and Silicon Valley Toxics Coalition, the video can be ordered from BAN's website, www.ban.org.

Williams, Eric. 'Residential Computer Usage Patterns, Reuse and Life Cycle Energy Consumption in Japan' (oral presentation), 2005 ACEEE (American Council for an Energy Efficient Economy) Summer Study on Energy Efficiency in Industry, PANEL 4 – Industrial Energy Efficiency and Sustainability, www.aceee.org/conf/05ss/panel4.htm.

Paper products

The dream of a paperless office has yet to materialize. In fact, the proliferation of computers and printers has only increased the rate at which we convert trees into refuse.

Copy paper. Choosing among a wall of paper reams at an office suppliers can be a daunting task. How much recycled content is in the product? Is it pre- or post-consumer? What's the difference between elemental chlorine-free and chlorine free? Let's make this easy: from an environmental perspective, generally the higher the recycled content, the better; post-consumer is better than pre-consumer; 'process chlorine free (PCP)' is better than elemental chlorine free.

Toilet paper. You'd never imagine how uppity people can get about their toilet paper. They assume that recycled toilet paper will chafe. So when a property management firm in Portland, Oregon, decided to switch, they didn't tell anyone at first. A blissful month went by with no complaints. Then they admitted they'd switched to recycled tissue, and suddenly people complained. The moral to this story: don't ask; don't tell.

Paper towels. Certainly you can choose paper towels with a high post-consumer recycled content. You may also want to investigate the ecological trade-offs between towels and hand dryers. Progressive Investment Management decided that it was silly to use trees or electricity to dry your hands. So they provided cotton towels for their small office which one employee was willing to take home once a week to add to her laundry.

Printing. When you print fliers, booklets, posters and the like, use recycled paper and soya-based inks whenever possible. You may also want to experiment with tree-free papers. At AXIS Performance Advisors, we sent out our 2003 holiday greetings cards on paper made from kenaf (a lovely herbaceous annual in the mallow family) along with a poorly metered poem that began, 'Treeless papers may make you laugh, But this was printed on kenaf.'

RESOURCES

Conservatree provides information and sources for environmentally preferable paper, www.conservatree.com.

Break room

One of the visible places to make sustainability real to people is in the break room. Buying Energy Star appliances and eliminating disposable cups are two obvious actions. You can also purchase fair-trade, shade-grown and/or organic coffee. Leave a few old plastic containers in the cabinets for people to use for their leftovers. Provide recycling or perhaps a worm bin or compost bin for food scraps. (A worm bin produces material with more fertilization value than a compost pile and can easily be kept inside without an odour problem if properly set up. Worm bins don't need to be turned like a compost pile but do require occasional maintenance to remove the old worm castings – which can be used for your potted plants. You can toss in your used paper towels and old newspapers to provide worm bedding.)

- After a six-month planning process involving a cross-section of the organization, SERA Architects in Portland, Oregon launched their sustainability efforts by holding a briefing for all employees to discuss their vision for creating fully sustainable buildings. During the briefing, they presented their plan, educated staff on what sustainability means, recruited their involvement in their various project teams and symbolically handed each person their own set of eating utensils, bought from thrift stores, packaged in lovely carrying cases sewn from the office's outdated fabric samples.

- Norm Thompson, a US catalogue retailer, targeted the plastic coffee cups their vending machines were spewing out. They approached the vendor to get a machine that would dispense coffee into mugs instead and then issued every employee with a ceramic mug. Eliminating the disposable cups saved Norm Thompson $10,000 a year, not counting the savings in waste disposal.[3]

Take responsibility for your ripples

As we have already mentioned, a service business's largest impact often comes not from its own operations but from its impact on others. Some businesses may chose to ignore those 'externalities', but you can often differentiate yourself and build a positive image by ensuring your impacts are positive instead of negative. Negative impacts have a way of catching up on you eventually. The well-publicized example of Wal-Mart putting the fate of a new store into voters' hands in Inglewood, California and *losing* after spending $1 million on the campaign is but one example. Increasingly, the public holds you accountable not only for what you do but also for your ripple effect.

- Shorebank Pacific is a small bank based on the coast of Washington State. They were founded to fund restoration and other environmentally sound investments. Their unique mission has helped them attract deposits from all over the country. They employ a rating system adapted from The Natural Step framework to rate their loans. This rating system helps them invest in projects that will have the greatest environmental and social benefits.
- Bon Appétit runs cafeterias for a number of businesses and universities. They have staked out a niche by providing healthy food from local organic and in-season produce. They have adopted the Monterey Bay Aquarium's Seafood Watch List, only buying species that are plentiful (while over 70 per cent of the commercially harvested species are in serious decline). They boycott farmers who do not provide appropriate living conditions for migrant workers. They take good care of their employees as well, paying above-market wages and providing health benefits to all employees.
- Burgerville, a northwest fast-food chain, has committed to buying all their hamburgers from Country Natural Beef (formerly Oregon Country Beef), a cooperative of over 40 sustainable family ranches dedicated to raising cattle in harmony with nature, without the use of hormones, antibiotics, genetically modified grain or any animal by-products. This cooperative has saved a number of family farms in the area by providing a premium product. Burgerville worked with this cooperative for several years to help them increase their production so that this arrangement would be possible. Burgerville also features delicious seasonal shakes and sundaes from locally sourced, seasonal

produce. They purchase green power for all of their electricity usage in their stores between Albany and Portland, Oregon.

- Staples, the office products retailer, worked with Metafore, a non-profit organization, to support responsible forest practices. Now most of Staples' paper products boast 30 per cent or more recycled content. They participated in the Paper Working Group, a collaborative effort including 11 other companies, FedEx Kinko's, Starbucks and Time among them, to create an assessment tool for buyers and suppliers of paper. They also provide recycling services for electronics, ink cartridges and other office products.

- McDonald's recently issued notices to their suppliers, specifying a humane minimum cage size for chickens that produce their Egg McMuffins and discouraging the practice of withholding water to increase egg production. They are also addressing the profligate use of antibiotics, which are showing up in our rivers and creating super-germs resistant to treatment. Approximately 70 per cent of the antibiotics produced in the US are given to livestock, mostly to promote growth, not treat illness.[4] By setting this policy against the use of growth-promoting antibiotics, they are putting pressure on the agricultural sector to change their practices worldwide.

- Gerding/Edlen Developers in Portland, Oregon have gained national recognition for their green building efforts. They've been interviewed on Public Broadcasting, highlighted in *USA Today* and touted in a host of industry journals. How did they get all this attention? While the owners have always been interested in socially responsible business practices, the turning point was when Dennis Wilde participated in a peer learning group convened by the Oregon Natural Step Network. With the help of others in the industry, they used The Natural Step's 'backcasting' process to write a white paper describing the attributes of a fully sustainable building: creates more energy than it uses, keeps all rainwater on site, etc. On each of their own projects, Gerding/Edlen raises the bar towards this ideal. Their commitment towards innovation has paid off handsomely, not only in public recognition but also in decreased operating costs and demand for premium-priced properties.

- Ashforth Pacific, a property management firm, promotes the use of alternative transportation by its employees. It provides free bus passes, bike parking and two parking spots for their FlexCar (a membership service that charges for car use by the hour and mile). They even offer a half-day of personal time to employees who commute 80 per cent or more by alternative transportation in a month.

- Norm Thompson, a US catalogue retailer, wanted to reduce the impact of shipping products, so they started up a 'Ship All Together' programme. If a customer orders several items, one or more of which is out-of-stock but expected to be in within a week, the customer is asked if he or she is willing to wait for the items to be shipped all together. This simple change is saving them over $200,000 per year and 30,000 shipping boxes or bags, along with all the other packing materials.[5]

Evaluate strategic threats

The insurance industry makes a business out of accurately assessing risks. So it's no surprise that they are the first service industry to be taking a strong stand on global climate change. Both Munich Re (the largest reinsurance company in the world) and Swiss Re (the second largest) have been studying this issue with growing concern.

Swiss Re created a tongue-in-cheek video of men in suits embracing trees and twirling in fields. The punch line: 'Now it's really time for business and nature to fall in love.' Insurance companies are not known for their senses of humour, so what possessed them to make such a video? The answer is that they see storm clouds gathering over all their major business lines. Because climate change is expected to increase the frequency and severity of freak weather events, insurers anticipate higher damage claims. Unless they revise their rates, this will translate into less profit. Some even fear climate change may bankrupt the industry.

Climate change is also expected to facilitate the spread of disease. Diseases that have traditionally been limited to remote, tropical regions – malaria, ebola and dengue, for example – will expand as the globe warms, facilitated by international travel. The West Nile virus demonstrates how quickly diseases can spread, spanning the US in about two years. What happens to life insurance claims if people start dropping like flies from diseases against which we have little immunity? What happens when super-bacteria, created from our overuse of antibiotics, hit a population centre? Since 40 per cent of Swiss Re's business is life insurance, they need their actuarial tables to factor in these increased risks.

In addition to increased property damage and reduced life expectancy, Swiss Re is also concerned about legal risk. They see climate change as the next great corporate litigation theatre, following in the footsteps of asbestos and tobacco. Many of the companies they insure are major emitters of greenhouse gases, key targets for such lawsuits. Shareholders are restless. There has been a dramatic rise in shareholder resolutions, many of which relate to climate change, and through proxies they are voting out directors at an unprecedented rate. Swiss Re has already sent out the word: they may not protect directors from litigation if the company is not doing enough to avert global warming. Since directors can be held *personally* liable for environmental judgements, this gets their attention.

Explore emerging opportunities

Beyond merely protecting themselves from these threats, Swiss Re is also examining the potential business opportunities. They want to play a role in brokering carbon credits. At the moment, a carbon reduction project may achieve only a small return in the form of carbon credits as there is a great deal of uncertainty about the market. Will the project actually produce the CO_2 reductions as advertised? Will the project pass muster once the audit criteria are finally standardized? Swiss Re sees its role as buying up a large number of projects, thus spreading the risk across them. This should improve the liquidity and price of carbon offsets, speeding the rate at which organizations take action against climate change.

Sustainability may help you discover new markets. Economically speaking the world can be divided up into three sectors:

1   the consumer economy (1 billion people);
2   emerging markets (2 billion people); and
3   the survival economy (3 billion people).

Traditionally, business has focused predominately on the first two, ignoring half the world! This is even more noteworthy because much of the future population growth will be in this part of the world.[6]

Do not assume that serving the survival economy is unprofitable. While these people do not have a lot of cash to spend, products packaged to meet their needs can improve their lives and also provide a viable business model. Michigan Business School professor C. K. Prahalad challenged a group of business analysts to find a way to sell ice cream to India's poor at a price they could afford – 1 rupee (or about 2 cents). Of course, the analysts initially thought it couldn't be done. They soon discovered, however, that much of the cost

---

RESOURCES

Hart, Stuart L. and Mark B. Milstein (1999) 'Global Sustainability and Creative Destruction of Industries', *MIT Sloan Management Review*, Fall.

Hall, Jeremy and Harrie Vrendenburg (2003) 'The Challenges of Innovating for Sustainable Development', *MIT Sloan Management Review*, Fall.

Young, Stephen (2003) *Moral Capitalism: Reconciling Private Interest with the Public Good*. San Francisco: Berrett-Koehler.

United Nations Environmental Programme (2002) *Global Environment Outlook 3: Past, Present and Future Perspectives*. UNEP and Earthscan.

Rees, Martin (2003) *Our Final Hour: A Scientist's Warning: How Terror, Error and Environmental Disaster Threaten Humankind's Future in this Century – on Earth and Beyond*. NY: Basic Books.

Huntington, Samuel P. (1996) *The Clash of Civilizations and the Remaking of World Order*. Simon & Schuster.

Suzuki, David and Holly Dressel (2002) *Good News for a Change: Hope for a Troubled Planet*. Toronto: Stoddart Publishing.

Intergovernmental Panel on Climate Change, www.ipcc.pr.

of ice cream is from refrigeration. So they sidestepped electricity and used an innovative technology and employed dry ice instead. Now, people in India are buying scoops at 2–3 rupees and Prahalad expects the price to be down to 1 rupee soon. Similarly, Unilever has made *more* profits from selling cheaper versions of detergent to India's poor than selling the premium product to the more affluent. Aravind Eye Hospitals manages to perform 250,000 cataract operations at a cost of US$10 each and still make a 200 per cent profit. The trick is to use technology and innovation to find cheaper ways to provide the same service. 'Turning India's poor into a viable market requires a rethinking. You need to marry low cost, good quality, profitability and sustainability,' advises Prahalad.[7]

Conclusion

As you can see, the responsibilities of service organizations go far beyond recycling their paper and reducing energy use. There are a host of threats and opportunities to be considered. But service companies must look beyond the walls of their own organization to take advantage of these insights. They must both examine the potential threats to their own image and to the viability of their customer base and take into account demographic changes around the world.

SCORE SERVICES AND OFFICE PRACTICES

See page 31 for how to complete this assessment and page 33 for how to interpret your score.

INTERNAL OFFICE OPERATIONS				
Practice	Pilot *1 point*	Initiative *3 points*	Systemic *9 points*	Points
Office supplies and equipment: Minimize impacts associated with office supplies, furnishings and equipment.	Identify targeted purchasing categories and more sustainable options.	Have a system in place for routinely assessing the impacts of purchases and working on finding better options.	80% or more of office supplies and equipment come from sustainable sources (ie from a certified sustainable source, 100% post-consumer waste, recyclable, product take-back).	

INTERNAL OFFICE OPERATIONS				
Practice	Pilot *1 point*	Initiative *3 points*	Systemic *9 points*	Points
Energy: Improve energy efficiency and transition to renewables (see related practices under Facilities).	At least every 5 years, conduct an energy audit on office operations and act on the results.	Have a system in place for monitoring and communicating energy efficiency, including behavioural changes. Purchase 10% or more renewable power (or the equivalent carbon offsets).	Achieve climate neutrality for electricity, heating and cooling (eg via generating energy, purchasing 100% green power and/or purchasing carbon offsets).	
Transportation: Actively promote the reduction of climate impacts associated with transportation of people and documents/materials (see related practices under Human Resources).	Encourage alternative transportation for commuting through incentives and other means (eg paid parking, car-share). For correspondence, freight and business travel, use the lowest impact carrier that will meet the needs of the parties involved.	Offer incentives to contractors and customers to reduce fossil fuel use.	Be climate neutral for all organizational transportation and for at least 25% of commuting impacts.	
Contract services: Use contractors (banks, cleaners, landscaping, couriers, catering) that share a commitment to sustainability (see related practices under Purchasing).	Notify all major contractors/ suppliers of your commitment to sustainability.	Implement a tool for evaluating contractors on their sustainability practices. Write sustainability criteria and requirements into contract language for all contractors.	Actively influence contractors not hired directly (eg work with building owners or create collaborative purchasing programmes with building tenants).	

INTERNAL OFFICE OPERATIONS				
Practice	Pilot *1 point*	Initiative *3 points*	Systemic *9 points*	Points
Food Services: Ensure access to healthy, sustainable food and minimize waste (cafeterias, vending machines, etc.)	Use non-disposable tableware and energy-saving devices.	Label and promote the sale of healthy foods (organic produce, low-fat, etc.) Use green or sustainable cleaning products.	Only provide locally sourced, in-season, sustainable food items. All food waste is composted.	
Remodels: Employ green building principles when choosing a new site or remodelling an existing one (see related practices under Facilities).	Achieve LEED certified or equivalent.	Achieve LEED silver or equivalent.	Achieve LEED platinum or equivalent.	
			Total	
			Average	

SERVICE INDUSTRY				
Practice	Pilot *1 point*	Initiative *3 points*	Systemic *9 points*	Points
Strategy: Develop a business strategy related to sustainability that identifies your opportunities and threats.	Develop a formal business case for adopting sustainability and take initial steps to implement the insights.	Sustainability is part of formal strategic and business planning processes; sustainability is seen as an important element of the organization's competitive advantage.	Actively working to affect customers, suppliers and others in our industry to solve sustainability-related problems.	

SERVICE INDUSTRY				
Practice	Pilot *1 point*	Initiative *3 points*	Systemic *9 points*	Points
Service delivery: Embed sustainability into the core service.	Conduct a sustainability analysis of your core service and identify sustainable targets for all major impacts. Work on at least one sustainability initiative per year.	Redesign service to eliminate all major internal impacts (eg use 100% recycled paper or paper from sustainable sources).	Change the service delivery such that customers change behaviour to support sustainability.	
			Total	
			Average	

Sustainability in Manufacturing and Product Design

Several decades ago, the quality revolution hit the manufacturing sector before the others, crippling the US auto sector, whose leaders didn't see it coming, and creating an economic boom in Asia. Similarly, the sustainability movement is affecting the manufacturing sector first. The reasons are straightforward. Manufacturing often deals with hazardous chemicals, uses a lot of energy, depletes natural resources, generates tons of waste and employs factories around the globe. Usually, those most in the cross-sights, and thus prompted to be more active in the sustainability movement, are multinational corporations selling branded products to the general public (eg Nike, Toyota) or industries formerly reviled by environmentalists, whether associated with energy and fossil fuels (BP, Royal Dutch Shell), natural resources (Louisiana Pacific, the Collins Companies) or the chemical industry (Monsanto, DuPont). Just as with the quality revolution, those who got on board first have tended to benefit the most and those who wait risk losing market share.

WHAT YOU SHOULD KNOW ABOUT SUSTAINABILITY

Manufacturing companies are implementing sustainability for a variety of reasons. Here are a few of the benefits they have realized:

Uncovering innovations that provide competitive advantage. When you examine your product through the lens of sustainability, you unleash creative thinking that often results in startling innovations. C&A Floorcoverings, for example, was getting uncomfortable questions from their customers about end-of-life issues associated with carpeting, since construction waste is a significant percentage of what goes into landfills and carpeting may last 20,000 years there. When they set a goal of creating new carpet from old carpet, they had to challenge a number of long-standing assumptions in the industry. One such assumption was that to recycle commercial carpet, you needed to separate the vinyl backing from the nylon nap. When one of their operators decided to melt down and extrude the whole carpet, combining both materials, they discovered the resulting carpet performed better and, after some tinkering, actually cost less to manufacture. Now they are eager to take back used carpeting instead of having it go to the landfill.

Saving energy. Even if your organization implemented energy conservation measures half a dozen years ago, you should do it again. Technologies are changing so fast that you are undoubtedly leaving money on the shop floor. For example, BP set a goal of meeting the Kyoto Protocol in ten years and achieved that in only two years at no net expense. The energy savings they discovered are going straight to their bottom line, giving them an edge over their competitors. If an energy company had this many opportunities to conserve, you have to wonder about the rest of us!

Improving product reliability. Philips Microelectronics designs a 'flagship' green product in every product category. While trying to decide how to eliminate fire retardants (which are accumulating in human body tissue) in TV housings, they discovered a simple way to eliminate the hot spots in the unit. Since heat is the major cause of electronic failure, they simultaneously improved the life span of their products.

Reducing hazardous materials. The use of toxic materials costs you more than you probably realize. Unless you have an activity-based cost accounting model, you may have never added up all the costs associated with training, spill response, special equipment, permits, disposal fees, community outreach, health-related expenses and insurance costs. Eliminating a toxic material can save you money in many budget line items.

Eliminating waste. A number of organizations have achieved the goal of zero waste to landfill, so don't need dumpsters (or skips, to use the British term). Even more have at least reduced their waste by 90 per cent. While all processes have some residual by-products, that doesn't mean the resulting material is necessarily waste. An Epson plant in Hillsboro, Oregon diverted all of their waste from landfill and saved about $300,000 in the first year. As a manager of an electronics manufacturer once said, 'If you haven't found someone to take all your waste, you're not trying hard enough.' In some cases, the recipients will pay for the material as well as removing it, turning a waste stream into a revenue stream.

Manufacturers also pursue sustainability to manage their risks. Here are some examples of situations that could have been avoided had the manufacturer been more aware of sustainability and its implications:

Losing a customer. Electrolux, the largest white goods manufacturer in the world, became interested in sustainability and The Natural Step framework only after having a major customer tell them they would not buy Electrolux's refrigeration units because they used ozone-depleting CFCs (Freon). When Electrolux said they had solved that problem by switching to HCFCs, the customer informed them that replacing one persistent chemical with another was not a long-term solution.

Bad press. Nike was raked over the coals by the media for their international labour practices. Nike don't manufacture anything themselves – they use suppliers, mostly in Asia, to manufacture shoes and clothing. They had assumed that they were not responsible for the practices of their suppliers. The public disagreed. After stories about worker abuses hit the papers, Nike's image took a dive. This experience drove them to wonder what other issues might catch them off guard. Sarah Severn, director of corporate responsibility, decided that the environmental arm of sustainability could be their next public relations debacle unless they did more.

Shut out of large markets. Sony experienced an expensive embarrassment in 2001 when, just in time for the holiday season, The Netherlands banned Sony Playstations because their cables contained too much cadmium, causing a media uproar and earning Sony a hefty fine. But their biggest problem was one of corporate image: do you want to buy your child a toxic toy for Christmas? The European Union in particular is passing more and more legislation about toxics in products. (See, for example, the Restriction of Hazardous Substances (RoHS) Directive and the Registration, Evaluation and Authorisation of Chemicals (REACH) Directive, which switches the burden of proof regarding the safety of a chemical on to the manufacturer.)

Harassment by an NGO. In 1995 Royal Dutch Shell became the focus of international controversy for their plan to scuttle the Brent Spar platform, an oil storage platform in the North Sea. Even though the plan had been carefully developed by scientists to minimize environmental impacts and all the appropriate ministries had approved the plan, Greenpeace staged a made-for-TV protest. The intensity of the public reaction stunned Shell executives. In Germany, the sales at some Shell petrol stations dropped by 50 per cent. Phil Watts, Shell Group's regional coordinator in Europe at the time, called this 'a life-changing experience in business terms'. Even though Greenpeace later acknowledged that their statements about the toxicity of the platform were inaccurate, his 'awareness level on the broader, softer issues went up by a factor of 10 to 100'. The experience left a lasting impression on Shell employees. '[It was] like being in a plane crash,' said Watts.[1]

Pressured by customers. It's not just the large multinationals that are being affected – the shock waves cascade down the supply chain. Royal Philips Electronics recently extended their own sustainability principles to their 50,000 suppliers. This goes far beyond just expecting them to have an environmental management system, something many manufacturers already expect of their vendors. Their criteria include minimum expectations on the environment, health and safety, and labour issues. 'Adhering to these minimum requirements will be an important factor in the company's decisions to enter into or remain in business relationships. In 2004, a self-assessment tool and audit methodology will be introduced to Philips' suppliers.'[2]

Proliferation of regulations. E-waste is a current battleground. Certain countries and US states are banning electronics, especially monitors and batteries, from landfills because of the high levels of hazardous materials, in particular heavy metals, which could leach into groundwater. Several US states are already considering imposing 'take-back' legislation similar to regulations in place in Europe to force manufacturers to take responsibility for their products at the end of their useful life. But in the US, manufacturers have not been able to reach a consensus on a product stewardship strategy. Until they do, or until the government imposes a solution, recycling seems like a logical response. In the interim, most of the equipment is sent to China, where environmental protection is nil. There, they burn off the plastic, generating dioxin, and let toxic sludge flow into their rivers. All this was documented in a damning video, 'Exporting Harm: The High-tech Trashing of Asia'.

Losing insurance coverage. Similarly, the issue of greenhouse gases and global climate change is generating attention. Even before the Kyoto Protocol was ratified, insurance companies and regulators were worrying about the risks. Swiss Re, the largest property and life insurance reinsurer in the US (and second largest worldwide) considers climate change the next big litigation risk, following asbestos and tobacco. They worry not only about property damage from weather events but also possible disease outbreaks associated with climate change. To manage their own risks, they are targeting the energy industry and large emitters of greenhouse gases:

> *Company executives could find themselves losing protection against climate change-related liability claims brought by shareholders. Swiss Re has announced it will withdraw coverage against such claims for senior executives of companies that fail to adopt adequate climate change policies.*[3]

Being sued. When the wells ran dry in Kerala, India, citizens were quick to blame Coca Cola's recently opened bottling plant for misuse of water resources. While lower courts have sided with the company, the case is still working its way through the appeals process. The incident led Coca Cola to do some soul-searching. 'We realize that the world's operating environment is much smaller than it used to be. With today's communication technology, everything you do is known all over the world very quickly,' says Perry Cutshall, director of operations, global public affairs.[4]

STRATEGIES YOU CAN USE

As you can see, there are a host of sustainability-related issues affecting the manufacturing sector. To counteract these threats and take advantage of the opportunities, industry is pursuing a number of practices that we have loosely organized into two categories: product design and operations.

Product design

Most of the impacts of a product are determined in its design. A Ford Explorer will never get the same mileage as a hybrid Toyota Prius, no matter how carefully the owner drives or maintains the vehicle. So it comes as no surprise that most of the strategies for producing sustainable products are related to design.

Design for environment

Design for environment (DfE) is a set of practices that strive to reduce the environmental impacts of a product in its production as well as in its end use. It includes, at the front end, choosing materials with the lowest impact to achieve a certain outcome. This may include considering such factors as recycled content, recyclability, embodied energy (how much energy it took to create the material), more abundant materials (especially metals), toxicity and harvesting practices (as in the case of natural resources that have been certified as sustainable). Some designers try to 'demassify' a product, ie to get the same results using less material in order to reduce both the pressure on natural resources and costs associated with shipping. They consider ways to eliminate the use of persistent or toxic chemicals such as fire retardants, wood preservatives and industrial solvents.

Sustainable designers are not daunted by what at first appears to be a price premium for greener alternatives. For example, Nike discovered that while water-based cleaning solvents cost more per gallon to buy, they didn't evaporate as quickly as petroleum-based ones. The water-based ones ended up costing less when functionality was considered.

DfE also considers the efficiency and eco-effectiveness of the manufacturing process. How much energy is required? How can we use waste heat? Can water be reused? Are the most benign chemicals being used? How much of the raw material actually ends up in the end-product?

And last, DfE considers waste not only in the manufacturing process but also to some extent in what happens at the end of the product's useful life. Can production by-products (also known as waste) be sold as an input to some other manufacturing process? Are all the plastic parts labelled and is each part made from only one type of plastic so that it can be recycled? Can the products be easily disassembled? Often, designing for disassembly speeds the manufacturing process because it makes the product easier to make as well as take apart.

Philips, the Dutch electronics giant, which manufactures TVs, CDs, DVDs and a host of other alphabet-soup electronics, has pioneered DfE practices. They choose a 'green flagship' product in each product category and seek to maximize the environmental features of the product. This practice usually not only produces a product that can be marketed on its environmental benefits but almost always uncovers insights and innovations that can be applied across the product line.

For example, as we mentioned before, Philips wanted to find a way to eliminate the fire retardants in their TV housings, since these chemicals have been found to be endocrine disruptors, mimicking hormones. The fire retardants are there to prevent the TV set from combusting. Philips designers asked themselves why TV sets caught fire at such relatively low temperatures. They discovered that their units had 'hot spots'. Just as the logs in your fireplace flare when you push them together and the flames die down when you separate them, Philips rearranged the components in their TVs to reduce the hot spots. Since heat is a primary cause of failure of electronic components, this strategy also improved the quality and longevity of their products.

Aveda, a manufacturer of natural personal care products, provides designers with a list of guiding questions. Notice the bookend questions:

- Do we need it? Can we do without it?
- Can we borrow, rent or get it gently used?
- Is the project designed to minimize waste? Can it be smaller, lighter, or made from fewer materials?
- Is it designed to be durable or multi-functional?
- Is it available in a less toxic form? Can it be made with less toxic materials?
- Does it use renewable resources?
- Is reuse practical and encouraged?
- Is the product and/or packaging refillable, recyclable or repairable?
- Is it made with post-consumer recycled or reclaimed materials? How much?
- Is it available from a socially and environmentally responsible company?
- Is it made locally?
- Do we need it? Can we live without it?[5]

RESOURCES

Lewis, Helen and John Gertsakis (2001). *Design + Environment*. Sheffield: Greenleaf Publishing.
US EPA website, www.epa.gov/dfe.
Design for Environment Guide published by the Minnesota Office of Environmental Assistance, www.moea.state.mn.us.
The Ecodesign Section of the Industrial Designers Society of America has produced Okala, a tool for assessing the impacts of various materials. Visit the ISDA website for a White Paper on the curriculum, www.idsa.org/webmodules/articles/anmviewer.asp?a=516.
White, Philip (ed.) *Business Ecodesign Tools: Ecodesign Methods for Industrial Designers*. Industrial Designers. Society of America Environmental Responsibility Section, www.idsa.org/whatsnew/sections/ecosection/pdfs/IDSA_Business_Ecodesign_Tools.
Hannover Principles, www.virginia.edu/~arch/pub/hannover_list.html.
Fuad-Luke, Alastair (2002) *EcoDesign: The Sourcebook*. San Francisco, CA.

This list provides a way to choose between options. Often, trade-offs must be made between one criterion and another. However, a list like this does prompt designers to look beyond their existing set of suppliers for more responsibly produced materials.

Life cycle assessment and life cycle costing

Life cycle assessment (LCA) is a process of examining the impacts of a product over its entire lifetime: Where do the raw materials come from? How are they transported? How is the product manufactured? How is the product transported and sold to a customer? How does the customer use the product? What happens at the end of its useful life? LCA quantifies the environmental impacts at each step in this life cycle. You can use LCA to design products so that they have the least negative environmental and social impacts.

Doing a full-blown LCA can be a daunting and complicated process, fraught with embedded assumptions, and unfortunately the results are often not easily transferable from place to place because the energy, transportation and use profile may differ greatly from country to country. If you hope to make public claims that your product is environmentally better than a competitor's, such a thorough analysis may be necessary. However, a more cursory analysis can still yield useful insights.

Electrolux, after solving their customer challenge mentioned at the beginning of the chapter, began to wonder what they should do to improve the environmental performance of their other products. When they examined their washing machines, they asked, where is the biggest impact of this product? Is it in the manufacture, use or disposal? Based on their analysis, they discovered that most of the impact was in the use of the product, the many years of laundry loads, using 40 gallons or so of water, and often energy-intensive hot water, a time.

So they developed new, now common, front-load washers that use a fraction of the water needed by traditional machines. This new design also reduced energy use and lengthened the lifetime of the clothes being laundered. The innovation gave them early access to the burgeoning Chinese market. And over the past several years, their environmentally preferable products have been making up a larger and larger percentage of sales, and with higher profit margins than their traditional lines.

Related to LCA is life cycle costing (LCC), examining the costs (as opposed to the environmental impacts) over the life cycle of a product: from research and development and manufacturing to maintenance and disposal. Similar to activity-based costing, LCC helps you get a clearer picture of the true costs of several product options. Through LCC, it becomes clear that the cheapest first cost is often not the cheapest in the long term. LCC allows you to take into account such factors as the longevity of the product, associated safety precautions and disposal costs.

For example, vinyl flooring is usually one of the cheapest first-cost flooring options. However, many other flooring options last longer, avoiding the cost of buying more flooring and the associated installation. Over the lifetime of the floor, in other words, vinyl is often not the best choice.

LCC can help you determine the best overall return between options in capital projects. For example, most of the cost of a building is in its operation, not its construction, so LCC can help you determine which environmental features make financial sense over the long term, even if they add up-front costs. LCC can also help you work out which of your product lines is really most profitable. Once you factor in training, safety equipment, hazardous waste permits and disposal costs, a product you thought was profitable might turn out not to be.

LCA and LCC can be combined to help you sell your products: you can emphasize the life cycle benefits of your products over those of competitors which may initially cost less (see the Finance and Accounting chapter for more information).

RESOURCES

Schenck, Rita (2000) *LCA for Mere Mortals.* Vashon, WA: Institute for Environmental Research and Education, www.iere.org/mortals.html.

'Life Cycle Assessment, Integrated Environmental Management, Information Series 9' (2004). Pretoria: Department of Environmental Affairs and Tourism (DEAT), www.environment.gov.za/Documents/Publications/2005Jan7/Book4.pdf.

American Center for LCA, www.aclca.org.

Sustainable Assessment Model developed by BP, Genesis Oil and Gas Consultants, and the University of Aberdeen is a tool for life cycle or full-cost accounting, calculating the social and environmental costs and benefits of different scenarios, www.abdn.ac.uk/oilgas/research/man3.shtml.

Building for Environmental and Economic Sustainability (BEES) is a software tool to help you select environmentally preferable building products, www.epa.gov/oppt/epp/tools/bees.htm and www.bfrl.nist.gov/oae/software/bees.html.

'The Ecoindicator 95 – Weighting Method for Environmental Effects that Damage Ecosystems or Human Health on European Scale' (1996), NOH report 9523, The Netherlands.

Sustainable Products Purchasing Coalition, www.sppcoalition.org/.

ISO 14040, www.iso.org.

The Ecodesign Section of the Industrial Designers Society of America has produced Okala, a tool for assessing the impacts of various materials. Visit the ISDA website for a White Paper on the curriculum: http://new.idsa.org/webmodules/articles/anmviewer.asp?a=516.

Grey lists, black lists and supply chain management

A number of countries and customers are publishing grey lists (of chemicals that they want phased out) and black lists (of chemicals they will not permit in their products). This is where Sony ran into conflict with the European Union by having too much cadmium in certain components of its Playstation. Of course, to know what is in your product, you must also know what is in the components, dyes and other inputs that you purchase from suppliers. And if you *make* a product such as PVC plastic that is commonly being listed, you have a major business threat.

What gets a chemical on to one of these lists? Usually it possesses, or its manufacture creates as a by-product with, one or more of the following attributes:

- carcinogen – causes cancer;
- teratogen – causes birth defects;
- endocrine disruptor – mimics hormones (often also a teratogen);
- mutagen – causes mutations of genetic code, thus passing on the problem to future generations;
- persistent bioaccumulative toxin (PBT) – A chemical that is not easily broken down by biological processes which accumulates in body tissue.

William McDonough and Michael Braungart worked with a Swiss textile mill, Rohner, to produce upholstery for DesignTex furniture products. They collaborated to create a high-fashion fabric that was created and dyed with a limited array of chemicals. Rohner had been informed by Swiss authorities that the trimmings from the factory were now classified as hazardous waste and that the closest waste disposal site was in Spain. McDonough and Braungart examined the roughly 1600 dyes in use, eliminating those that caused cancer or other health problems, and identified 16 that were safe. From these 16 chemicals, they could make virtually any colour at a competitive price. They designed a new fabric made

RESOURCES

Forging New Links: Enhancing Supply Chain Value through Environmental Excellence, published by the Global Environmental Management Initiative, www.gemi.org.

McDonough, William and Michael Braungart (2002) *Cradle to Cradle: Remaking the Way We Make Things.* NY: North Point Press.

The Zero Waste Alliance has developed a software system called CARS which can compare chemicals using multiple lists to rank them based on their environmental impacts (eg as carcinogens, PBTs or ozone depleters), www.zerowaste.org.

from benign inputs that performed better than the traditional fabrics, was biodegradable and won them design awards. The waste trimmings can now be converted into mulch and weed fabric, a new product line. When the inspectors came to check their factory, they thought their equipment was broken – the water leaving the factory was as clean or cleaner than the water coming in! The process of making fabric was actually filtering the water. As William McDonough says, 'Here, the filters of the future will be in our heads, not on the ends of pipes. They will be intelligence filters.'[6]

Green chemistry

Closely related to grey lists and black lists is the emerging field of green chemistry. Whenever you produce something, you create not only a product but also unintended by-products. Until recently, chemists never concerned themselves with how toxic these by-products were. This led to odd ironies such as pharmaceutical companies making carcinogens and other toxic by-products in the process of producing medicines, potentially making us sick while they make us well.

Environmental risk has long been seen to be a function of the hazard as well as exposure:

Risk = Hazard × Exposure

To manage the risk, most effort to date has been put into reducing or eliminating exposure: protective clothing, scrubbers, filters, warning labels, training, etc. Green chemistry, on the other hand, addresses the hazard portion of the equation. Even with our best efforts, accidents happen. According to the Toxics Release Inventory (which only covers about 650 chemicals out of the 80,000–100,000 we produce and only larger emitters operating in the US), we released 6.16 billion pounds of these chemicals in 2001, 45 per cent of this contributed by the mining industry.[7]

The costs of managing environmental and health risks through regulations and compliance are enormous. In 1996 DuPont's environmental compliance budget equalled that for research and development! Together these two items represented 41 per cent of chemical sales revenues. But managers are often blind to these costs because they are usually buried in different accounting line items – training, permitting, protective gear, insurance, health costs, paperwork, fines, legal fees, etc. – instead of being linked directly to specific products or production lines.

The old response – the solution to pollution is dilution – doesn't work when the chemicals are persistent and bioaccumulative. Studies around the world confirm that people of all nations are carrying a 'body burden' of hundreds of synthetic chemicals – wood preservatives, industrial solvents, pesticides, fire retardants – and that these are being passed on to our children via, among other things, breast milk. So we are warned against eating certain types of fish because of the high levels of mercury. Where is the mercury coming from? Mostly from coal-burning power plants. Entropy happens. Everything spreads.

Green chemists recognize that the best way to control these emissions is to not make them in the first place. And often changing the production process yields other benefits. For example the BHC Company (Boots, Hoechst-Celanese) in Bishop, Texas, applied green chemistry principles to the manufacture of ibuprofen, a common painkiller. The old 'stoichiometric' process took six steps and roughly 60 per cent of what was created was by-product, not ibuprofen. They switched to a process using a catalyst that can be recovered and reused after the chemical reactions. This green chemistry process took only three steps (versus six) and 99 per cent of what is created is either product (80 per cent, twice as much as before), recovered catalyst (which can be used again to make more ibuprofen) or a by-product, acetic acid, which is the dominant ingredient in vinegar.[8]

RESOURCES

The University of Oregon specializes in green chemistry, www.uoregon.edu/~hutchlab/greenchem/.

Green Chemistry Institute, www.lanl.gov/greenchemistry.

US EPA website, www.epa.gov/opptintr/greenchemistry/.

The Toxics Network has information on various chemicals, www.oztoxics.org.

Converting products to services

One of the reasons our manufacturing processes are so problematic is that the incentives are wrong. If you view yourself as a product company, then the way to make more money is to sell more products, regardless of how hazardous such products may be. Functional obsolescence is the key to profitability. The sooner the customer throws it away and needs a new one, the better.

However, some progressive companies are seeing a better business model, both for themselves and for the environment. The answer is sometimes to convert a product into a service. Usually the customer doesn't really want to *own* the product; instead they want the service it provides. I don't want a drill bit; I want holes.

In a business-to-business situation, a number of organizations are using service contracts where they align their own interests with those of their supplier. This is most commonly used in resource management and haulage contracts or in purchases of toxic chemicals (paints, cleaning products, etc.). DuPont, for example, has changed its relationships with auto companies. They used to sell car paint, and thus were rewarded the more they sold. Now they are selling the service of painting cars. The car maker specifies the level of quality and the price they are willing to pay; DuPont operates a paint shop on the car maker's own factory floor. The car maker never has to take possession of the paint, which means they don't bear the responsibility for storing, handling, clean-up or disposal. And DuPont is now rewarded for conserving the amount of paint used, as long as quality levels are maintained.

In a business-to-customer situation, Interface, one of the largest makers of commercial carpet tiles, offers the Evergreen Lease programme. Customers don't buy carpet but lease it. Interface monitors the carpet, removing tiles as they show wear. The customer benefits by saving the initial capital investment, converting it instead to an expense item. Interface benefits because they level out their revenues across the boom-and-bust construction cycles. They turn the old carpet into new carpet, saving on raw material costs, and they maintain a long-term relationship with their customer.

RESOURCES

'Servicizing: The Quiet Transition to Extended Product Responsibility' by Mark Stoughton, www.epa.gov/nrmrl/std/mtb/pdf/stoughton.pdf.
Anderson, Ray C. (1999) *Mid-Course Correction: Toward a Sustainable Enterprise.* Chelsea Green Publishers.

Biomimicry

If you compare humans' approach to making things to that of nature, nature is far more elegant and efficient. Engineers have long talked in terms of three processes: heat, beat and treat. In comparison to nature, our approach to manufacturing typically consumes huge amounts of energy and results in piles of toxic waste.

Nature cannot be so profligate. It can't harness 'ancient sunlight', as fossil fuels are sometimes called, and nature is careful not to foul its own nest.

Biomimicry, using nature as an inspiration for design, can yield surprising insights. Most of what we want to do nature also does, only better: compute, colour, cleanse, build, fortify, and so on. Spiders' webs are stronger than Kevlar, and more flexible. Mussels create a glue that works under water and then biodegrades. Geckos can adhere to glass. Slugs create their own highway over rough terrain. Janine Benyus, the biologist who coined the term 'biomimicry', does not envision industrial slug farms or spider factories. Instead, she and other 'biomimics' learn from nature's ingenuity to inspire their own designs.

Much of this research is years away from saleable products, but one of the more promising lessons comes from the lotus plant. How does it manage to keep its leaves so clean that it has become the symbol of purity? The answer is not by being smooth but, surprisingly, by being rough, so that water droplets form and pull down any dust or pollen. Coming soon to a store near you: exterior paint that sheds dirt; cars you don't have to wash.

Benyus provides the following advice: invite a biologist to your design meetings and ask him or her to consider what in nature has the same problem and how does that organism solve the problem? We should ask: how does nature do this? How would nature want us to do this?

RESOURCES

Benyus, Janine M. (1997) *Biomimicry: Innovation Inspired by Nature*. NY: Wm Morrow.

Operations

While much of a product's impact is decided during design, everyday operational decisions also have an impact. Here are some of the most common strategies to improve your sustainability performance.

Energy and greenhouse gases

A few years ago, we were asked by the Oregon Department of Energy and the Portland Office of Sustainable Development to do research on resource efficiency strategies for certain manufacturing sectors. We interviewed many local plant managers and engineers. We were shocked to find that many did not understand the connection between energy use and greenhouse gases. When asked about carbon dioxide (CO_2) emissions and greenhouse gases, the interviewees often said they had none. It was as if they expected to find a tank out back with CO_2 written on the side. So let's get this straight, if you don't already understand: if you use energy made from oil, natural gas or coal, you emit greenhouse gases, indirectly perhaps, but it still counts.

Your process may also directly create CO_2 (as in the manufacture of cement), or you may emit methane, which is 21 times more powerful as a greenhouse gas per molecule, through anaerobic processes (cows, rice paddies, landfills and forest practices that increase the population of termites). Then there are designer, man-made greenhouse gases such as perfluorocarbons, mostly from aluminium smelting, and sulphur hexafluoride (SF_6), used in utility switchgear and substations and, for a while, Nike Air Jordans.

The Kyoto Protocol lists six greenhouse gases and the Intergovernmental Panel on Climate Change has assigned each a factor to make their molecules equivalent to CO_2:

- carbon dioxide (CO_2);
- methane (CH_4; 21 times CO_2);
- nitrous oxide (N_2O; 310 times CO_2);
- hydrofluorocarbons (HFCs; 1300 times CO_2);
- perfluorocarbons (PFCs; 6500 times CO_2); and
- sulphur hexafluoride (SF_6; 23,900 times CO_2).

For most, however, your biggest climate contribution is likely to be energy: transportation, space heating and cooling, and energy related to producing your products. Of course, every organization is convinced that they are extremely lean and mean. Most carried out energy efficiency measures back in the 1970s and 1980s and now assume that they've already achieved all the efficiencies they can.

Dow's experience would suggest otherwise. In 1982 their Louisiana Division started a contest to find energy-saving projects with a high rate of return. In the first year, 27 winners, with projects requiring capital expenditures of $1.7 million, provided an average annual rate of return of 173 per cent. For the next six years, during a period of declining fuel prices, the ideas kept rolling in and, by 1988, productivity gains from the ideas were exceeding the environmental gains. After ten years and over 700 project winners, one might think all the best ideas had been tapped, but the contests in 1991–1993 yielded over 100 ideas per year with an average return on investment of 300 per cent, saving Dow over $75 million a year just for the projects in those years.[9] Over the years, employees became increasingly sophisticated in their ability to identify and fix inefficiencies.

You'd think at least an energy company would be wise enough not to waste energy. In the past few years, during which BP formally changed their name to no longer stand for British Petroleum, and also branded themselves 'Beyond Petroleum', they set a goal of becoming Kyoto compliant, meeting the goals of the international climate change agreement for reductions in greenhouse gas emissions. They gave themselves ten years, but reported having achieved the goal in only two years *at no net cost* to the company. The ease with which they met the Kyoto goals shows how unnecessarily wasteful their practices had been in the past. They achieved their target by creating an internal carbon trading system similar to that proposed in the Kyoto Protocol.

Sometimes you can not only save money by eliminating inefficiencies, you can also tap into new funding sources. For example, the Gerding/Edlen Development Company in Portland, Oregon is developing a number of blocks in an old industrial district. Passionate about the environment, they invested in extra green features in their Brewery Block project. The extra construction costs they incurred for green design were around $600,000–700,000, but this was offset *twice over* by grants, technical assistance and tax credits.[10] Now they benefit from the reduced operations and maintenance costs.

Some of the funding may be linked to energy so, in the US, check out both the Environmental Protection Agency and your state energy department; elsewhere similar grants are almost certainly available. Other sources may come from the developing market in carbon credits and carbon offsets. Even without the ratification of the Kyoto Protocol, these markets are developing, for example in Australia, the European Union and in Chicago. If you have a project that can be audited to show a significant reduction in greenhouse gases (eg through energy reduction or carbon sequestration), you may be able to sell carbon credits, usually to a middleman/broker such as Natsource or The Climate Trust or through one of the emerging regional or national exchanges. Other organizations may then purchase these carbon offsets, often as a way of hedging against the eventual ratification of the Kyoto Protocol or other regulatory mechanisms such as carbon taxes.

RESOURCES

Aston, A. and B. Helm (2005) 'The Race Against Climate Change', *Business Week*, 12 December, pp59–66. Also see case studies at www.businessweek.com/go/carbon.

Romm, Joseph J. (1999) *Cool Companies: How the Best Businesses Boost Profits and Productivity by Cutting Greenhouse Gas Emissions.* Washington DC: Island Press.

The Intergovernmental Panel on Climate Change is the UN body coordinating research on climate change. Their summary papers on the scientific consensus, likely impacts and possible mitigation measures can be downloaded from their website, www.ipcc.ch.

The Greenhouse Gas Protocol is the emerging standard for reporting on greenhouse gas emissions. Go to www.ghgprotocol.org.

Collaborate with the supply chain

Managing your supply chain has become increasingly important as a business strategy, not only to reduce environmental impacts but also to manage costs and uncertainty. In 'The Supply-Chain Management Effect' Kopczak and Johnson identify six different shifts in thinking in supply chain management, all of which imply or require collaboration across organizational boundaries:

1 from functional integration to cross-enterprise integration (ie outside your own organization);
2 from physical efficiency to market mediation (eg matching market demand with supply);
3 from supply focus to demand focus;

4   from single-company product design to collaborative, concurrent design;
5   from cost reduction to breakthrough business models (eg Dell, IKEA); and
6   from mass market to tailored offerings.[11]

Because manufacturers are now being asked about and held responsible for what is in their product, many organizations are trying to 'green' their supply chain. Sometimes this takes the form of sending questionnaires to suppliers or switching to more environmentally preferable vendors. Some organizations require first-tier suppliers to have an environmental management system or to be ISO 14000 certified. These actions help a business understand what risks they are assuming when they buy components. Furthermore, in this age of just-in-time manufacturing and sole-sourcing, these actions help build confidence that the suppliers have robust management systems to prevent environmental disasters which could disrupt the supply chain and reflect poorly on their own company.

One of the most powerful and profitable practices is often overlooked: sitting down face to face to explore opportunities to improve the overall supply chain process to address quality, environmental or other concerns. According to a study done by Business for Social Responsibility, waste and inefficiencies across organizational boundaries can be staggering: inefficiencies across the supply chain can waste up to 25 per cent of a company's operating costs and a 5 per cent reduction in waste throughout the supply chain can double a typical company's profit margin.[12]

General Motors, for example, discovered that by requiring their supplier of ignition sets to manufacture different versions for different cars, they inadvertently had added significant costs for themselves and their supplier.

You don't have to be a large corporation to initiate or benefit from supply chain changes. NACHI Technology in Greenwood, Indiana manufactures ball bearings for the automotive industry. Though tiny by comparison, with only 115 employees, they approached GM about greening the supply chain. They eventually focused on making changes in their packaging. It took some convincing and some testing, but eventually they were able to get GM to agree to a smaller, standardized pallet size (so they could use the pallets they got from their own vendors) and reusable shipping containers. This has saved them about $55,000 per year.

Product certification

A number of third-party certification systems intended to give purchasers certain assurances about the products they buy are being developed for natural-resource-based products. These may include aspects of both the product itself and the way it is manufactured or harvested. Some even take into account the social impacts of the

---

RESOURCES

'Forging New Links: Enhancing Supply Chain Value through Environmental Excellence', Global Environmental Management Initiative (GEMI).

The Pollution Prevention Resource Center provides an overview of the topic as well as links to resources, www.pprc.org/pubs/topics/grnchain/index.html.

Hitchcock, Darcy (2004) *Partnering with Vendors: Supplier Workshops for Mutual Gain.* Portland, OR: AXIS Performance Advisors. Part of the Sustainability Series™, www.axisperformance.com.

'Suppliers' Perspectives on Greening the Supply Chain', Business for Social Responsibility, www.bsr.org.

'The Lean and Green Supply Chain', US Environmental Protection Agency, www.epa.gov/wastewise.

Going Green, Upstream: The Promise of Supply Chain Environmental Management (2001), Washington DC: National Environmental Education and Training Foundation (NEETF), www.neetf.org.

---

operation on the surrounding communities. In agriculture, 'organic' has been defined by the US Department of Agriculture, but other labelling systems exist such as that of the Food Alliance, which allows some pesticide use but emphasizes social and other factors. Green Seal certifies a wide range of mostly household products – cleaners, showerheads and paper towels – and also alternative fuel vehicles. They also have programmes for government and the hospitality industry. Wood products may be certified, most commonly by the Forest Stewardship Council or the Sustainable Forest Initiative. Similar schemes are emerging for fisheries and other natural resources. The construction industry has LEED, which stipulates tiers of building performance.

If you are in a natural-resource-intensive industry, you will need to evaluate the relevant certification options for your products. Typically, the costs associated with third-party certifications can be high. Maintaining a chain of custody can be complicated if your business is not vertically integrated (eg if you don't grow and process your own trees). But the absence of certification may lock you out of certain markets, especially in the European Union or certain Asian countries (Japan, for example).

Non-governmental organizations have been targeting the major retailers of certain products. For example, the Rainforest Alliance targeted Home Depot, which sells a large percentage of timber in the US. Once educated about the issues (the hard way), Home Depot made a commitment to give preference to certified wood products. At the time, they had trouble finding an adequate supply. Still, very quietly, without waving a green flag in front of customers or giving them green options, they have been identifying the source of all their wood (from 2×4s to hammer handles) and taking off the shelves products with wood from illegal, ecologically sensitive or over-harvested sources. It is actions like these that led the infamous Indonesian timber giant, Sumalindo Lestari Jaya, known for it rapacious forest practices and devastating impacts on indigenous peoples, to partner The Nature Conservancy for fear they would lose out entirely on US and European markets.[13]

If you are not in a natural-resource-intensive industry, you can still purchase certified products. While they may cost more, this not only builds the market for the certified products but may also provide you with opportunities for new, higher margin profit lines. For example, Neil Kelly Company, a design/build firm specializing in residential remodels in Portland, Oregon, got virtually all their income locally. When they started looking into sustainability and networking with other companies with the same interest, they developed a line of sustainable furniture using wood from the Collins Company, the first timber company in the US to have all their forests certified. Today, in addition to their local remodelling business, they sell furniture to customers across the country, giving them access to a market they could never have tapped under their traditional business model.[14]

RESOURCES

General information can be found at the Consumer Reports eco-label website, www.eco-label.org/home.cfm.

See Appendix B for common certification schemes in use around the world.

Zero waste

Nature operates on the principle that the waste of one organism becomes food for another. The industrial revolution was built on quite a different, linear model, what Paul Hawken and others have referred to as Take–Make–Waste. Manufacturers were not expected to consider what happened to a product after its useful life. That was an externality, a cost imposed on municipalities and their citizens. But all that is changing.

Zero waste strives to eliminate all forms of waste in an organization. Like the 'zero defect' policies of the quality movement, this bold goal drives radical innovation and improvement in efficiencies. Zero waste does not mean that you produce no by-products; instead it implies that you think of waste as a resource and find markets for all your residual products. Some people use the term 'zero waste to landfill', which helps to make this distinction, but this term only relates to solid waste and does not look at other forms of waste (eg air emissions, energy). Any manufacturing process is likely to have by-products that are not needed in the process. Zero waste simply means that none of those by-products go to waste.

If you have any waste, then you are also wasting money. This isn't just bad for nature; it's bad for your bottom line! Remember, waste is something you paid for and then were not able to sell. One study of 'material throughput' in US manufacturing discovered that only 6 per cent of the cumulative inputs ended up in the final product! The remaining 94 per cent generated in the extraction, manufacture and transportation can be thought of as waste.[15] In addition, waste costs you even more because you often have to pay to dispose of it or pay for permits to emit it. As the Grassroots Recycling Network likes to quip, 'If you're not for zero waste, how much waste are you for?'

So how do you really eliminate the concept of waste? Is it possible to get to zero waste? To some degree it may depend on how you define 'zero waste'. The Grassroots Recycling Network lists organizations that have eliminated 90 per cent or more of their waste streams. As an example they cite Hewlett Packard in Roseville, California, which reduced its waste by 95 per cent and saved $870,564 in 1998. One action that contributed to this savings was switching from pallets to reusable slip-sheets to transport products.

Certainly zero waste to landfill is easier to achieve than zero waste in everything. Imagine no skips. In 2000 Epson in Portland, Oregon reduced its waste to landfill to zero and saved over $300,000 in the first year (through avoided disposal fees and income from the sale of residual products). They bought a compactor to compress foam packaging so that it could be manufactured into floor moulding by another company. Excess printer ink was used as pigment by paint manufacturers. Ninety per cent of their waste was reused, recycled or sold as input to someone else's product. The 10 per cent that was left was shipped off to a power plant to be burned for electricity.[16]

Of course, if you do sell or give your residual products to others, make sure they will be used for safe purposes along their entire life cycle. Unbelievably, for decades industry has *legally* turned hazardous waste into fertilizer, spreading arsenic, lead, cadmium, chromium, dioxins and radioactive ingredients on to agricultural lands, some of which got absorbed by crops and showed up on our dinner tables. This practice has also been implicated in clusters of health problems in farming communities (it is linked to cancer and lung disease) and is alleged to have rendered some farms incapable of growing anything for years.[17] Just because a practice is legal doesn't make it right.

Extended producer responsibility, product stewardship and product take-back

Product stewardship is basically synonymous with EPR (extended producer responsibility in the EU or extended product responsibility in the US). Product stewardship involves taking responsibility for your product for its entire lifetime. Planning for proper management and handling at the end of its useful life is one aspect of this, usually the part that gets the most attention, which is why we consider it under the operations category rather than design. But what we are really talking about is a full life cycle approach.

RESOURCES

Hitchcock, Darcy and Larry Chalfan (2001) *Approaching Zero Waste.* Portland, OR: AXIS Performance Advisors. Part of the Sustainability Series™, www.axisperformance.com.

See the GrassRoots Recycling Network website for information on what they did and how much they saved: www.grrn.org.

Biocycle is a journal on compostables and recycling organic waste, www.jgpress.com/biocycle.htm.

Environmental Building News is a magazine on green building practices, www.buildinggreen.com.

The Xerox Business Guide to Waste Reduction and Recycling and its companion workbook are available from the Xerox website, www.xerox.com/environment.html.

The California Waste Management Board has information on waste profiles, laws, loans, etc., www.ciwmb.ca.gov.

Zero Emissions Research Initiatives focuses on air, land and water and so provides resources especially helpful for those working on issues other than solid waste, www.zeri.org.

At its core is a fundamental shift in responsibility, one that many in industry have resisted. In the past, companies were held responsible for the manufacturing of their goods and also the performance of those goods. Did you cause effluent to flow into the river? Did the disposal of your hazardous waste cause people to become ill? Were the safety features of your product adequate to prevent injury in use? But until recently no one asked who was responsible for managing the disposal of a product at the end of its useful life.

To be fair, the 'bottle bills' in Oregon and California during the early 1970s set a precedent for EPR at least in the US. But it has only become a hot issue as a result of the massive rise in electronic waste. Suddenly, municipalities with waning budgets and an impending tidal wave of hazardous e-waste filled with lead and other rare metals are baulking at having to manage its disposal.

Germany was one of the first countries to go to the manufacturers to ask them to foot the bill. Not surprisingly they declined. So the municipalities refused to accept certain types of waste and compelled the manufacturers to come up with a system for disposing of it responsibly. At present, EPR regulations vary from country to country. The European Waste Electrical and Electronic Equipment (WEEE) Directive covers basically anything with a cord. Even packaging must be taken back. In Canada, British Columbia passed legislation that covers paints, pesticides, pharmaceuticals and other household products.

Once the genie was out of the bottle, other municipalities piled in and the manufacturers will probably never be able to put the responsibility for disposal back on the taxpayer. While Europe is far ahead of the US in this matter, the US has begun to address carpeting waste and e-waste. Producers of nickel-cadmium batteries set up a voluntary but poorly advertised programme. The National Electronic Product Stewardship Initiative is working on take-back product stewardship systems. In our estimation, it is only a matter of time before most products are required to be taken back. Many businesses look at this as a Pandora's box situation and wonder what products will be affected next.

The first reaction from manufacturers when their product is targeted is panic – what are we going to do with all this refuse? But then they begin to understand how to mine the waste stream. Xerox has excelled at this. Since they leased many of their copiers, the product already tended to come back to them. At least in part to save jobs, they created a disassembly plant. Now they carefully test the components that come out of the old copiers. If the recycled parts match the performance of new parts, they are put into 'new' copiers. Xerox has saved more than US$2 billion since 1990 and diverted the equivalent of 2 million printers and copiers from the landfill.

To make this work, they have had to develop sophisticated systems for forecasting when these recycled parts will be available. This has also had an impact on product design. As Elizabeth Graves, environmental health and safety regulatory affairs manager at Xerox, explains:

> Our engineers design product components for durability over multiple lives and commonality with a wide range of models. As a result, components can not only be reused in the same model but also in the next-generation models (through a process some call 'up-cycling').[18]

The Japanese computer manufacturer NEC has created a new business refurbishing old computers. They purchase their old computers (2000 or later models) from customers, fix them up, load new software, and then resell them as 'NEC Refreshed PCs' with a six-month warranty. Noboru Ozawa, group manager of the refreshed PC sales group, said they expected to lose money, at least initially, but instead, the operation has been profitable from the first year: 'It's often said that environmentalism does not generate profits, but we were actually

---

RESOURCES

National Electronic Product Stewardship Initiative, www.nepsi.org.
    Product Stewardship Institute at www.productstewardship.us.
    WEEE (Waste Electrical and Electronic Equipment) Directive, www.europa.eu.int/comm/ environment/waste/weee_index.htm.
    For British Columbia's EPR programmes, see Driedger, R. J. (2001) 'From Cradle to Grave: Extended Producer Responsibility for Household Hazardous Wastes in British Columbia', *Journal of Industrial Ecology*, Vol 5, No 2, Spring, p89.

able to successfully reduce environmental impact while contributing to our bottom line.' While one might expect this business to undermine their new computer sales, they have found the opposite. New PC buyers and second-hand buyers are different pools of people, so they have actually expanded their user base. Each refreshed PC is estimated to save 100 kg of greenhouse gases. In addition, for every second-hand computer they purchase, NEC also pays for one tree to be planted in the Kangaroo Island, Australia reforestation effort.[19]

Conclusion

As you can see from the examples above, there is a lot of profit being left on the table by manufacturers still oblivious to sustainable business practices. Sustainability, on the one hand, is a risk management issue, protecting against legal liability, new regulations, shareholder initiatives and NGO publicity stunts. On the other it is a strategic issue, honing competitiveness, gaining access to high-margin markets, and developing innovative new products.

When you can, eliminate negative social and environmental impacts in the design process. Since design tends to be episodic, however, also investigate the practices associated with operations and waste management. See the following checklists for possible actions that could improve your triple bottom line.

SCORE MANUFACTURING

See page 31 for how to complete this assessment and page 33 for how to interpret your score.

NOTE: Manufacturing businesses should also take the services assessment (page 48) to capture their office and service-related activities.

DESIGN				
Practice	Pilot *1 point*	Initiative *3 points*	Systemic *9 points*	Points
Design for environment: Redesign your product to maximize sustainability benefits using the best available technology.	At least every 5 years, redesign one product with sustainability in mind. Disseminate lessons learned from other related products.	At least every 5 years, redesign most products.	Have products third-party certified as sustainable.	

DESIGN				
Practice	Pilot *1 point*	Initiative *3 points*	Systemic *9 points*	Points
Packaging: Minimize packaging and its associated impacts.	Conduct a life cycle analysis on packaging and take appropriate action.	Reduce packaging by at least 20% (weight and/or volume).	Convert to packaging that is 100% reusable, recyclable and/or biodegradable.	
Supplier influence: Engage suppliers in a formal process for redesigning products and processes.	Engage at least one first-tier supplier.	Engage all first-tier suppliers (eg materials declaration, supplier workshops, technical support).	Work to change the entire supply chain to achieve sustainability	
Life cycle thinking: Apply life cycle thinking to your products, processes, packaging and distribution.	At least every 5 years, conduct a life cycle analysis on prevalent product components and/or packaging.	At least every 5 years, conduct and publish a life cycle assessment paper on one or more products.	Make available independent LCA comparisons on your and your competitors' products.	
			Total Score	
			Average	

OPERATIONS				
Practice	Pilot *1 point*	Initiative *3 points*	Systemic *9 points*	Points
Energy efficiency and renewables: Conduct a process energy audit and implement the best available technology.	Reduce energy by up to 10% per unit of production.	Reduce energy by 11–25%.	Reduce energy by 25% or more with at least 25% from renewables.	
Climate change: Conduct a process greenhouse gas audit and take appropriate action to reduce greenhouse gases.	Reduce greenhouse gases to 1990 levels.	Exceed Kyoto Protocol standards.	Be climate neutral (through reductions and offsets).	

OPERATIONS				
Practice	Pilot *1 point*	Initiative *3 points*	Systemic *9 points*	Points
Resource efficiency: Conduct a (non-energy) resource process efficiency audit and act on the results.	Reduce inputs of raw materials (water and other natural resources) by 10%.	Reduce inputs by over 10%.	Reduce inputs by 25% or more and source at least 50% (by volume or weight) from certified sustainable sources.	
Transportation and distribution: Reduce impacts associated with moving raw materials and products.	Factor in distance when sourcing supplies. Install best available technology to enhance fuel efficiency.	Switch to at least 50% bio-fuels.	Redesign the distribution systems and logistics to minimize transportation.	
Social impacts: Ensure fair and humane working conditions.	At least every 2 years, conduct an internal work climate survey and act on results.	Conduct social audits of some major suppliers.	Require all suppliers to adhere to SA 8000 or equivalent standards.	
Chemicals: Reduce exposure risks to all toxic chemicals.	Complete a chemical inventory that ranks or rates them. Reduce toxic and hazardous materials by 25%. All material safety data sheets are available, easy to access and up to date.	Eliminate all hazardous chemicals and persistent bioaccumulative toxins (PBTs). If appropriate, implement a chemical pharmacy system.	Eliminate all toxic chemicals on all customer grey lists.	

OPERATIONS				
Practice	Pilot *1 point*	Initiative *3 points*	Systemic *9 points*	Points
Product stewardship: Implement a product stewardship strategy.	Take responsibility for your product at the end of its useful life (eg reverse distribution systems). Dispose of any waste responsibly.	Work with industry to eliminate waste.	Turn product into a service; cradle to cradle.	
Waste management: Eliminate the concept of waste.	Reduce solid waste by 20–50%.	Reduce solid waste by 50–89%.	Achieve zero waste to landfill (90–100% reduction).	
			Total Score	
			Average	

5

Sustainability in Government Agencies

Government has a huge role to play in sustainability. Administrations use a large amount of resources and employ a lot of people, but more importantly they are also responsible for protecting the 'commons': air-sheds, watersheds, fisheries and huge tracts of publicly owned land. Through infrastructure and incentives, they set the stage upon which the rest of civilization acts. Their decisions determine to a large extent the liveability of our communities and the environmental impacts of our lifestyles. For example, China has been heralded as having dramatic economic growth, but the World Bank recently estimated that they are losing 8 per cent of gross domestic product (GDP) in environmental costs. Governments must see their communities as a whole system and make decisions that simultaneously improve the health of the community, the economy and the environment.

Often, the necessary vision and courage is not in evidence. And even when the vision is there, it can be hard for government to make significant changes. Bombarded by competing interests, public servants often retreat to safe, tried-and-tested but unsustainable practices. In the US much of the public no longer respects or values the role of government, yet they still want good roads, great schools and better security, exactly the services government provides. The US is caught in a Catch-22 situation: people need more leadership from government but government waits for pressure from its constituents, many of whom have a vested interest in the status quo. In this chapter, we highlight those who have taken risks and made at times unpopular decisions to drive us toward a more sustainable world. We need more heroes like these!

According to Susan Anderson at Portland, Oregon's Office of Sustainable Development, partnerships are key. Government plays a host of roles – modelling, facilitating, educating, regulating – but can only go so far on their own. The most successful efforts integrate government, non-profit organizations and business.

WHAT YOU SHOULD KNOW ABOUT SUSTAINABILITY

What do we need and expect of government in order to move toward a sustainable society? The list is long and the challenges daunting.

Spending revenue wisely, maximizing the benefits to society. We want government to provide its services efficiently. However, governments operate within a tangle of legislative rules and mandates. Ideas that sound great on the floor of the legislature often cause problems in practice. For example, when a homeowner in Oregon installs a new furnace, the job is inspected twice. The electrical and gas pressure test are done before the system is turned over to the homeowner for use. But the homeowner may get a call several months later by another inspector required to look at furnaces and air conditioners prompted by paperwork turned in by the contractor. In these cases, the inspection is completely redundant. Right now, a supervisor is trying to find a way around this, but it takes initiative to overcome the stupidity of certain rules.

Agencies, acting within their own narrow frame of reference, often pass on costs and problems to other agencies, leading to sub-optimal results. For example, consider the problem of rainwater. Traditionally, buildings are constructed with gutters that dump huge quantities of water into the rainwater system. At the same time, roads funnel rainwater into the same pipes. As more and more impermeable surfaces expand on the landscape, wastewater treatment centres become overloaded. Treating all this water is expensive. Because we rarely use the rainwater, we also need large potable water systems and reservoirs. The solution should not be bigger pipes, more dams and larger wastewater treatment centres. Instead we need to rethink how we construct buildings, communities and roads. In Portland, Oregon, some houses have been legally permitted to use rainwater in the home, including for drinking water. With the area's legendary rainfall, these homes easily provide enough storage for most of the year. They simultaneously reduce the pulse of rainwater and reduce the need for drinking water supplies. Bioswales could collect street run-off. The technologies exist to solve this problem. It's a matter of design. Agencies need to collaborate and understand their interdependencies.

Providing infrastructure and security. Enrique Peñalosa, the former mayor of Bogotá, Colombia, said that solving traffic congestion by building more roads was like solving obesity by giving people larger belts. But this is exactly the strategy of many transportation departments. Already in many US cities 50 per cent or more of the urban landscape – streets and parking lots – is devoted to cars.[1] The choices governments make determine the quality of neighbourhoods, the viability of public transportation, air quality and the fitness of citizens. By building roads, they create suburban sprawl, which is more expensive for government to serve with infrastructure.

When people think about security, they think about the military and first responders. Certainly these are critical pieces of our security system; however, the military, in particular, is responsible for a significant amount of pollution and human misery. The range of security issues is also expanding. In the US, the CIA has warned that certain environmental issues may destabilize the world. Global warming and fresh water are on the top of their list of such concerns. Social, economic and cultural issues are feeding terrorism. Sustainability provides a framework for the Pentagon and first responders to anticipate future problems.

Protecting the commons. Government is the guardian of all public resources, those things critical for life but which may not have been assigned a market value or owner. Without sufficient regulation, protection and enforcement, we can experience a 'tragedy of the commons', the tendency to overexploit public resources. Sometimes governments make things worse rather than better. Take fisheries for example: when stocks of cod, which had been abundant for centuries off the coast of Canada, began to decline, the actions of government actually precipitated the collapse. To shore up the economies based on the cod, government subsidized the fishermen, keeping prices low and harvest high. Now the fishery is closed and few expect it *ever* to recover.

Creating a level playing field. Government sets the stage for commerce, but often the stage is tilted, and not toward the audience. Government is rife with perverse incentives. As Paul Hawken, author of *Natural Capitalism* explains, 'The US government subsidizes energy costs so that farmers can deplete aquifers to grow alfalfa to feed cows that make milk that is stored in warehouses as surplus cheese that does not feed the hungry.' Conservative estimates calculate the total cost of subsidies as $2.6 trillion per year, approximately five times corporate profits. By some estimates, around 77 per cent of these are perverse, having serious, unintended negative side effects.[2]

Protecting and helping people who need it. Here again, problems get passed from agency to agency. In the US, mental institutions have been closed to protect the rights of those inside, paradoxically resulting in many becoming homeless, shivering on the streets and begging for food. Overwhelmed social service agencies lose track of at-risk children who end up in foster homes, correction facilities or on the police roster of missing persons. Even the progressive Oregon Health Plan, providing health insurance to the neediest Oregonians, lost funding during an economic downturn; but the savings may have been illusory because more people ended up in emergency rooms and jails after losing their access to essential prescriptions and health services. These costs were paid out of different budgets but may have cost the state even more.

Guiding us towards a better future. Government is the only institution clearly tasked to attend to the long term. Community growth plans are drawn up for a period of 20 years. Energy policy sets the direction for half a century. Schools prepare students for their lifetimes. Too often, vested interests preserve the status quo; many communities, however, like those cited below, have set in place visionary goals that have affected the quality of life for generations.

RESOURCES

If you want to know how your country compares to others, Yale University publishes an Environmental Sustainability Index, www.yale.edu/esi. In 2005 Finland, Norway and Uruguay were at the top; North Korea was at the bottom. Major US cities can see how they rank in the SustainLane ranking; San Francisco, California and Portland, Oregon were at the top of their list in 2005, www.sustainlane.com/cityindex/citypage/ranking/.

The Millennium Ecosystem Assessment was commissioned by the UN and involved thousands of scientists from around the globe. Their report (and an easy-to-read summary) identifies the biggest environmental-related issues facing our planet, www.millenniumassessment.org. See also the Millennium Goals, www.un.org/millenniumgoals/.

United Nations Environmental Programme (2002) 'Global Environment Outlook 3: Past, present and future perspectives', UNEP and Earthscan.

Hammond, Allen (1998) *Which World: Scenarios for the 21st Century.* Washington DC: Island Press.

World Business Council on Sustainable Development (2002) 'The Business Case for Sustainable Development', www.wbcsd.org. Outlines the reasons why their 150 international companies think sustainability should be pursued.

Huntington, Samuel P. (1996) *The Clash of Civilizations and the Remaking of World Order.* Simon & Schuster. Provides an interesting theory of how power is shifting in the world and explores both social and environmental issues in that context.

Jacobs, Jane (2000) *The Nature of Economies.* NY: The Modern Library.

Kinsley, Michael J. (1997) *Economic Renewal Guide: A Collaborative Process for Sustainable Community Development.* Snowmass, CO: Rocky Mountain Institute.

The 'Agency Sustainability Planning and Implementation Guide' was designed to help Massachusetts state agencies develop internal sustainability plans and programmes but will also be of interest for other governments developing sustainability plans. It includes sections on waste reduction and recycling; mercury and PBTs (persistent bioaccumulative toxins) reduction; sustainable design and construction; and environmentally preferable purchasing. For each section, the report includes a one-page sheet of 'Action Steps', a list of 8–12 short-term actions that state facilities can take to reduce their environmental impacts, www.state.ma.us/envir/sustainable/pdf/ss_guide_web.pdf.

Federal Government (US) web addresses:

www.sustainable.doe.gov

www.gsa.gov/environmentalservices

www.federalsustainability.org

www.ofce.gov

www.epa.gov/sustainability

www.federalelectronicchallenge.net.

State and local governments:

ICLEI: Local Governments for Sustainability, www.iclei.org.

European Campaign of Sustainable Cities and Towns, www.global-vision.org/city/aalborg.html.

National League of Cities, www.nlc.org/home.

EKOS (2000) 'Urban Sustainability: Leading Approaches, Tangible Results'. This report, written for the City of Seattle by a consulting firm, contains profiles of the efforts of a variety of cities. It can be ordered from the EKOS website, www.ekosi.com.

Amarillo, Texas has a demonstration village. www.globalecovillage.com

Curitiba, Brazil, www.solstice.crest.org/sustainable/curitiba.

Madison, Wisconsin, www.sustaindane.org.

Oregon, www.sustainableoregon.net.

Portland, Oregon, www.sustainableportland.org.

Santa Monica, California, www.santa-monica.org/edp/scp.

Seattle, Washington, www.sustainableseattle.org.

Whistler, British Columbia, www.awarewhistler.org.

STRATEGIES YOU CAN USE

Let's start by providing positive examples of ways in which governments have promoted a more sustainable future. Hopefully these examples will spark actions your administrations might take. If you are in the private sector, these stories may inspire policy changes to suggest to your representatives. You may even uncover strategies you can use inside your own organization.

Spend tax revenue wisely, maximizing the benefit to society

Taxpayers want the biggest benefits for their money, not inefficiencies and red tape. Smart agencies have found ways to provide multiple benefits from the same tax revenue. These agencies not only attempt to be cost-effective, they also track their overall impact on the economy as their investments cycle through the community. Here are a few examples from the western US.

Conserving energy

Like many prison systems in the US, the Oregon Department of Corrections has been swamped with prisoners, following the three-strikes-and-you're-out legislation. They struggle to house all these people without commensurate funding increases. Prematurely releasing prisoners for lack of space did not endear them to the public. They needed to find a way to get more services for the same amount of money.

One answer was to focus on energy efficiency. Many prisons have large boilers used for laundry, showers and sometimes also heating. They take municipal water in the 50 to 60°F range and heat it to 230° or so. In Oregon one prison discovered thermal solar systems (designed to heat water as opposed to generating electricity) were quite cost-effective. By letting the sun preheat the water during the summer months to close to 125°, they reduced their natural gas consumption by 10 to 20 per cent. They are working with an out-of-state manufacturer of one of the components to use prison labour to manufacture these simple systems. They realize that many other government buildings also use boilers, as does most of the industrial sector. By testing these units, the Department of Corrections may lay the foundation for a new industry in the state and simultaneously improve the efficiency and competitiveness of organizations there as well.

RESOURCES

Romm, Joseph (1999) *Cool Companies*. Island Press.
US Environmental Protection Agency, www.epa.gov.
Better Bricks green building site, www.betterbricks.com.
Energy Star programme for energy-efficient equipment and appliances, www.energystar.gov.
Urban Consortium Energy Task Force (1992) 'Sustainable Energy: A Local Government Planning Guide for a Sustainable Future'.

Take advantage of wasted resources

The Oregon Department of Corrections is also seeking ways to improve its image with its host communities. Someone realized one day that the vehicles used to transport prisoners from the cities to the prison in Pendleton, Oregon, which is in the sparsely populated eastern portion of the state, usually returned to urban areas empty. At the same time, farmers around Pendleton were ploughing-under surplus produce. So they have set up a system to take tax-deductible donations of surplus produce from farmers, use prisoners to sort and bag it, and transport it in the empty buses to the Food Bank in Portland for distribution across the Pacific northwest. The prison gets a boost to its image, the prisoners do something they can be proud of, the farmers get a tax deduction and the hungry get fed.

RESOURCES

GrassRoots Recycling Network, www.grrn.org.

Streamline red tape

Red tape usually translates into increased costs and long lag times. Plans go from agency to agency for approval and any one can stop the process. Contractors hate it. So the Oregon Department of Transportation, preparing to rebuild many of the state's crumbling bridges, pulled all the relevant regulating agencies – state and federal – together to define the criteria and specifications for the work. When they issued their requests for proposals, sustainability criteria were embedded in the requirements. A contractor submitting a proposal can be assured of immediate approval unless they wish to suggest a different way of constructing a bridge. On one project alone, they saved 100 days and over $1 million.

Streamlining usually involves analysing the work process to find redundant and wasteful steps. The total quality movement has created many of these tools, the most useful of which is likely to be process mapping.

RESOURCES

Brassard, Michael (1989) *The Memory Jogger Plus.* Methuen, MA: Goal/QPC.

Employ green building practices

According to the National Research Council, 60 to 85 per cent of a building's real costs are related to operations; the initial construction cost is 10 per cent or less. Since many government buildings are owner-occupied, you may want to pay a little extra for 'green' features so that you can save operating costs over the long term. The California Department of Finance, with the help of Capital E Group and Lawrence Berkeley Laboratory, studied national data on 100 green buildings. They concluded that the financial benefits of a LEED-rated green building are $50–70 per square foot, more than ten times the additional construction costs. The cost savings come not only from conserving energy and water but also from productivity and health-related human benefits.[3]

For more on this topic, see Chapter 7.

RESOURCES

Morton, Steven (2002) 'Business Case for Green Design', Building Operating Management, FacilitiesNet, November 2002, www.facilitiesnet.com.

The Green Building Council's LEED rating system is available at www.worldgbc.org, www.usgbc.org.

California study, www.colorado.gov/rebuildco/services/highperformance/Costs_and_Benefits_of_Green_Buildings.pdf.

Better Bricks, a programme under the Northwest Energy Efficiency Alliance, www.betterbricks.com.

Portland, Oregon's G/Rated programme and their Tenant Improvement Guide, www.green-rated.org.

Find new funding sources

Occasionally, agencies can catalyse new business models. One irrigation district funded by the Oregon Watershed Enhancement Board invented a new type of fish screen to prevent fish from moving into irrigation canals. Typically these screens clog and need to be cleaned out, sometimes several times a day. Their new design rarely clogs and has no moving parts. Farmers Irrigation District has now patented the fish screen and the Farmers' Conservation Alliance is promoting the screens. They will use all of the profits to further their mission of developing solutions to ensure fish, farms and families thrive.

Revolving loan funds have been used successfully to fund expensive upgrades in wastewater treatment plants. Unlike grants that go to the first in the pipeline, revolving loan funds continue to provide resources for change and may grow over time.

See the municipality as a whole system

Too often, organizational silos represent mental barriers. When you look at your municipality as a whole system, though, new opportunities become apparent. Think about closing the loops, living off what is available within your boundaries, and getting more benefits from each function. For example, Portland, Oregon uses their drinking water system to generate electricity. They installed a micro-hydro system in the water pipes leading from a reservoir. Most water departments would never think about generating electricity; energy isn't their responsibility. But with creative thinking, many cross-organizational efficiencies can be uncovered.

Industrial ecology prompts us to think even across sectors. Eco-industrial parks are popular in Europe. Kalundborg, Denmark is probably the most famous example, where steam, water, fly ash, sludge, fuels and sulphur are traded among the different entities, the waste of one becoming the input for another. China has grasped this concept and implemented a 'circular economy initiative'. 'China can no longer afford to follow the West's resources-hungry model of development and it should encourage its citizens to avoid adopting the developed world's consumer habits,' says Pan Yue, Deputy Minister, State Environmental Protection Administration. 'It's important to make Chinese people not blatantly imitate Western consumer habits so as not to repeat the mistakes made by the industrial development of the West over the past 300 years.[4]

RESOURCES

Allenby, B. R. (1995) *Industrial Ecology – Policy Framework and Implementation,* Prentice Hall, New Jersey.
    International Society for Industrial Ecology, www.is4ie.org.
    Journal of Industrial Ecology, www.yale.edu/jie/.
    The Economic Policy Institute makes policy recommendations, for example their published report on 'Clean Energy and Jobs', http://epinet.org.

Provide infrastructure and security

Government is responsible for the planning, design and construction of our infrastructure, the framework that supports our society. Infrastructure comes in many forms. Urban planning, roads, public transportation and utilities are all interdependent but housed in different agencies. The trick is to design them to optimize their collective effectiveness.

Ensure security
In the past, the US Defense Department used to be one of the worst polluters in the country. However, many in the military are proving that security can go hand in hand with sustainability. Lieutenant General Hill at the US Army Base in Fort Lewis, Washington recognized that in order to continue as a good neighbour in the community they needed to clean up their act. He set goals of zero net waste and an 85 per cent reduction in air emissions within 25 years. They have reduced the amount of hazardous materials used by 54 metric tons (from 2001 to 2004) and reduced their air emissions from 333 tons in 2000 to 175 tons in 2004. Their sustainability programme is projected to reduce their operating costs by over $1 million annually in direct cost savings and cost avoidance.

In designing logistics exercises, the Alaska National Guard decided to solve a real-world problem at the same time. They gathered up abandoned cars and unwanted appliances for recycling. The exercise provided skills in recon and logistics while contributing a valuable service to the Mat Su Valley.

It's important to look beyond the typical actors that provide security. What about energy, water and food? Berkeley, California is one of the first cities in the US to undertake an assessment of the security and sustainability of their food system. In 2001 their city council passed the Berkeley Food and Nutrition Policy, which provides a framework for moving them towards sustainable regional agriculture while fostering a local economy.

With the combined threat of biological weapons and the spread of disease from global warming and international travel, the Center for Disease Control may be an equally important player. Since ecological problems can cause mass migrations of people, destabilizing nearby countries, foreign policy and foreign aid also play a role. Security is not just about getting the bad guys. It also has to be about preventing people from becoming so desperate they become bad guys. To that end, city, state and national climate strategies are part of security. International aid for family planning is part of security. Renewable energy standards are part of security. Security is not just intelligence, border guards and special forces. Health, social services, energy and environmental departments also play a role. Take this into account when you allocate funds.

Design efficient, vibrant urban spaces

In 1971 Curitiba, Brazil elected Jaime Lerner, an architect schooled in urban planning, to his first of three terms as mayor. Like many cities in developing countries, Curitiba has been subjected to an 'invasion' of people hoping for a better life. But Lerner did not want Curitiba to become like Sao Paulo and other large cities, inundated with traffic, pollution, crime and squalid *favelas* (shanty towns).

One of his insights was that cities usually expand from the centre out in all directions, like an inflating balloon, becoming increasingly dense and clogged. To avoid this, he and his colleagues hypothesized it would be better to define corridors of high-density development which could be efficiently served by public transit and other city services. While this layout looks odd from the air, with skyscrapers extending out like tentacles, it provides a number of benefits. In addition to providing efficient transportation, which we will describe in the next section, it also ensures that those in the high-density areas have easy access, visually and physically, to less dense areas including Curitiba's many public parks.

Most of the parks were created to solve a problem. Curitiba's eastern border is the Iguaçu River, which floods from Brazil's tropical rains on a regular basis. Rather than using federal funding to build embankments, Lerner used the money to purchase the land along the river for their largest park. In addition to recreation, it provides natural, cost-effective flood control. It also prevents development in an area that would otherwise cause human suffering and property losses from the inevitable flooding on a regular basis.

Sometimes disasters provide opportunities to correct past mistakes. Soldiers Grove in Wisconsin flooded repeatedly. The US Army Corps of Engineers looked into a technical solution – building embankments – but realized that just the upkeep on them would be twice the annual tax receipts. So instead of fighting nature, they moved the town, completing the work in 1983. It cost $1 million to move the town but that resulted in annual savings of $127,000, a reasonable rate of return. Furthermore, they used this opportunity to make radical improvements in energy efficiency. They passed new ordinances that specified tough thermal performance standards and required that at least

50 per cent of heating had to be served by solar systems. They passed a solar access ordinance so that new structures couldn't block the sun for existing structures. As in Curitiba, the floodplain became a popular park.[5] These examples should provide food for thought in the rebuilding of New Orleans and the rest of the Gulf Coast. Instead of spending a fortune to fight nature, it is often wiser to work with it.

RESOURCES

The American Planning Association's 'Policy Guide on Planning for Sustainability' can be found at www.planning.org/policyguides/sustainability.htm.
  James, Sarah and Torbjorn Lahti (2004) *The Natural Step for Communities: How Cities and Towns Can Change Sustainable Practices.* New Society Publishers.
  European Campaign of Sustainable Cities and Towns.
  US Department of Energy, www.sustainable.doe.gov.

Design effective public transportation

The corridor-style urban design facilitates an incredibly efficient public transportation system. While Curitibans have a high rate of car ownership, most trips are by public transport, so much so that government does not have to subsidize the bus system. (In the US, it is typical for more than half the cost of a ride to be funded through tax subsidies.)

Not having the funds for an expensive rail or underground system, Curitiba has pushed its bus system to carry the equivalent number of passengers at one-hundredth the cost of an underground rail system and 10–20 times cheaper than light rail. Their red express buses run along dedicated streets through the high-density corridors. During peak time, they arrive every 56 seconds. These special triple-reticulated buses with five oversized doors stop at the large plexiglass stations that passengers enter (known locally as tube stations), where the passengers have already paid their fares and people in wheelchairs have already been elevated to floor level. The buses stop for 15 seconds to disgorge and load passengers out of different doors.

Green buses travel a loop around the city, so you don't have to travel into the centre to get to a different *barrio* (district). Other colour-coded buses perform other functions, including one that zips across town, stopping infrequently, another that serves tourist destinations and a third for disabled people. Low-density areas are served by minivans so that they can maintain a service at least every 15 minutes, a benchmark they consider key to maintaining passenger levels. With only a few exceptions, the same fare works on all the lines. The government only manages the system; the buses are owned and operated by a host of different companies. Curitiba pays them based on kilometres travelled to maintain the frequent service.

This system has developed over time, using existing streets, by taking advantage of opportunities as they arose. They have not built expensive freeways that isolate neighbourhoods. They haven't had to waste precious downtown plots for parking structures. Those who do drive generally find few traffic jams. And everyone breathes easier for the lack of air pollution.

These innovations produce a higher quality of life. Based on a community survey, 99 per cent of Curitibans are happy with their town (compared to 70 percent of people in Sao Paulo, who think Curitibans have it better). They have a high per capita ratio of green space. They boast a 95 per cent literacy rate and 98 per cent of their children attend school. Their biggest problem seems to be an influx of poor people who have been encouraged to leave by surrounding communities that don't want to fund social programmes for them.

These benefits are just as relevant in richer nations. While Atlanta, Georgia and Portland, Oregon experienced similar population and income growth in the past decades, their experiences were vastly different. Portland has a good public transportation system and is encircled by an urban growth boundary intended to preserve agricultural and forested lands. In his book, *The Eco-Economy*, Lester Brown compares their experiences:[6]

Table 5.1 *Liveability for Portland, Oregon versus Atlanta, Georgia*

Indicator	Portland	Atlanta
Population	+26%	+32%
Income	+72%	+60%
Vehicle miles	+2%	+17%
Single occupant vehicle	−13%	+15%
Commute time per week	−9% (34 hrs)	+1% (53 hrs)
Air pollution (ozone)	−86%	+5%
Energy consumption	−8%	+11%
Neighbourhood quality	+19%	−11%

Note: percentages refer to change from mid-1980s to mid-1990s.

It's clear from these figures that sustainability is also a liveability issue. People in Portland spent less time in traffic jams, breathed cleaner air and saw their neighbourhoods improve.

Protect the commons

Nature provides a host of services upon which we depend. Gretchen Daily of Stanford's Center for Environmental Sciences and Policy provides the following list:[7]

- purification of air and water;
- mitigation of droughts and floods;
- generation and preservation of soils and renewal of their fertility;
- detoxification and decomposition of wastes;
- pollination of crops and natural vegetation;
- dispersal of seeds;
- cycling and movement of nutrients;
- control of vast majority of potential agricultural pests;
- maintenance of biodiversity;
- protection of coastal shores from erosion by waves;
- protection from sun's harmful ultraviolet rays;
- stabilization of the climate;
- moderation of weather extremes and their impacts; and
- provision of aesthetic beauty and intellectual stimulation that lift the human spirit.

To Daily's list, we would add the production of food, fibre and fish – even with genetic engineering, we cannot make a tomato, tree or tilapia without nature's help. While these services are provided for free, they are clearly not worthless! In fact, by some albeit controversial estimates published in an article by Robert Costanza in *Nature Magazine*, if we were to provide these same services through human engineering (where we could) it would cost more that the entire world's gross national product!

When nature's capacity to deliver these services is compromised, it can cost taxpayers dearly. New York City used to have such good quality water that it bottled it. After development and agricultural uses degraded the watershed, the city was faced with having to build a $8 billion water treatment facility. Fortunately, someone had the wisdom to ask first how much it would cost to restore the watershed, letting nature do the work. The answer was $1–2 billion. So in an experimental effort under the Environmental Protection Agency's watchful eye, New York City is hoping to save not only three-quarters of the capital costs but also the $300 million per year to operate the plant.[8]

You can be affected by actions outside your borders. For example, deforestation in China has caused massive sandstorms that have disrupted air traffic as far away as Korea and Japan. According to the World Health Organization, air pollution associated with industry and automobiles is killing more than 500,000 Asians each year.[9] Pulses of pollution cross the Pacific and affect the Pacific northwest. African dust storms are affecting coral in the Caribbean.

In the Western world, the most common way of protecting something is through private ownership. But by and large, no one owns these services and there is no market to manage their efficient distribution or use. These are public goods, the commons, services often not included in cost–benefit calculations. So we end up with 'externalities', impacts not accounted for by the companies that cause them, and perverse incentives that encourage the continuation of unsustainable practices.

Part of the challenge is to get a handle on what your impacts are. One method is the ecological footprint. Basically the inverse of carrying capacity, the ecological footprint quantifies the average amount of land needed per person to provide the resources and ecosystem services we use. To understand this concept, imagine someone placed a glass bubble over your city, not allowing anything in or out. You would quickly run out of certain resources (water, timber, food, etc.) and the wastes (organic waste, carbon dioxide, etc.) would begin to build up. So the ecological footprint of a city is actually much larger than its physical boundaries. The ecological footprint quantifies those flows using the number of acres per person as the measure. Santa Monica, California, used this model, along with The Natural Step framework, to quantify their improvements. They reduced their ecological footprint by 5.7 per cent in 1990–2000, requiring four fewer acres per person than the US average. Unfortunately, this still represents a lifestyle that is far beyond the Earth's ability to provide if everyone alive enjoyed that same standard of living.

Government is centre-stage in this drama. Progressive agencies are using a variety of regulatory and market-based solutions to protect the commons. One such example is Abottsford, British Columbia. As part of their land use planning, they protected areas of farmland from development through their Bill 42 Agricultural Land Reserve. In addition to preserving green space, it increased food security for their residents.

RESOURCES

Costanza, Robert, et al (1997) 'The Value of the World's Ecosystem Services and Natural Capital', *Nature Magazine*, May, pp202–209.

Cities for Climate Protection, www.iclei.org.

The Center for a Sustainable Economy provides economic models to determine the impact of environmental market-based tools, http://sustainableeconomy.org.

Redefining Progress (Ecological Footprint), www.rprogress.org.

Ostrom et al (1999) 'Revisiting the Commons: Local Lessons, Global Challenges', *Science*, No 284, pp278–282.

Engineer market-based incentives

According to a Pollution Prevention Northwest article (Fall, 2004), a US Environmental Protection Agency study in 1999 found that the agency could save almost $50 billion per year (a quarter of the $200 billion spent annually on environmental management) by increasing the use of economic incentives in environmental regulation. When acid rain became a known threat to forests, lakes and buildings, the government might have instituted tough prescriptive regulations for the major emitters of nitrogen oxides and sulphur dioxides (fondly referred to as NO_x and SO_x). Instead the US government set up a cap and a trading system whereby polluters could either clean up their own act or purchase the rights to other companies' improvements. This method allowed investments to flow to the best opportunities and rewarded the companies that did the most. As a result, emissions dropped much faster than expected at a fraction of the cost to industry that was initially expected.

Based on the success of this programme, many other systems, including those to reduce greenhouse gases, are being modelled on it. The US Fish and Wildlife Department, for example, is using this approach to protect endangered species. They have set up bankable permits for breeding pairs of red-cockaded woodpeckers. 'International Paper currently believes that it can sell banked breeding pairs for about $100,000 each. If several pairs can nest on each acre, this means that the value of land for breeding woodpeckers is greatly in excess of its value as a source of timber.'[10]

Green taxes, more common in Europe than in the US, are another way of getting the incentives right. For example, in the UK, excise duties on leaded petrol were raised compared to those on unleaded over time, helping to reduce lead emissions by 70 per cent in a decade. Get the incentives right and you can change behaviour quickly. A Swedish tax on the sulphur content in diesel resulted in a tenfold increase in the use of clean diesel in only 18 months.[11]

Sometimes you just need to educate the citizens. A number of cities in the US are realizing that the loss of forest cover is costing them dearly. For example, in the Atlanta, Georgia area a study showed that the cities reportedly would need to spend $2 billion on new rainwater treatment facilities to deal with the run-off resulting from the loss of tree cover over 25 years. In Cincinnati, Ohio the government is having success reversing this trend by telling homeowners if they plant two trees, they can save $55 per year in air conditioning bills.

Public policy is also an important lever. Susan Anderson at the Portland, Oregon Office of Sustainable Development advises looking for the action that can create a tipping point. Portland adopted a green building policy that stated, in effect, that any city buildings or any housing or commercial buildings receiving local tax benefits or subsidized loans had to be to LEED-certified. Suddenly, a large volume of work was subject to this requirement, far beyond the city's own set of buildings. Anderson commented:

> We didn't need to do much else, architects and developers are a creative bunch. We provide training, technical help and product information, but they know it's to their advantage to learn what they need to know to get the job done. And now, many of these firms are providing development services throughout the US using sustainable construction practices related to LEED. It has been a great partnership between the city and local builders, architects and ensgineers.

RESOURCES

The Center for a Sustainable Economy provides economic models to determine the impact of environmental market-based tools, http://sustainableeconomy.org.

Reclaim public goods and charge the full cost

While economists often have the most to say in favour of privatization, even *The Economist* magazine has concluded that for certain public goods, this is not the best solution. Water is one example. Life is not possible without it, so privatizing water resources might lead to only the rich being able to afford it, an untenable policy. Furthermore, private water companies have not always proved to be more efficient than their public counterparts. Instead, *The Economist* advocates raising prices to reflect the full cost of water, including environmental impacts. California steeply raised prices for irrigation and added the needs of the environment into the equation, and they also set up a California Water Bank. Chile charges everyone the full cost of water but gives poor people stamps to redeem against their bills. *The Economist* also advocates changing how water rights are distributed, making these rights tradable so that they can go to serve the highest value purposes. South Africa, for example, abolished riparian rights and made water allocations temporary and tradable. Australia separated water rights from property rights, making water a public good, and then instituted a system of trading, which now crosses state boundaries.[12]

Why should public goods – water, radio frequencies, microwave bands, fishing rights, etc. – be sold once and then traded in the private sector when the government can lease them instead, providing an ongoing income stream for society?

Create preserves

Often the best way to preserve ecosystem services is to protect vast tracts of habitat. Dr Daniel Pauly, a world-renowned fisheries scientist, believes that marine preserves are going to be key to regenerating fish stocks. To make this point in presentations, he shows a slide of the North Atlantic from roughly the equator to beyond the Arctic Circle. The title of the slide informs the audience that all the areas in green are protected from fishing; everything is red, nothing is green at the scale of his map. We don't need international agreements, he asserts, since most of the fisheries are within the 200-mile boundary along coastlines. So nations already have the ability to protect portions of their marine habitat to help stocks recover.

In Curitiba, Brazil authorities recognized that their city was dependent upon the health of habitats outside their municipality. They are experimenting with transferring building rights to protect sensitive habitats both inside and outside its boundaries. If a developer wants to construct a building with more floors than zoning permits, he or she can protect one of these lands and, in exchange, the city will grant a variance. This ensures their citizens can benefit from the ecosystem services (clean water, flood control, etc.) that stem from lands outside their jurisdiction.

Adopt the precautionary principle

The precautionary principle to some extent switches the burden of proof. In most situations, the government has to prove that something is unsafe to stop it. The precautionary principle instead asks manufacturers to prove that their products are safe. The Precautionary Principle Project defines the concept as 'acting to avoid serious or irreversible potential harm, despite lack of scientific certainty as to the likelihood, magnitude, or causation of that harm'. While it is not feasible to prove that a product is safe in every situation for every organism on Earth, it is possible to invoke the precautionary principle when evidence begins to suggest there is a negative impact. At least in the US, the usual protocol is for companies to continue to sell their products while their corporate lawyers spend years fighting it out with government officials. Adopting the precautionary principle in public policy means that a product's use can be stopped or phased out until the manufacturers can prove it is safe.

The precautionary principle was used in the Montreal Protocol, an international agreement to phase out ozone-depleting substances. Because it was believed that the ozone hole would pose a serious cancer threat, the precautionary principle was made the decision rule. Why wait for more data when the effects could be so catastrophic? The Montreal Protocol was quickly adopted for several reasons. It was a media-capturing event when the ozone hole was discovered, creating a sense of urgency. It was framed as a human health issue, making it more personal than vague threats to the environment. It also didn't hurt that DuPont had declared they could manufacture alternatives to Freon if a market could be assured.

Both municipalities and nation states – San Francisco, California, Hungary and Brazil among them – are adopting the precautionary principle as public policy. Jacques Chirac has recently added an environmental charter to the French constitution whose 10 articles include the precautionary principle.

RESOURCES

The Precautionary Principle Project, www.pprinciple.net/.

The Precautionary Principle in Action: A Handbook was written for the Science and Environmental Health Network by Joel Tickner, Carolyn Raffensperger and Nancy Myers, www.biotech-info.net/precautionary.html#defining.

Appell, David (2001) 'The New Uncertainty Principle', *Scientific American*, January.

Implement regulations

Regulations have been successfully used around the world, especially in Europe, to shift behaviour patterns, and while the approach is currently out of favour in the US, it still has an important role to play even there. Examples of landmark European legislation include:

- the WEEE (Waste Electrical and Electronic Equipment) Directive requiring manufacturers to take responsibility for many products and their packaging at the end of their useful life;
- the RoHS Directive (eliminating various hazardous substances in electronic components, including lead, mercury and cadmium); and
- the REACH (Registration, Evaluation and Authorisation of Chemicals) Directive, intended to help control chemicals.

Europe is using its significant buying power to change the behaviour of corporations around the world. Evidence is accumulating that these regulations are already having a positive impact on human health. Europeans, for example, have significantly lower levels of synthetic chemicals associated with fire retardants in their bodies than US citizens.

Create a level playing field

Too often, the playing field is tilted toward the unsustainable players. Why else should virgin-fibre paper cost less than recycled? How can mining virgin aluminium be viable as long as there are cans to be recovered? In most cases, the answer is that the full cost to society is not factored into the prices. Businesses count some costs (eg harvesting trees, making pulp and drying paper) but can ignore others (eg loss of habitat, stream degradation, landslides and the destruction of fisheries).

Privatize the resource within the right boundaries

People who support privatization often point out that you never wash or change the oil in a rental car. Why bother? Ownership, if the boundaries are right, can produce better long-term protection of a resource. However, for this to work owners, to the extent that this is possible, must be made to internalize their externalities.

For example, imagine a timber company. Their land produces more than trees – it provides a habitat for plants and animals; it may protect streams and downstream fisheries and it anchors topsoil. However, traditionally timber companies have only been able to generate revenue from cutting and selling trees, so there are strong financial incentives to clear-cut as much as the laws allow. The traditional governmental approach has been to regulate what they could, for example forbidding harvesting inside riparian zone buffers. But timber owners, both large corporations and small woodland owners, tend to bristle at these restrictions. Many clamour to be paid for these 'losses'.

Geoffrey Heal, in *Nature and the Marketplace*, presents a different approach. While it might not be possible to develop markets for all the services timberland might provide, you can redraw the boundaries of an owner's responsibilities. Why not combine a timber company and a water company? Let the hybrid organization get income not only from trees but also from water quality. Then the proper financial incentives would be in place for them to protect the ecosystem services of their land.[13]

RESOURCES

Heal, Geoffrey (2000) *Nature and the Marketplace: Capturing the Value of Ecosystem Services.* Washington DC: Island Press.

Get the numbers right

Government (ie society) picks up the cost for many impacts caused by business. These 'externalities' are not included in the price of products or services. Without the right prices, markets will make the wrong decisions. Some have suggested that we assign 'green taxes' to correct the market signals, to internalize the cost to society in the product price. And in some situations these have been effective. For example, Ireland assigned a PlasTax to plastic bags. In short order, this move reduced demand for plastic bags by 90 per cent and earned 3.5 million euros for other environmental projects.

However, Herman Daly, the former World Bank economist, is not a fan of green taxes. He worries we'd spend all our time trying to get the numbers just right. Instead, he advocates taxing resources more than income. He feels that getting most of our government revenues from natural resources would create the same result with a lot less effort.

Governments also use broad societal measures to monitor the health of their societies. Here again Daly highlights major problems with the methods they use: gross domestic product (GDP) is the benchmark generally used, but GDP only measures money moving around. It doesn't distinguish between what most would consider good things (education, food, housing, etc.) and costs associated with bad things (eg prisons, environmental clean-up, domestic abuse and antidepressants) which, to some extent, are unintended negative side effects of our society. It's like a calculator with only a plus sign. He states, '… empirical evidence that GNP growth has increased economic welfare in the United States since about 1970 is nonexistent.'

Most measures of economic growth such as GDP (which has now replaced GNP as the measure of choice) and traditional economics are blind to nature's inputs. They may count the costs of cutting trees, transporting them and milling them but give no value to the tree itself (the input). Yet without this natural capital, the other steps would be valueless. Likewise, they do not count the impacts of the outputs and waste on climate change, water quality, soil erosion and the like.

Daly acknowledges that markets (which GDP does measure) do provide *efficient* allocation of resources. However, they don't deal at all well with justice (redistribution of wealth) or issues of scale (which deals with sustainability). He says we must begin to view the economy as a subset of the environment, not separate from it, and as such the issue then becomes the optimal size of the economy (at least in terms of its use of natural resources for inputs or outputs/waste). The economy cannot grow forever, especially in terms of material throughput. And the service/information economy is no saviour because it too relies on natural resources. As Frederick Soddy put it, 'No phosphorus, no thought.' We need natural resources to build cells and proteins so that we can think.

Daly also emphasizes that we must stop counting natural capital as income. At present, when a timber company harvests trees, it generates revenues, making its financial statements look healthier. But in fact it has depleted its holdings. Depleting natural and non-renewable resources should be treated as depreciation. Daly recommends using a portion of the income from non-renewable resources to finance renewable substitutes.[14]

RESOURCES

Cobb, C. et al (1995) 'If the GDP is Up, Why is America Down?', *The Atlantic Monthly*, October.
Daly, Herman, E. (1996) *Beyond Growth: The Economics of Sustainable Development*. Boston: Beacon Press.

Eliminate perverse subsidies

Subsidies are, in the words of Norman Myers and Jennifer Kent, 'a form of government support extended to an economic sector, generally with the aim of promoting an activity that the government considers beneficial to the economy overall and to society at large'. These can be direct (eg federal or state tax deductions or credits for energy-efficient appliances) or indirect (eg free parking and roads subsidize the auto industry). In *Perverse Subsidies*, Myers and Kent define a perverse subsidy as one that not only hurts the environment but also comes back to bite the economy. There are a shockingly large number of these, as cited earlier.

The table below represents Myers and Kent's best estimates of global subsidies by type and sector. Note that perverse subsidies are a subset of the total, so you can get a sense of the percentage of each subsidy type that is having perverse effects.[15]

<h3 style="text-align:center">Table 5.2 Perverse subsidies</h3>

Sector	Conventional subsidies (US$ billion)	Externalities (US$ billion)	Total subsidies (US$ billion)	Perverse subsidies (US$ billion)
Agriculture	385	250	635	510
Fossil fuel/ nuclear	131	200	331	300
Road transport	800	380	1180	780
Water	67	180	247	230
Fisheries	25	NA	25	25
Forestry	14	78	92	92
TOTAL (rounded)	1420	1090	2510	1950

These perverse subsidies lead us to make investments that are counter-productive. One interesting battleground today is electronic waste. Until recently, companies were not held responsible for the costs associated with managing the disposal of their products. However, electronics are filled with heavy metals, which can leach into groundwater in a typical landfill. European countries were some of the first to refuse to take on the responsibility for managing this waste, banning TVs, computers and other electronics from their landfills. Initially, the manufacturers baulked. Until it becomes their responsibility, manufactures have few incentives to improve the environmental impacts of their products. Wayne Rifer, a member of the National Electronics Product Stewardship Initiative, points out that traditionally, 'During the whole lifecycle of the product, manufacturers take responsibility only until the point of sale. And after use when the value of the product becomes negative, traditionally it then becomes the responsibility of government.' Making manufacturers responsible for the product through to end of life prevents them from externalizing disposal costs on to governments and citizens. Instead, product stewardship legislation creates an incentive to redesign products to maximize the value of the materials for reuse and recycling.

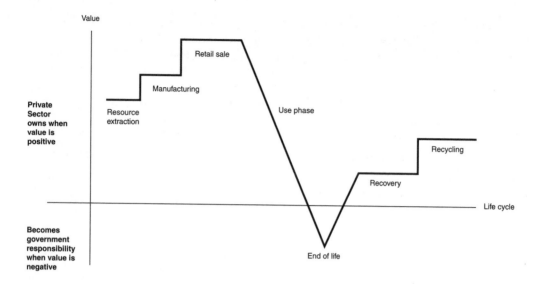

Figure 5.1 *Value, ownership and product life cycle*

Source: courtesy of Rifer Environmental. Permission granted.

What is the solution? Product stewardship has the potential to solve the particular problem Rifer mentions above. (See more in the Manufacturing chapter.) Beyond that, Myers and Kent advocate making subsidies transparent. Since subsidies are often unpopular, this helps to balance out those who have a vested interest in maintaining subsidies. It also helps to build collaboration across constituencies. For example, environmentalists, deficit hawks and neo-conservatives can agree we shouldn't borrow from our children's future. The Sierra Club, Friends of the Earth and the Wilderness Society banded with Citizens for Tax Justice, Taxpayers for the Common Cause and the US Public Interest Research Group to expose perverse subsidies. Myers and Kent also recommend using regulations, user charges, tradable permits and green taxes where appropriate. Sunset clauses should be included in new subsidies to ensure that they come up for review periodically, so they can be removed when they are no longer needed or have become perverse.

Protect and help people who need it

In the early part of the last century taking care of the needy was largely a task for churches and communities. Now, however, many citizens expect governments to take care of homelessness, hunger, illiteracy, drug abuse, child abuse, gangs and domestic violence. It's a tall order, especially in times of reduced funding. The developed world can learn a lot

---

RESOURCES

Myers, Norman and Jennifer Kent (2001) *Perverse Subsidies: How Tax Dollars Can Undercut the Environment and the Economy.* Washington: Island Press.

Subsidy Watch, www.iisd.org/subsidywatch.

The Product Stewardship Institute at www.productstewardship.us is a non-profit organization of governmental entities that sets priorities for product stewardship initiatives in the US.

The National Electronic Product Stewardship Initiative, see www.nepsi.org/, is a US initiative to solve end-of-life issues for electronic products.

WEEE (Waste Electrical and Electronic Equipment) Directive, www.europa.eu.int/comm/environment/waste/weee_index.htm.

For British Columbia's extended product responsibility (EPR) programmes, see Driedger R.J. (2001) 'From Cradle to Grave: Extended Producer Responsibility for Household Hazardous Wastes in British Columbia', *Journal of Industrial Ecology,* Vol 5, No 2, Spring, p89.

---

from the developing world in this area, as people there have more profound problems and even less money. We'll use Curitiba again as a source of inspiration.

Perform triage

On a recent visit to Curitiba, one of the authors saw no homeless people, a dramatic contrast to her home in Portland, Oregon. Certainly, some people lived in conditions that many in the developed world would find unacceptable, but no one was wandering the streets, pushing stolen shopping trolleys or urinating in alleys. How had this relatively favourable situation been accomplished? In Curitiba, if you see someone on the street who appears to need help – perhaps you see a homeless man or a runaway teenager – there's a central number to call. A social worker is dispatched to offer assistance. That is one entry point to their network of public–private partnerships to address social needs, everything from food and housing to job training and substance-abuse programmes. The authorities provide free rent in business incubators, where they also provide training in marketing and other business skills. They also set up markets for people to sell their wares. Curitibans are working hard to move away from a care-taking philosophy where government is responsible for taking care of people to one where individuals and communities share in the responsibility to make things better.

Combat hunger

Curitiba's programmes emphasize good nutrition. Instead of just providing food stamps, there are a number of ways to put fresh fruits and vegetables into the hands of the poor. In the *favelas*, a waste-for-food exchange as a way of cleaning up the shanty towns and reducing disease was implemented. People bring refuse and recyclables to the edge of the *favela* (an area with streets too narrow for the refuse collection vehicles to manoeuvre) and exchange them for surplus produce. There are also low-cost groceries at Citizenship Streets, buildings along the major transportation routes which house, in a decentralized fashion, the city services people are likely to need: job training, legal assistance, business licences, social services, etc. When people come to pick up their packet of staples (rice, beans, flour, etc.), they are asked to spend an hour in training where they learn to read, develop job skills, discover how to make meals from kitchen scraps, and hone their parenting skills.

RESOURCES

Smith, Stephen C. (2005) *Ending Global Poverty: A Guide to What Works*. Palgrave Macmillan.

Provide housing

As in any city, providing affordable housing is a challenge. One mechanism Curitiba uses to fund new projects is transferring building rights. Similar to the programme mentioned earlier in this chapter where they used building rights to preserve precious habitat, in some situations they allow builders to construct a taller building than zoning allows. The developer pays a fee for the additional floors that goes into a low-income housing fund.

RESOURCES

Bullard, Robert (2005) *The Quest for Environmental Justice: Human Rights and the Politics of Pollution*. San Francisco, CA: Sierra Club Books.

Sachs, Jeffrey D. (2005) *The End of Poverty: Economic Possibilities for Our Time*. New York: Penguin Press.

For a fascinating example of creating healthy communities in the poorest communities and settings (in Colombia), see Weisman, Alan (1995) *Gaviotas: A Village to Reinvent the World*. White River Junction, VT: Chelsea Green Publishing.

Guide us toward a better future

We all hope that our governments have the foresight to set into motion policies that will lead us toward a better future. In addition to all the strategies we have already mentioned, there are many ways, both big and small, for government to use its clout. Here are a few to consider.

Model and encourage new behaviour

Habits are hard to break. Sometimes government needs to model new patterns of behaviour. For example, Japan wanted to change energy use patterns to achieve their Kyoto greenhouse gas goals. So their prime minister, Jurichiro Koizumi, built a campaign to encourage workers to dress casually during the summer. To be without a coat and tie was considered unprofessional, so this represented a major cultural shift. He told his cabinet ministers to show up in shirtsleeves and was photographed in casual attire with US President George Bush. He decreed that air conditioning thermostats be set to 28°C (82°F). He even sponsored a Cool Biz Collection fashion show that he hoped would result in a boost to the economy, resulting in an estimated US$92 million in consumer purchases.

Educating the community is also a critical task. The resort community of Whistler, British Columbia convened a group of community leaders and businesses to create the Whistler: It's Our Nature programme. The members included the municipality of Whistler-Blackcomb, the Fairmont Chateau Whistler, Tourism Whistler and the Association of Whistler Area Residents for the Environment. They developed four toolkits: a household kit, a small business kit, a kit for schools and a community sustainability kit. These were funded in part by foundations and were distributed in the community to build awareness.

Use purchasing as a way to drive markets

The high-tech industry was launched a few decades ago by the military. Their long-term demand accelerated production, drove down costs and inspired research and development. Similarly, governmental purchasing guidelines for recycled-content paper and LEED-rated green buildings have created a cost-effective market for those products and services. Oregon's Department of Administrative Services is trying to enlarge their influence and bulk purchasing power by encouraging schools to use the state's purchasing programmes.

Recently, the City of Portland in Oregon issued a request for proposal (RFP) to purchase all their electricity on the open market from wind farms rather than through their local utility. To protect the interests of their taxpayers, the RFP stated that it couldn't cost a cent more than what the City was paying now, even though the green power programmes in the area all cost a premium. The City is currently in negotiations with a company and it appears that the power will actually cost less. The main benefit to the community, though, is this contract creates a larger market for renewable energy. It also helps to heal the urban–rural divide. In Oregon, there has historically been friction between the conservative rural areas and the more liberal, populated and powerful urban areas. Since the wind farms will be in the rural parts of Oregon, this is a way to benefit these economically challenged regions. Also, it may be possible, once this contract is in place, for other communities and large power users to be added to this groundbreaking agreement, multiplying the market effects.

Don't underestimate the power of putting the word 'sustainability' in your RFPs. Making it one of many criteria sends a strong signal to potential respondents and it will create a ripple of learning. Axis Performance Advisors was once asked to become part of a team proposing on a waste treatment job. We have no experience in that field but the engineering firm needed someone on the team with knowledge of sustainability since it was mentioned in the RFP. By the time the proposal was written, our firm had provided them with a grounding in the concept.

Write sustainability-related terms into your contracts as well, perhaps as add-on options. For more information about using purchasing as a lever, see the chapter on purchasing later in this book.

Develop social capital

To a large extent, the social fabric of a community is defined by the connectedness among its members – what social researchers call the social capital of a community. Government can play a significant role in developing social capital by providing an infrastructure that promotes interaction and involvement. Robert Putnam, noted professor at Harvard and author of *Bowling Alone* and *Better Together*, has documented an interesting phenomenon in the US. His research shows a steady decline in civic participation and social connectedness in the US since the 1970s as measured by a drop in membership in civic organizations and clubs, attendance at public meetings, involvement in school groups, voter registration and even a decline in social gatherings like picnics and card parties. He draws compelling correlations between these indicators and other trends such as increasing crime rates.

Interestingly this trend has been consistently documented in every American city save one. Portland, Oregon has succeeded where every other American city has failed in engaging its population and actually increasing civic involvement. Steven Johnson, a professor in the Urban and Public Affairs department at Portland State University, built on Putnam's research to examine what was going on in Oregon. Though the reasons for the countervailing trend are complex, Johnson cites the state's opportunities for involvement in formal activities such as neighbourhood associations (that have surprising authority over neighbourhood governance), watershed councils (that work across territories and agency jurisdictions to protect and restore Oregon waterways) and a multitude of public hearings that give citizens a voice in major decisions such as school management, urban growth boundaries and civic projects. Johnson also believes that along with these formal opportunities communities need to create informal gatherings that bring people together in social settings to enable them to develop holistic relationships. People who have had a social relationship understand each other better and are less likely to fight with one another when it comes to doing the formal work of shaping community policies.[16] While this level of involvement often seems cumbersome and time-consuming, the result is actually less government as the community takes more direct responsibility for its governance, requiring less regulation and interference.

Denmark also has a strong system for civic involvement. Danish citizens engage in dialogue about the impacts of policy decisions, giving them a voice in shaping their communities on important public policy issues.

> *When a new technology is presented to the Danish government for approval, the Board of Technology invites a number of ordinary people, from various backgrounds, to serve as a sort of jury. In 1992, for example, such a jury tackled the question of genetic engineering in animal breeding. The jurors sat through two background briefings, then went on to hear and cross-examine witnesses for and against: scientists, experts on the social effects of technology and representatives of interest groups. After due deliberation, they gave their verdict to a national press conference. Among other things, they found against using genetic manipulation to make new kinds of pets, but in favour of using it to help find a cure for human cancer. Though their decision was not binding, it had enough moral weight to sway parliamentary votes on the matter.*[17]

Processes like these can ensure that policy decisions are thoroughly weighed and can also provide a means of educating the public.

RESOURCES

Putnam, Robert D. (2000) *Bowling Alone: The Collapse and Revival of American Community.* New York: Simon and Schuster.

ICLEI is working on methods to reduce violence, insecurity and conflict in communities. Go to www.iclei.org/index.php?id=806.

Provide incentives and grants for needed research

Government in the US used to be a major source of funding for research. Over the last couple of decades, however, this task has increasingly devolved to the private sector. There are areas where business is well suited to this task. But there are a number of drawbacks in government taking a back seat. First, company research is focused on those areas where they expect to make huge profits. This has tended to ignore important issues where there may not be a lucrative market, for example diseases of the poor such as malaria, which in turn causes human misery in the developing world. Second, business prefers patentable solutions over natural ones, creating even more synthetic or genetically modified products to worry about. And third, and perhaps more problematic, businesses focus on issues that are likely to pay off relatively quickly, while it will require long-term research and development to solve some of our sustainability-related challenges. Solar photovoltaics, for example, are still not cost-competitive in many markets (as long as externalities are ignored) except in remote areas far from existing power lines. We need to increase the efficiency of these solar cells and also ramp up production to bring the costs down. Similar problems have been encountered with social issues. Governments around the world are currently having to spur funding for the development of vaccines and antiviral drugs to combat the threat of a bird flu pandemic.

The Golden Carrot was a programme in 1993 that jump-started research on more efficient appliances in the US. While it was initiated by utility companies, it still provides one successful model. Rather than offsetting the cost of research and development, they offered an incentive of $30.7 million to a single manufacturer that could design, build and distribute refrigerators that were 25–50 per cent more energy efficient than comparable models. This incentive got the attention of the entire industry. Today refrigerators are 30 per cent more energy efficient than they were prior to this programme.

Create audacious goals and policies
A clear compelling vision gets people excited and also provides business with some certainty about the future. At least 13 US states and a number of nations have set renewable electricity standards, goals for the percentage of energy which must come from such cleaner sources as wind, geothermal and solar.[18] Iceland has upped the ante by setting a goal to be the first hydrogen economy. Governor Arnold Schwarzenegger committed California to reducing greenhouse gases by 80 per cent below 1990 levels by 2050. Portland, Oregon has a goal to have the city government served by 100 per cent renewable power by 2010. These goals often generate excitement and coalesce different groups so that they can collaborate.

Government is also in a position to clarify priorities and create a context for a high quality of life. The US has the dubious honour of having edged ahead of Japan as the most workaholic nation. Compare that with policies in the European Union, where a directive prescribes four weeks of vacation for all. The Netherlands has a '1.5 jobs' policy for parents with children, encouraging them to have at least one parent stay home at least part-time. They offer five to seven weeks' paid holiday *plus* ten days' unpaid personal time. Part-time work is encouraged instead of being a blight on your career, with approximately 40 per cent of the workforce working this way. Benefits are prorated but the national health plan protects workers if they become ill. It is not policy to maximize GDP; instead the goal is to maximize quality of life. In the US people seem to have forgotten what an economy is for. Those who say that Europe, with these 'socialistic' practices, can't compete should consider that many US companies invest heavily in Europe. If Europe's practices were really that unprofitable, it's unlikely this would be the case.

RESOURCES

Pollar, Odette (1999) *Take Back Your Life*. Conair Press.
    Sustainable Communities Network.
    Healthy Cities Network (World Health Organization).
    ICLEI: Local Governments for Sustainability, www.iclei.org, and the Local Agenda 21 Campaign, www.iclei.org/index.php?id=798.

Sponsor award programmes

Award programmes can often help get a new concept anchored. In the US the Malcolm Baldrige National Quality Award created a lot of interest in total quality management practices while also providing a useful self-assessment tool. The Environmental Protection Agency's green chemistry award programme is serving this same need and generating inspiring stories. Individual states or local governments have also created their own award programmes. For example, New Mexico created the Green Zia programme, an environmental performance award modelled on the Malcolm Baldrige National Quality Award.

RESOURCES

Green Zia, www.mnenv.state.nm.us/Green_Zia_website.
    The European Campaign of Sustainable Cities and Towns sponsors a Sustainable City Award, www.global-vision.org.

Make information visible

Sometimes all government needs to do is to make certain data easily retrievable. The Toxic Release Inventory forced US companies to report their emissions. While the method of reporting was in some ways misleading, no company wanted to be at the top of the list: just the threat of the information becoming public prompted changes in behaviour.

Similarly, labelling requirements can make a difference. Many fast-food outlets have eliminated trans-fatty acids, associated with coronary heart disease, after the US Food and Drug Administration proposed listing them on food labels. Agricultural interests have fought hard to prevent genetically modified organisms from being identified for the same reason. But information is empowering.

Portland and surrounding Multnomah County, Oregon have been tracking and reporting on greenhouse gas emissions. In conjunction with their energy policy (the first was written in 1979) and action plan, these measures have helped the area achieve the Kyoto Protocol goals. The area has reduced its climate impact almost to 1990 levels despite a significant increase in population (whereas the trend nationally is up by 13 per cent). On a per capita basis, the area has reduced greenhouse gases by 12.5 per cent. This received significant coverage in the media. Policy, measures, action plans and education can come together to get results.

Similarly, Oregon measures the overall health of the state with its Oregon benchmarks. These measures track social, environmental and economic indicators over the long term, including everything from teenage pregnancy to air quality and job creation. These benchmarks are linked to agencies that can affect them, with local jurisdictions having their own set of measures. In practice, these do not drive public policy and legislation to the degree they could, but they do provide a scorecard for how the state is doing.

RESOURCES

ICLEI: Local Governments for Sustainability, www.iclei.org, and their Cities for Climate Protection Campaign, www.iclei.org/index.php?id=800.
Oregon Benchmarks/Oregon Progress Board, www.egov.oregon.gov/DAS/OPB/obm.shtml.

Integrate sustainability into education

Sustainability requires systems thinking, the ability to envision how things are interconnected. It also requires some scientific understanding. So embedding sustainability into curricula, beginning at an early age, will be key to its success.

Massachusetts Institute of Technology (MIT) has created activities for elementary and secondary schoolteachers to impart systems thinking skills to children. Many universities are now carving out niches relating to sustainability: the University of Oregon in green chemistry, Portland State University in urban design, Iowa State in sustainable agriculture, for example. Some have developed partnerships. For example, MIT, The University of Tokyo, Chalmers University of Technology and the Swiss Federal Institute of Technology have formed the Alliance for Global Sustainability to 'promote joint research projects that will result in realistic policy proposals for the development of a civilization that can be sustained within the limitations required to preserve the global environment.'[19]

RESOURCES

University Leaders for a Sustainable Future, www.ulsf.org.
   Talloires Declaration, www.ulsf.org/programs_talloires.html.
   National Wildlife Federation's 'Campus Ecology' programme, www.nwf.org/campusecology.
   Education for Sustainability Western Network, www.efswest.org.
   Good Company's self-assessment 'toolkit', www.goodcompany.com.
   Reimagine Education, www.reimagineeducation.org.
   Cloud Institute for Sustainability Education, www.sustainabilityed.org.
   Center for Ecoliteracy, www.ecoliteracy.org.

Equalize opportunities

Government is supposed to benefit all people, but campaign financing gives undue weight to the big, rich players who are often wedded to the status quo. Sometimes, however, their interests are not mutually exclusive. When Jaime Lerner, the former mayor of Curitiba, Brazil, decided to give preference to public transportation over those who could afford cars, he didn't just make life better for the poor, he made the city more liveable for everyone. He invested in infrastructure for public transportation which could benefit everyone, instead of infrastructure for personal vehicles alone.

   One way government can improve the life of the majority of its citizens is to promote policies that broaden ownership. In *The Ownership Solution* Jeff Gates tries to answer the question, why does capitalism create so few capitalists? Why does such a small percentage of the population benefit wildly, while the rest struggle with comparative insecurity?

> *One of today's most profound tests – morally, economically and socially – is whether global capitalism can be coaxed to create more haves and fewer have-nots. That, in turn, may well determine the fate of democracy – which will never realize its full potential until based on an economically just foundation in which its constituents are full participants, not simply wage earners and occasional voters.*

Company share purchase plans and retirement plans are insufficient. According to a Harvard study, 71 per cent of US households hold less than $2000 of shares in any form. Gates again:

> *Expecting a broad base of wage earners to buy their way into significant*
> *ownership (ie from their already stretched paychecks) is what I call 'Marie*
> *Antoinette Capitalism' – only instead of urging, 'Let them eat cake', the modern*
> *refrain is, 'Let them buy shares'. Today's closed system of finance has much the*
> *same economic effect as the enclosure movement of the eighteenth century –*
> *creating pools of people who, deprived of any realistic chance to own, find*
> *themselves competing against each other for an ever dwindling number of*
> *well-paid jobs.*

Gates presents a number of different options to increase the level of ownership of everyday people. For example, in Jamaica they developed related enterprise share ownership plans (RESOPs) that allowed employees not only to acquire shares in their small enterprises (which are notoriously unstable) but also in their suppliers and distributors (which could allow them to gain shares in larger firms). Under programmes like this, even migrant farm workers can build a portfolio so their wealth is not just based on the number of hours of back-breaking work they can do. Customer Stock Ownership Plans allow customers to gain shares in such organizations as local utilities. Alaska's oil fund, which pays money to all residents annually, is another example where the benefits of a natural resource are shared by the community. Local, barter-based currencies also tend to favour small, local enterprises. Perhaps the best-known example of this is in Ithaca, New York. There citizens created their own local currency called Ithaca Hours. These pay for everything from groceries to professional services but can only be redeemed at local businesses.

Gates calls into question our slavish attention to job growth as an economic strategy when real wealth and economic security is more likely to be created through ownership and capital. He asks good questions in his book. We have environmental impact assessments on public investment; why don't we have ownership impact assessments? Why do most of the growth benefits go to institutional investors instead of employees? Why not offer preferential tax treatment to employee-owned ventures including cooperatives, which are used extensively in Costa Rica, for example, as an economic development strategy?[20]

RESOURCES

Gates, Jeff (1998) *The Ownership Solution: Toward a Shared Capitalism for the 21st Century.*
Reading, MA: Addison-Wesley.

Use public pension funds as a signal to business

Socially responsible investing is the fastest growing sector on Wall Street. Government pension funds have on occasion played an important role, for example in protesting against apartheid South Africa. The California Public Employees' Pension System (CalPERS) has even worked to oust directors of corporations. As their Global Proxy Voting Principles (19 March 2001) shows, they use their clout intentionally.

> *However, actions taken by CalPERS as a shareowner can be instrumental in encouraging action as a responsible corporate citizen by the companies in which the Fund invests. Moreover, through its Economically Targeted Investment (ETI) policy, the Board has recognized that the interests of CalPERS' beneficiaries can be served by considering – in addition to maximizing investment returns to the Fund – collateral benefits to the national, regional and state economies.*[21]

Conclusion

Government has such an important role to play in driving us towards a sustainable future. Whether you work in a small, local department or in regional or national government, you can facilitate the emergence of new markets through your purchasing and contracting practices and use sustainability to uncover ways to do more with less. Emphasize positive incentives to encourage performance beyond compliance. In the core work of your agency, keep the long, sustainable view in mind and seek ways to deliver even greater benefits. Take risks, even though your workplace may discourage it – we can't get to sustainability without your leadership.

SCORE GOVERNMENT

See page 31 for how to complete this assessment and page 33 for how to interpret your score.

NOTE: This assessment focuses on the larger impacts government has on its community. This assessment is intended to be used at a municipality, regional or national level, although an individual agency may want to score itself on a practice that directly relates to its mission. Governmental agencies should also take the services assessment (on page 48) to capture their internal impacts and the appropriate functional assessments.

GOVERNMENT				
Practice	Pilot *1 point*	Initiative *3 points*	Systemic *9 points*	Points
Energy: Promote energy efficiency, conservation and renewables.	Offer and promote free energy audits to constituency.	Have a system of incentives that encourage organizations and individuals to conserve energy and switch to renewables.	Have set a renewable standard of at least 30% renewables by 2020.	
Land use: Promote sustainable land use practices.	Use smart growth and associated principles and policies in new development and redevelopment projects. Provide outreach and education.	Have in place long-term land use plans that protect important natural services (clean water, carbon sequestration, etc.) and natural resources (agriculture/ forests/ fisheries).	Base the long-term land use planning on an estimate of population growth and carrying capacity such that if needed the community could provide for 80% of its critical needs (food, water, fibre, etc.)	
Transportation: Actively promote the reduction of climate, air-quality and congestion impacts associated with transportation.	Transportation planning is integrated with land use planning. All public transportation vehicles use clean fuels. Provide outreach and education to the community.	Give preference and support to public and alternative transportation through investments, incentives and regulations.	Require major employers to reduce one-person-per-car commuting through a variety of incentives.	
Contract services: Use purchasing power to influence the marketplace.	Include sustainability as a selection criterion in all requests for proposals.	Write sustainability criteria and requirements into contract language for all contractors hired.	Develop systems to help others identify vendors/suppliers with effective sustainable practices (eg award programmes or a database of sustainable organizations).	

GOVERNMENT				
Practice	Pilot *1 point*	Initiative *3 points*	Systemic *9 points*	Points
Buildings: Promote green building practices.	Set a better-than-code standard for all new government buildings (LEED silver or equivalent); use green building principles when remodelling existing facilities.	Actively promote green building practices in the community through education, incentives, technical assistance, etc.	Increase building code requirements to LEED silver or equivalent.	
Waste management: Move toward a 'zero waste' society.	Provide convenient recycling services for organizations and the public for all recyclable/ compostable materials.	Build markets for recyclable materials through economic development incentives, technical assistance, and purchasing practices; provide convenient hazardous waste collection systems for all toxic products including electronics, batteries, pharmaceuticals, paints, pesticides, etc.	Implement product stewardship/ EPR legislation for all toxic materials, requiring some form of product take-back, that creates incentives to manufacturers to create more sustainable alternatives.	
Economic development: Encourage sustainable development.	Use sustainability as a criterion for selecting targeted industries.	Educate existing businesses about sustainability and provide services to develop effective business clusters.	Create legislation, regulations and other mechanisms to eliminate unsustainable practices in the community.	
Human health: Promote human health and well-being for all citizens.	Ensure all citizens have access to basic health care and basic services (shelter, food, drug/alcohol prevention, mental health services, etc.)	Actively promote healthy lifestyle choices (diet, exercise, stress management, etc.) through education, events, labelling and incentives.	Adopt the precautionary principle as policy.	

GOVERNMENT				
Practice	Pilot *1 point*	Initiative *3 points*	Systemic *9 points*	Points
Education: Ensure all citizens have the knowledge and skills necessary to participate in a sustainable society.	Include some sustainability content in primary and secondary educational materials, including systems thinking. Assess schools on their sustainability performance and act on the results.	Embed sustainability into the curriculum of primary and secondary education and create sustainability demonstration and community service projects. In higher education, develop strong academic and research programmes.	Sustainability education is required in high school and higher education, linked to social, economic and environmental subject matter. Ensure that every citizen (children and adults) receives regular messages about how to be more sustainable and gets meaningful feedback on the overall performance of their community.	
Tolerance and diversity: Promote practices that enable all citizens to reach their potential.	Actively recruit and hire from disadvantaged populations. Provide job and literacy training.	Have programmes that teach tolerance and conflict resolution. Provide mediation and arbitration services.	At least every 5 years, systematically evaluate the community's well-being and have effective systems in place to increase social capital and civic engagement (eg neighbourhood associations, citizen advisory committees, and community mixers).	
Global peace and prosperity: Promote practices that avoid war, de-escalate tensions and prevent mass migrations due to famine, natural disasters, or political strife.	Provide outreach and education to help local citizens understand global sustainability challenges and the impacts their decisions can have on other peoples.	Screen purchases and investments so as not to support regimes or organizations that contribute to world problems. Give preference to organizations that actively work to prevent world problems.	Actively support sustainable economic development throughout the world through education, exchange programmes, participation in sustainability-related organizations, technical assistance, aid and trade.	

GOVERNMENT				
Practice	Pilot *1 point*	Initiative *3 points*	Systemic *9 points*	Points
Emergency preparedness: Have effective plans in place to protect citizens, property and the environment in the case of natural or man-made disaster.	Regularly educate citizens about potential threats and what to do to protect themselves. Have programmes that help them put together an emergency preparedness plan and kit.	Have an effective network of trained disaster relief workers spread throughout the community and a robust communication system; have a well-tested plan for foreseeable disasters.	Have systems for handling sewage and containing hazardous materials without electricity or other major infrastructure elements such that there will be no harmful releases into the environment.	
			Total Score	
			Average	

Part 3

Sustainability by Organizational Function

6

Senior Management: How to Lead the Sustainability Effort

Senior management acts as the antennae of the organization, sensing and making sense of changes in the world. They must foresee both continuous and discontinuous change and then develop strategies to steer around looming problems.

Sustainability can be a particularly useful tool for top management to organize their thinking and explore issues that are currently off their radar screen. Because sustainability is rooted in long-term worldwide trends and science, it can make strategic planning more tangible and urgent.

WHAT YOU SHOULD KNOW ABOUT SUSTAINABILITY

According to PricewaterhouseCoopers' sixth annual survey of 1000 chief executive officers (CEOs) from 43 countries, 79 per cent of these executives agreed that 'sustainability is vital to the profitability of any company', 71 per cent said they would consider sacrificing short-term profitability, if needed, in exchange for long-term shareholder value when implementing a sustainability programme and 67 per cent thought that sustainability was not just a public relations issue. Most were driven by a desire to enhance their brand, attract employees and provide improved shareholder value. Some of the most commonly mentioned practices they were putting into place included writing codes of conduct, evaluating environmental impacts of their operations and working on the sustainability performance of their entire supply chain. (The entire report can be downloaded from www.pwcglobal.com/gx/eng/ins-sol/survey-rept/ceo6/index.html.)[1]

Top management must juggle the competing interests of different stakeholder groups: customers who want good value, shareholders who want quarterly profits, employees who want meaningful work and regulators who want safety for employees and the environment. Sustainability can help management come up with creative strategies that meet multiple needs, turning 'ors' into 'ands'.

In today's complex world, the biggest and most common mistake executives make is to ignore the relevance of certain points of view: Nike thinking that their suppliers' employment practices were not their concern; Monsanto thinking that religious and moral questions were not as important as technological prowess; OPEC thinking they could continue to control oil prices while the world's demand, in large part driven by China, outstripped their ability to pump; the US military's assumption that the people of Iraq would react like Kuwaitis when the US 'liberated' their country. It is normal to want to filter out information to make sense of things, but this is a dangerous tendency in an interconnected world. A better understanding of sustainability and the questions it might have prompted could have helped all these organizations avoid embarrassing and expensive oversights.

One misconception that prevents many executives from pursuing sustainability is the assumption that it will end up costing more. In fact, as long as you filter ideas through a normal 'does this make sense for us to do now?' decision process, the sustainable action often saves money, yielding unanticipated benefits as well. Consider the following:

- Green buildings can now be constructed at about the same cost as traditionally constructed buildings but save over 30 per cent in operating costs.
- Organizations that adopt a zero waste strategy usually find lucrative markets for their 'residual products'.
- The Domini 400 Social Index, a stock index of socially responsible companies, has performed as well or better than the Standard and Poors, a broad market index, for many time periods.
- A recent award-winning study concluded that organizations that focus on the concepts of eco-efficiency increase their market valuation as well as financial performance.[2]

In addition, and perhaps even more important, sustainability can help you manage risk to your operation and your image. Consider that:

- The number of corporate social responsibility (CSR) shareholder resolutions in the US leapt to around 800 in 2002 and was expected to increase by 20 per cent in 2003.
- Six European countries (the UK, France, Sweden, German, The Netherlands and Switzerland) have adopted laws requiring pension funds to consider the environmental, ethical and social performance of companies they want to invest in.
- NGO and activist groups now number over 28,000 worldwide.

If your company is publicly traded, you want to be in the good books of important stakeholders.

In addition to using sustainability to scope out threats and opportunities, senior management may also want to use sustainability to imbue its mission with more meaning.

As Collins and Porras assert in *Built to Last*, the difference between highly successful companies and their peers is often a strong, shared set of guiding values:

> *Contrary to business school doctrine, 'maximizing shareholder wealth' or 'profit maximization' has not been the dominant driving force or primary objective through the history of visionary companies. Visionary companies pursue a cluster of objectives, of which making money is only one – and not necessarily the primary one. Yes, they seek profits, but they're guided by a core ideology, values and a sense of purpose beyond just making money. Yet, paradoxically, the visionary companies make more money than the more purely profit-driving comparison companies.*[3]

Sustainability can be a powerful framework for harnessing employee commitment and energy. Saving nature for future generations, solving social problems people care about – these are issues that get people's blood flowing. Even employees who flip burgers, make pizza or pour coffee for a living can feel they are saving the world through their actions. It may be hard to quantify the impact on productivity but many organizations have anecdotally reported that adopting sustainability has meant that they now attract a higher quality of employee and that morale and retention have improved.

It's not only important for organizations to adopt sustainability as a strategy; they must also execute the strategy artfully. Companies that try to implement sustainability but do it poorly can find themselves no better off. Monsanto is probably the best-known example. Monsanto was one of the first companies to publicize sustainability in the management literature. In a 1997 Harvard Business Review article entitled 'Growth through Global Sustainability', CEO Robert Shapiro explained how sustainability was a key strategic issue that should be examined during strategic planning:

> *Years ago, we would approach strategic planning by considering 'the environment' – that is, the economic, technological and competitive context of the business – and we'd forecast how it would change over the planning horizon ... extrapolating recent trends. So we almost never predicted the critical discontinuities in which the real money was made and lost ... But every consumer marketer knows that you can rely on demographics. Many market discontinuities were predictable and future ones can still be predicted – based on observable, incontrovertible facts ... Sustainable development is one of those discontinuities. Far from being a soft issue grounded in emotion or ethics, sustainable development involves cold, rational business logic.*[4]

However, their execution of this strategy, with an emphasis on genetically modified organisms, brought them even more bad press. The public was not impressed with

Monsanto's new genetically modified soya beans that could be nuked with even more Round-Up. People were further concerned about embedding Bt, a natural pesticide in a wind-pollinated crop, and were outraged when Monsanto sued a small farmer for patent infringement because his rapeseed plants (canola) became infected with their GM seeds. By Monsanto's own admission, they have at least failed the public relations effort:

> *We've learned that there is often a very fine line between scientific confidence, on the one hand, and corporate arrogance, on the other ... It was natural for us to see this as a scientific issue. We didn't listen very well to people who insisted there were relevant ethical, religious, cultural, social and economic issues as well.*[5]

RESOURCES

World Business Council on Sustainable Development (2002) 'The Business Case for Sustainable Development', www.wbcsd.org. This report outlines the reasons why their 150 international companies think sustainability should be pursued.

Hollender, Jeffrey (2004) *What Matters Most: How a Small Group of Pioneers is Teaching Social Responsibility to Big Business, and Why Big Business is Listening*. Basic Books.

Aston, A. and B. Helm (2005) 'The Race Against Climate Change', *Business* Week, 12 December, pp59–66. Also see case studies at www.businessweek.com/go/carbon.

Elkington, John (2001) 'Buried Treasure: Uncover the Business Case for Corporate Sustainability', www.sustainability.org.

Elkington, John (1998). *Cannibals with Forks: The Triple Bottom Line of the 21st Century*. Stony Creek, CT: New Society Publishers.

McDonough, William and Michael Braungart (2001) 'The Next Industrial Revolution' (video), Stevenson, Maryland: Earthome Productions. There is also an *Atlantic Monthly* article of the same name.

Romm, Joseph (1999) *Cool Companies: How the Best Businesses Boost Profits and Productivity by Cutting Greenhouse Gases*. Island Press.

Willard, Bob (2002) *The Sustainability Advantage: Seven Business Case Benefits of a Triple Bottom Line*. Gabriola Island, BC: New Society Publishers.

Willard, Bob (2005) *The Next Sustainability Wave: Building Boardroom Buy-in*. Gabriola Island, BC: New Society Publishers.

STRATEGIES YOU CAN USE

So what should the management team be doing vis-à-vis sustainability? We break the task down into five elements:

1   assessing threats, opportunities and constraints;
2   choosing frameworks and terms;
3   devising an implementation strategy and enlisting support;
4   aligning business systems; and
5   providing for transparency and stakeholder involvement.

These are some of the tasks of managers as a matter of course, but here we explore how they are used in the context of sustainability.

Assess threats, opportunities and constraints

In the last 50 years, we have undergone a number of seismic shifts in organizational models. In the post-World War II mass-production world, the standard response when something broke was that it was 'Made in Japan'. Then came the quality revolution, making Honda the best-selling car for years, crippling the US auto sector. Next came the information age, which made a geek by the name of Bill Gates the richest man in America. Globalization, spurred by transnational groups such as the World Trade Organization and International Monetary Fund, along with associated trade agreements such as the North American Free Trade Agreement (NAFTA), have exported white-collar work. In each of these shifts, winners in the old world became losers in the new. As Joel Barker, author of *The Power of Vision*, has long been saying, when the paradigm shifts, everyone goes back to zero. In other words, past successes in the old world are no guarantee of success, indeed often a liability, in the future.

Given the rate at which new business models are being created, executives must constantly keep an eye out for emerging trends. We believe, as do many others, that the next big shift will be toward sustainability. We laid out the case for this in the first chapter, so we will not reiterate the points here. Assuming that you believe that some elements of sustainability will be important in the future, the question to ask is how to systematically assess your threats and opportunities. Below are some useful methods, beginning with ones all executives will find familiar.

RESOURCES

To Whose Profit? published by the World Wildlife Fund and Cable & Wireless.
    'Global Warming: Why Business Is Taking It So Seriously', *BusinessWeek*, 16 August 2004, www.businessweek.com/magazine/content/04_33/b3896002_mz001.htm.

Strategic planning

Strategic planning has long attempted to take a broad view of the world. In the 'environmental scanning' portion of the process, executives are usually expected to examine trends in their industry, their customers, their communities, demographics and the physical environment. One common method is a SWOT analysis, where executives itemize their Strengths, Weaknesses, Opportunities and Threats. And one way to introduce sustainability into your organization, especially if the concept is new to many on the leadership team, is to examine sustainability as one of the many emerging trends.

To do this, you would want to provide a briefing on sustainability and then facilitate a discussion based on the potential implications. A number of organizational leaders, including Ray Anderson of Interface, have had an epiphany after being asked to speak on their environmental or sustainability policy, so invite one of the organizational leaders to research the topic and come prepared to speak. It can also help to bring in other industry leaders who are pursuing sustainability. As part of the strategic planning process, force executives to examine how certain seemingly irrelevant trends (eg HIV in Africa, freshwater supplies or global warming) could affect their organization – such conversations can often uncover important interdependencies.

RESOURCES

Senge, Peter and Goran Carstedt (2001) 'Innovating our Way to the Next Industrial Revolution', *MIT Sloan Management Review*, Winter.

James, Jennifer (1997) *Thinking in the Future Tense*. New York: Simon & Schuster.

Pfeiffer, William J., Leonard D. Goodstein and Timothy M. Nolan (1989) *Shaping Strategic Planning: Frogs, Dragons, Bees, and Turkey Tails*. Glenview, IL: Scott, Foresman and Co. in association with University Associates.

Scenario planning

Scenario planning involves creating discrete future scenarios and examining how the organization might fare in each. You could present a scenario where sustainability was becoming the dominant organizational model. Or you can use the three scenarios created by the World Business Council on Sustainable Development: FROG (First Raise Our Growth, basically business as usual), Geopolity (using international agreements) and Jazz (improvised voluntary actions). The UN Environmental Programme also laid out four discrete scenarios – market first, security first, policy first and sustainability first – providing an abundance of data on their likely effects.

RESOURCES

Speth, James Gustave (2004) *Red Sky at Morning: America and the Crisis on the Global Environment.* New Haven, CT: Yale University Press.
UNEP (2002) *Global Environment Outlook 3: Past, Present and Future Perspectives,* UNEP and Earthscan.
World Business Council on Sustainable Development, www.wbcsd.ch.
Schwartz, Peter (1991) *The Art of the Long View.* New York: Doubleday Currency.

Stakeholder management

All organizations are buffeted by the competing needs of their various stakeholders. Businesses must address the concerns of owners, employees, customers, suppliers, regulators and NGOs. Governments must address the needs of taxpayers and other citizens, legislators, other governmental bodies, special interest groups and NGOs. So it is no surprise that stakeholder management has emerged as one way to deal with these relationships. This usually involves determining who your stakeholders are, learning more about their interests and expectations, engaging them in productive dialogues and keeping the channels of communication open.

This same framework can incorporate sustainability. Often the simplest way is just to add in any missing stakeholders (the environment, the world community, NGOs, future generations, etc.).

Another approach is to develop systematic audits of each of your stakeholders. The Body Shop has spearheaded this approach; detailed information about their methods can be found in *The Stakeholder Corporation* by David Wheeler and Maria Sillanpaa.

It is important in this process to assess the constraints each stakeholder places on you. Will your customers respond well to your involvement with sustainability, or, like Home Depot, do you want to keep your efforts off-stage? Will you raise red flags for some of your stakeholders? For example, when the AES Corporation stated that having fun was one of their core values, the Securities and Exchange Commission made them list their values as a potential risk factor in their annual reports! These points of view do not have to prevent your pursuing sustainability, but they may guide how you frame your efforts or determine whether you emphasize them publicly.

Backcasting

The problem with most strategic planning methods is they rely on projecting existing trends into the future. But not all change is continuous: a new technology or a disaster, for example, can completely change the rules of the game. So rather than just forecasting from an existing point in time, it can be instructive to do 'backcasting' from a desired future.

RESOURCES

Wheeler, David and Maria Sillanpaa (1997) *The Stakeholder Corporation: The Body Shop Blueprint for Maximizing Stakeholder Value.* London: Pitman Publishing.

   Elkington, John (1998) *Cannibals with Forks: The Triple Bottom Line.* Stony Creek, CT: New Society Publishers.

   The first of a two-volume series entitled 'From Words to Action: The Stakeholder Engagement Manual', published by the Stakeholder Research Associates in partnership with the UN Environment Programme and AccountAbility, *Practitioners' Perspectives on Stakeholder Engagement* examines the trends, processes, key success factors and challenges of stakeholder engagement based on the first-hand experiences of practitioners on the front lines.

The Natural Step has taken the concept of backcasting and given it traction. The Natural Step framework provides a simple, four-rule description of a sustainable society. The rules (referred to as 'system conditions'; see the more complete description later in this chapter) were created and vetted by a wide range of scientists. They deal mostly with environmental issues, requirements that nature places on us based on the laws of thermodynamics. The four rules can be used to describe the 'end-game', what we all must be able to do if we want a sustainable world. Executives go through a visioning process to image how their organization might operate in that sustainable state and then work backwards to figure out how to get there.

One of the advantages of backcasting is that it helps people get beyond current limitations. It often unveils entirely new directions and provides clear guidance for current decisions. It can help organizations avoid investing in dead-end technologies and instead show them how to invest in platforms for future ones.

RESOURCES

For information on backcasting, go to The Natural Step website for your country or www.naturalstep.org.nz/tns-f-implementation.asp.

Choose terms and frameworks

Assessing sustainability-related threats, opportunities and constraints should provide executives with a clearer focus. What sustainability issues are most pertinent to their organization? How urgent are the threats? Where are the most intriguing opportunities?

How do their primary stakeholders feel about sustainability? Answers to these questions provide a basis for selecting terms and frameworks.

Alternative terms

It matters what you call something. As George Lakoff, author of *Moral Politics*, points out, the choice of terms can invite or diffuse objections. Who wouldn't want 'tax relief' or 'healthy forests' or 'clear skies'? We are not advocating spin-doctoring, but why not choose terms which invite people in instead of scaring them away?

'Sustainability' may not be the best word to use in your organization. The term may seem too vague, abstract or academic for your audience. It also implies maintaining a status quo instead of restoring what has already been degraded. And like many popular terms, it has been co-opted (to mean 'sustaining my business').

We raised this issue in consultations with a client in Alaska. Alaska has had a highly extractive economy and 'environmentalists' are often viewed as obstacles rather than advocates. Since for many people, 'sustainability' equals 'environmentalism', it became important for this client to find an alternative term. We settled on 'sustainable economic renewal', keeping the term 'sustainability' embedded but linking it to economic development.

Be open to 'bridging terms', phrases that bridge the gap between where people are now and ultimate sustainability. Manufacturers, for example, may not like the term 'sustainability', but 'zero waste' may seem a logical next step to 'zero defects' and 'waste reduction' programmes they may already have. 'Sustainable communities' may bring to mind bearded hippies, but 'smart growth' sounds, well, smart.

In some situations, it makes most sense to adopt one issue under the sustainability banner. For example, the two largest reinsurance companies in the world, Munich Re and Swiss Re, have both adopted climate change as their focus. Certain industries may lend themselves to focusing on a particular practice, for example the construction industry talking in terms of 'high-performance buildings' or chemists focusing on 'green chemistry'.

In some situations, the framework you choose – CERES (Coalition for Environmentally Responsible Economies), The Natural Step framework or the Ecological Footprint, for example (see more about these common frameworks in the next section) – can provide the overarching term for your effort. Sometimes organizations develop their own terms, such as the Collins Company referring to their Journey to Sustainability programme to emphasize it is a process as much as a destination.

If you choose not to use the term 'sustainability', here are a few suggestions for alternatives:

- zero waste;
- green building or high-performance buildings;

- green chemistry;
- community health;
- social responsibility;
- triple bottom line;
- three-Es (economy, environment and social equity). Since 'equity' tends to leave out many other social-related issues, some replace 'social equity' with 'community' or 'social';
- resource efficiency or radical resource efficiency;
- risk management;
- product certification;
- product stewardship;
- stakeholder management;
- smart growth; and
- quality plus (enlarging the definition of quality to include the environment and other stakeholders).

Frameworks

A number of different frameworks or methods have been developed to explain sustainability. Depending on the work you do, some will seem more relevant or useful than others. You may choose to combine a couple, The Natural Step framework and zero waste, for example. Consider the pros and cons of several before selecting the language that will work best in your organization.

The usefulness of a framework is often best understood by analogy. Imagine you want to start a supermarket. Into your head pops a mental model that would, in its main characteristics, be shared by most people; a framework, organized by produce, dairy, frozen foods, canned goods, breakfast foods, etc. This framework makes it easy to know what you will need and see what you may have forgotten (perhaps a pet food aisle). Because this concept is so widely shared, it makes it easy for customers to find what they need and employees to know where to place things on the shelf. Everyone accepts that the grapefruit are in the produce section and not the breakfast aisle, even though most grapefruit are consumed at breakfast. This same framework is reflected not only in the layout of the supermarket but also the organizational structure (produce manager, butcher, baker, etc.), the computer system and vendor relationships.

Now, instead of building a supermarket, imagine you want to build a sustainability programme. What comes to mind? Wouldn't it be great if we had a shared mental model of what should be contained in such a programme, a framework that made it clear how to organize the effort?

There are a number of sustainability frameworks currently in use. None is perfect, but some are more appropriate for some situations than others. (See Appendix A for a list of common ones in use.) You will want to choose a framework or set of frameworks that will:

- ensure you are working on a complete set of issues, not forgetting anything important;
- be easy to understand and remember, will resonate with your employees and stakeholders;
- imply clear end-points, letting you know when you have reached a sustainable state; and
- provides or imply a process for moving forward.

To meet all these criteria, you may need to blend different frameworks. Frameworks exist in a hierarchy – some provide overarching principles of sustainability, describing what sustainability is; others are more related to specific methods or tools and as such are more prescriptive. As with any new field, the terms and frameworks are proliferating, so in Appendix A we have organized the most common terms into a hierarchy so that you can focus on the ones most likely to be relevant in your situation. You should be able to Google any of the terms to find more information.

In the building industry, for example, some use The Natural Step framework to inform their use of LEED, a green building scoring system. Some of our clients have adopted the triple bottom line (social, economic and environmental), which gives equal weight to the three elements, and then embedded The Natural Step system conditions into those three elements. Some in manufacturing and government have embedded either The Natural Step or triple bottom line into an existing environmental management system.

Ideally, the framework or frameworks you choose will be echoed in a sustainability policy, metrics, decision tools and your sustainability report. For more information on sustainability metrics and reporting, see the Finance and Accounting chapter.

Devise an implementation strategy and enlist support

After developing a business case for pursuing sustainability and identifying terms and frameworks, the next step is to develop an implementation strategy. Where are you going to start your efforts? Who needs to be involved? What do the executives need to do to demonstrate their support? The importance of this step cannot be overemphasized. In our experience, many of the mistakes organizations make regarding sustainability are not technical mistakes but mistakes in change to management:

- A catalogue retailer trained all employees on sustainability before having any systems in place to harness the ideas and energy that the training generated. They ended up with hundreds of employee suggestions languishing for over a year until they hired someone to head up the sustainability effort.
- A timber company also trained employees and then expected improvements to happen spontaneously. They soon discovered they needed a set of teams to provide structure and focus and a process to evaluate the ideas that were generated.

- A consultant associated with The Natural Step framework became so enamoured with the backcasting process that he was adamant about approaching all clients with this approach. He discovered the number of organizations willing to jump into sustainability 'whole hog' was quite limited.
- One company tried to apply the same exhaustive environmental management system that was used in their manufacturing group in their retail outlet, getting hopelessly bogged down in terminology and technique.
- A governmental agency decided to use a voluntary green team to spearhead their sustainability efforts. The team didn't have enough clout or the right members to be effective.

These are just a few of the organizational change mistakes we have witnessed, all examples of making the implementation of sustainability unnecessarily difficult. The following advice should help you avoid these and other problems.

Pick the best entry point

In many situations, organizations are better off starting their sustainability effort quietly, tucking it into something already in existence. This lets you gain some experience and avoid the eye-rolling usually associated with new organizational 'programmes' or 'initiatives'. The analysis of your threats and opportunities should imply likely places to begin. Find a place where those intersect with existing efforts you have planned:

- Are you planning any capital improvements (new/remodelled buildings or product lines)? The catalogue retailer, Norm Thompson, began their sustainability effort when they were constructing a new office building. Since buildings last for decades, the impacts of design decisions go on for years. After achieving their goals of making it as green as possible, they moved on to the next phase of their sustainability plan.
- Are you designing a new product, service or programme? Philips Microelectronics chooses a 'flagship' product within a product group and applies design for environment principles. Since most of the impacts of products are determined in design, this is a high-leverage opportunity.
- Where are your largest expenses and environmental impacts? Herman Miller ships their furniture in their own trucks. They discovered that by adding an aerodynamic scoop on to their truck cabs, the fuel savings paid for the upgrades in several months, reducing their climate impacts.
- Where is the 'low-hanging fruit', something you can pick off easily to show progress and save money? Many organizations find that energy/lighting upgrades and packaging changes can yield significant benefits with little effort.

- Do you have an existing process that could be tweaked to make it relate to sustainability (eg environmentally preferable purchasing policies or an environmental management system)? The Oregon Department of Administrative services used their purchasing power to reward those with more sustainable products and services.
- Do you have a waste stream that has potential to go somewhere other than the landfill? At the Klamath Falls, Oregon plant of wood products manufacturer Collins Companies, an employee wondered if the sawdust couldn't be put back into the product instead of burned for energy or hauled off. This single idea saved the company over a million dollars and actually improved the quality of their product.
- Is there a nuisance (to employees, customers or the community) that you could solve and thus generate future support for your work? A number of different property management firms have found that by changing to green cleaning products, they eliminated janitor complaints about skin irritation and allergic reactions.

Set up the best structure

Given your chosen entry point, you may need one or more of several common structures:

Sustainability coordinators or directors. Many organizations find it helpful to assign someone the responsibility for leading the sustainability effort. Ideally this person should report to top management. It can be impressive how much one person can make happen. Two women at Multnomah County, in Portland, Oregon have jump-started everything from eco-roofs to a global warming action plan to a food policy council. It is often wise, however, to make these positions long term but temporary, sending the message to managers that soon they will need to take over these functions.

Steering committees. Often the management team isn't yet ready to manage the sustainability effort. In these situations, a steering committee can provide supervision, coordination and leadership. The Oregon Museum of Science and Industry (OMSI) successfully used a steering committee for a year to increase front-line participation in and commitment to the effort.

Task forces. Steering committees, managers and/or sustainability coordinators often spawn task forces to work on specific projects: researching the best certification schemes, setting up environmentally preferable purchasing policies, redesigning the production process, etc. At OMSI the steering committee set up a zero waste team and a climate team to attack two of their largest environmental impacts.

Standing teams. In some situations, having standing teams that focus on certain elements of the organization can be useful. Collins Companies, for example, created an input–output diagram of their operation and then assigned teams to each of the inputs and outputs: an energy team, a raw materials team, a waste team, etc.

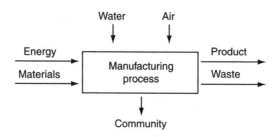

Figure 6.1 *Collins team structure*

When you set up any type of team, think long and hard about what you expect of it. We use a 'pre-launch' process of working through the why, who, what, when, where and how questions and, to really work, the process takes several hours. But taking the time up front saves many hours of team time and associated frustration. If you are clear enough about the boundaries, you should be able to give the team authority to make decisions.

Demonstrate support

Executives often think that all they need to do is tell people they support a new initiative and their work is done. In fact not only must they communicate the message regularly and repeatedly, they must align their actions. At the Oregon Museum of Science and Industry, the task force wanted to encourage employees to use alternative transportation for commuting. So when we talked to the executive director, we asked her to ride her bike to work and then parade around the office in her bike helmet until she was sure at least a dozen people had seen her. You must 'walk the talk'.

What you say is only effective to the degree that your actions support your words. So here are some effective ways to demonstrate support:

• Take symbolic action. Do something no one thinks you would do to demonstrate your commitment. This may be as simple as redesignating your hallowed parking spot for car-poolers or as big as dropping an environmentally or socially questionable product line.
• Do at least as much as you expect others to do. This may involve cycling to work, using teleconferences to avoid business travel, taking the most fuel-efficient fleet car, volunteering in the community, etc.
• Ask people about sustainability and what they have done to work towards it. Follow up on task forces. Ask for regular face-to-face reports from sustainability coordinators, steering committees and task forces.

- Promote people (perhaps the sustainability coordinator) in part because of their efforts on sustainability-related projects.
- Make it easy for employees to be more sustainable at work and at home. The Washington Park Zoo, in Portland, Oregon, for example, lets employees add difficult-to-recycle items like batteries to the organization's recycle bins. Quantec, a small consulting firm in Portland, Oregon, gives its 35 employees an incentive to buy Toyota Priuses; they have found this a powerful employee retention strategy since the bonus is paid out over several years. Portland State University lets employees and professors use the car-share programme for free during working hours to encourage alternative transportation.
- Bring in people from outside to show off what your employees have done. Give the teams visibility at important business functions.
- Put your money and your time where your mouth is. Join and attend appropriate professional associations. Send people to sustainability conferences and training. Expect people to work on sustainability tasks during working hours.
- Change your business systems to incorporate sustainability. (See below.)

RESOURCES

Sustainability Series™ booklets provide step-by-step instructions for how to move sustainability into your organization. www.axisperformance.com/booklets.html.

James, Jennifer (1997) *Thinking in the Future Tense*. New York: Simon & Schuster. This book includes wonderful questions to guide your assessment of your own culture.

Align business systems

Business systems are a powerful indicator of organizational priorities but they often hold back the organizational change effort, sending mixed signals. Below are some suggestions for how to incorporate sustainability into common business systems:

Strategic planning. Make sustainability one of the key trends you consider.

Operational planning. Expect every department to set at least one sustainability goal.

Budgeting. When sustainability-related projects can prove a return, let the department keep a portion of the return in their budget to use as they see fit.

Performance appraisals and compensation. Make sustainability a key part of executive and other employee reviews.

Orientation and training. Embed sustainability into employee orientation and management training.

Environmental management systems. If you have an EMS, incorporate sustainability into policy statements and the criteria for setting priorities.

RESOURCES

Embedding Sustainability into your EMS (Sustainability Series™ booklet produced by AXIS Performance Advisors, www.axisperformance.com/sust_series.html.)

Provide for transparency and stakeholder involvement

Many executives yearn for the days when all they had to do was make a profit and not break any laws. But those days are gone. Stakeholders (including investors, customers, suppliers, special interest groups and community members) are increasingly making their voices heard. Even Wal-Mart, which used to focus only on keeping prices cheap, is realizing the need to incorporate social responsibility and sustainability into its culture. They have realized that activists have been targeting retailers, not offshore manufacturers. 'We thought we could sit in Bentonville [Arkansas],' said Lee Scott, their CEO, 'take care of customers, take care of associates – and the world would leave us alone. It doesn't work that way any more.'[6]

Recently Wal-Mart announced sweeping and specific environmental goals to reduce energy consumption in its outlets and trucks, and reduce packaging.[7] Wal-Mart now recognizes the need to take responsibility for the social and environmental impacts of their entire supply chain. CEO Lee Scott again:

> *There will be a day of reckoning for retailers. If somebody wakes up and finds out that children that are down the river from that factory where you save three cents a foot in the cost of garden hose are developing cancers at a significant rate so that the American public can save three cents a foot, those things won't be tolerated, and they shouldn't be tolerated.*

One specific action they are taking is to begin buying organic cotton to remove many tons of pesticides from use.[8]

As already mentioned, shareholder resolutions are increasing. Environmental groups and other special interest groups can make their voices heard in uncomfortable ways if you don't involve them and listen to their concerns. Fortunately, many of these groups, even the most fringe ones, are now open to collaborating to find solutions.

In the aftermath of Enron, Worldcom, Tyco, Parmalat and other bad actors, there is an obvious need for transparency, accuracy and ethics. Just the hint of ethical breaches has already brought a number of companies down. In the US, the Sarbanes-Oxley Bill has at least made it clear 'where the buck stops'. It increases the responsibility of corporations to be transparent. But you will need to do much more.

Stakeholder involvement has progressed further in the UK and Europe than in the US. Below, we list a number of different resources to help provide guidance.

RESOURCES

ISO 26000 is a new standard for corporate social responsibility and stakeholder involvement. This effort is linked to the Global Reporting Initiative, which is creating standards for sustainability reporting.

AA1000 is a standard for ethics and stakeholder engagement, www.accountability.org.uk/aa1000/default.asp.

The UK has a Combined Code for Corporate Governance, www.fsa.gov.uk/pubs/ukla.

For checklists on stakeholder audits, see Wheeler, David and Maria Sillanpaa (1997) *The Stakeholder Corporation: The Body Shop Blueprint for Maximizing Stakeholder Value*. London: Pitman Publishing.

Hemmati, Minu (2002) *Multi-Stakeholder Processes for Governance and Sustainability*. London: Earthscan.

Paine, Lynn S. (2003) *Value Shift: Why Companies Must Merge Social and Financial Imperatives to Achieve Superior Performance*. New York: McGraw Hill.

Innovest is an environmental rating company, www.innovestgroup.com, rating large, publicly held companies based on their environmental performance and then selling this research to money managers, banks, insurance companies, industry and consultants. Many of the ratings apply to products and services that people use (eg petroleum, foods, retailers and banks). They have also published retail reports, which can be found at www.socialfunds.com under the section 'Corporate Social Responsibility'.

The Interfaith Center on Corporate Responsibility, www.iccr.org, provides a focus for corporate responsibility issues and campaigns.

Sustainability reports

With regard to transparency, one obvious option is to publish a sustainability report. This should cover all your major impacts and expose your warts as well as your successes. We cover reporting in more detail in the Finance and Accounting chapter.

Partner NGOs

Many organizations are finding it enormously helpful to use environmental or other non-governmental organizations as partners to help them improve their own performance. These NGOs can act as a proxy for certain stakeholder groups and can also provide technical assistance.

RESOURCES

The Global Reporting Initiative is attempting to develop international standards for sustainability reporting, www.gri.org.

If you're trying to convince your organization to publish an environmental or sustainability report, this article might help you make the case: '10 Reasons Why: The Surprising Truths about the Business Value of Sustainability Reporting', *Green at Work Magazine*, July/August 2001, p36.

Estes, Ralph (1996) *Tyranny of the Bottom Line: Why Corporations Make Good People Do Bad Things*. San Francisco: Berrett-Koehler Publishers, Inc.

For example, Norm Thompson, a catalogue retailer in the Pacific northwest, decided one of the best things they could do for the environment would be to shift the entire catalogue industry to using recycled content paper. Shockingly, most catalogues still use 100 per cent virgin paper, based on concerns about appearance. Norm Thompson's management figured they could switch their entire catalogues to 100 per cent recycled but they'd just represent a tiny blip on the environment's fluttering electrocardiogram. If they could instead convince the entire industry to shift to only 10 per cent recycled content, they could make a much bigger impact. In order to do this, they had to prove that 10 per cent recycled paper catalogues sold merchandise just as well as ones on virgin paper. Also they had to bring pressure on the paper manufacturers to offer the recycled content paper at the same price. To pull off this feat, they partnered the Alliance for Environmental Innovation, affiliated with Environmental Defense.

Other organizations have worked with the World Wildlife Fund, the National Resources Defense Council, The Nature Conservancy, even Greenpeace, which formerly had earned a reputation for confrontational rather than collaborative approaches. Starbucks worked with Conservation International. Ben Packard, director of environmental affairs, cautions:

> *It's critical that your interests and those of the NGO overlap because the organizations can be so different. It's not enough for them to be a great organization addressing an important issue. The issue [that the two of you are going to work on] must be centrally relevant to both you and the NGO. For example, we worked with Conservation International on shade-grown coffee where they were trying to protect biodiversity and local economies and we could provide a market for their product.[9]*

RESOURCES

Business for Social Responsibility has advice and papers on partnering NGOs. See for example *BSR Update*, March/April 1999.

Stakeholder engagement activities

There are a number of different ways that you can engage stakeholders in discussion and exploration: community meetings, public hearings, private interviews, by-invitation round-table discussions, etc. We recommend that you find a number of ways to engage them. One gutsy example is US office equipment manufacturer Pitney Bowes' long-standing practice of holding annual worker stakeholders meetings. 'Stockholders meetings are usually tame compared with the annual jobholders meetings,' they report. Held in auditoriums near their main sites, the meetings give every employee a chance to ask management questions or air personal gripes. Senior officers sit on the stage while groups of up to 500 attend. They also hand out prizes – $50 Savings Bonds – for the best questions.[10]

Stakeholder audits

Some organizations, The Body Shop among them, do formal stakeholder audits. In *The Stakeholder Corporation: The Body Shop Blueprint for Maximizing Stakeholder Value*, the authors identify different classifications of stakeholders:

- primary social stakeholders: local communities, suppliers and business partners, customers, investors, employees and managers;
- secondary social stakeholders: government and civil society, social and third world pressure groups, media and commentators, trade groups and competitors;
- secondary non-social stakeholders: environmental pressure groups, animal welfare pressure groups, etc; and
- primary non-social stakeholders: the natural environment, non-human species, future generations.

The book provides guidelines for how to audit each of these areas.

Conclusion

Sustainability is an important strategic trend. Your organization may be able to delay significant financial commitments associated with sustainability. There is no need to install uncompetitive equipment, for example. However, you do not want to delay the learning process. Just as with the quality revolution, where it took years to understand what quality meant, how to measure it, what customers expected, etc., so each organization must answer similar questions regarding sustainability. The more you and your employees understand about sustainability, the more sophisticated you will all become in identifying threats and opportunities. You may choose not to be first to market but don't be last to begin this journey.

SCORE SENIOR MANAGEMENT

See page 31 for how to complete this assessment and page 33 for how to interpret your score.

LEADERSHIP/SENIOR MANAGEMENT				
Practice	Pilot *1 point*	Initiative *3 points*	Systemic *9 points*	Points
Sustainability management system: Have in place a process to routinely set priorities for sustainability improvements, monitor the results and institutionalize best practices.	Have a parallel structure and process to identify and make sustainability improvements (eg a steering committee).	Have implemented an environmental management system (EMS) equivalent to ISO 14001.	Have an ISO-compliant EMS with sustainability policies, criteria and targets embedded.	
Vision: Have a clear vision for how sustainability relates to your organization's mission.	Establish vision and framework for sustainability that clearly defines the business case for pursuing it.	Have conducted a backcasting-like process to develop a clear long-term vision of sustainability and interim goals that take responsibility for all major externalities.	Have a long-term vision of your role in a fully sustainable society. Question basic assumptions of your mission or business model and engage in long-term efforts to transform your organization and sector.	
Strategy: Integrate sustainability into the strategy and mission.	Create a strategy to spread sustainable thinking throughout the organization.	Embed sustainability into the strategic and business planning process of the organization.	Actively work to transform your industry or supply chain.	
Communication and education: Clearly communicate the importance of the vision and strategy to all affected employees.	Explain the need for pursuing sustainability and take symbolic action to back up the rhetoric.	Train all employees in sustainability and your chosen framework(s). Provide frequent updates and ways to reinforce sustainability thinking.	Speak regularly to other groups about your efforts, encouraging them to adopt sustainable practices and learn from your experience.	

LEADERSHIP/SENIOR MANAGEMENT				
Practice	Pilot *1 point*	Initiative *3 points*	Systemic *9 points*	Points
Commitment: Demonstrate commitment to sustainability through accountability and resources.	Form a steering committee and/or create the position of sustainability coordinator.	Require each department to work on sustainability initiatives and goals.	Build sustainability into budgets, reviews, selection criteria and compensation.	
Implementation: Embed sustainability into the organization.	Implement pilot efforts with some measurable results achieved.	Embed sustainability in business processes (planning, budgeting, appraisal, rewards, standard operating procedures, etc.) and make it part of every department's and person's responsibility.	Undertake efforts to move sustainability into your suppliers', customers' and other stakeholders' operations.	
Transparency and stakeholder involvement: Operate in a transparent and involving manner.	Provide ready access to complete and accurate performance data to investors, regulators and the public.	Provide mechanisms to solicit input from all major stakeholder groups.	Conduct regular, formal assessments of stakeholder expectations and satisfaction levels.	
Sustainability reporting: Annually produce and review a sustainability report reflecting your goals and progress.	Produce an internal document used by managers and employees.	Produce reports available to the public.	Produce reports that meet standards such as the Global Reporting Initiative, Greenhouse Gas Protocol.	
			Total Score	
			Average	

Facilities: How to Save Energy and Water, Improve Productivity and Reduce Waste

Buildings, their construction and operation, are usually a significant cost for any organization. They both displace habitat and affect transportation and land use patterns. They also consume a large percentage of our energy and produce much of our waste.

> *Consider that US buildings, which represent about half of the nation's wealth, consume 70 per cent of the nation's electricity, generate 30 per cent of waste, and are responsible for more global warming than any other nation's economy except China. In contrast, green buildings – with more natural light, better air quality and greater comfort – typically also contribute to improved occupant health, comfort and productivity. A more complete accounting of these costs and benefits demonstrates that green buildings are generally cost effective today, with average financial benefits exceeding additional costs by a factor of ten to one.*[1]

Thus facilities managers have a tremendous opportunity to make their organizations more sustainable while also saving money. Because buildings last for decades if not centuries, their choices have long-term consequences for the building owners and occupants and the community at large.

WHAT YOU SHOULD KNOW ABOUT SUSTAINABILITY

Facilities managers often find it hard to believe that they are not already doing all they can. However, sustainability often uncovers new opportunities. Facilities managers need to guard against the following common mistakes:

Being pound foolish. Often facilities will choose the cheapest first-cost option. But this can end up costing more in the long run. For example, vinyl flooring is typically cheaper than linoleum. However, linoleum usually lasts about four times as long. If materials represent about half the cost of a flooring job, the cost of the vinyl should be multiplied by eight to give a true comparison. Looking at the life cycle costs can make the more expensive product seem cheaper!

Wasting energy. When building designers apply a sustainability lens to the creation of a building, they invariably identify efficiencies not previously revealed. A green building is designed with an integrated team approach with a focus on optimizing trade-offs. For example, the building orientation, insulation and glazing may substantially reduce the size of the heating, ventilation and air conditioning (HVAC) system required, saving both capital and operating costs. Similarly, laying the piping out first to minimize angles and maximize diameter can radically reduce the costs associated with pumping compressed air or water.

Making people sick. Indoor air quality is often six to seven times worse than outside, sometimes resulting in sick building syndrome. Carpets, vinyl flooring and plywood cabinets and work surfaces may 'off-gas' chemicals into the air. Toxic and fragranced cleaning products may also contribute to allergies and illness. Toxic mould, caused by inadequate ventilation, has forced the closure of many buildings.

Paying twice. Waste can be defined as something you paid for that you pay again to get rid of. Portland State University in Oregon discovered during a waste audit that they were disposing of 1400 paper cups a day. They bought them and then had to pay to dispose of them. Sometimes the waste is not as obvious: a refrigerator near an oven, a return air vent near a heating vent. The executives in one office building were so intolerant to fluctuations in temperature that they set the thermostat for such a narrow range that air conditioning and heating alternated on and off all day.

STRATEGIES YOU CAN USE

To help you identify opportunities for eliminating the waste in your building, we've organized this section around the functions a facilities manager typically performs:

- constructing/remodelling a high-performance building;
- operating the building;
- managing waste;
- providing green cleaning and landscaping services; and
- managing transportation issues.

Construct/remodel a high-performance building

It still comes as a surprise to many that so-called 'green building' practices do not necessarily increase building costs. Furthermore, buildings so constructed typically save 30 per cent or more on energy and related operating expenses. For owner-occupied buildings, green building practices are now a no-brainer. In many markets, it also makes sense for developers to use green building practices even if they intend to lease or sell the structure – tenants and buyers are often willing to pay somewhat more for the improved amenities and there is good evidence that such properties lease faster than their equivalent conventional competitors.

Green building (or high-performance building) is an emerging field, driven largely by the success of the US Green Building Council's LEED (Leadership in Energy and Environmental Design) scoring system. This system has now been adopted by Australia, Canada, Brazil, India, Mexico and Taiwan. Similar to the checklists at the end of each of our chapters, LEED provides a laundry list of things you can do, each with points assigned. A building or remodelling project can be certified at several levels (certified, silver, gold and platinum) based on the number of points the building is able to earn. The intention of the World Green Building Council and its affiliates is to keep pushing building practices toward sustainability as new methods and technologies become available.

The California Department of Finance commissioned a study by the Capital E group and Lawrence Berkeley Laboratory to determine whether green building practices paid off. After studying 100 buildings across the country and other studies, they concluded that the financial benefits of green design are between $50 and $70 per square foot in a LEED building, over ten times the additional cost associated with building green.

The subject of green building practices could fill a book of its own, so here we only provide a sample of tactics to give you a feel for what is possible.

RESOURCES

For some examples of green building and an understanding of why it is important, see McDonough, William and Michael Braungart (2001) 'The Next Industrial Revolution' (video), Stevenson, Maryland: Earthome Productions, www.thenextindustrialrevolution.org.

Here are several green building standards and tools:

LEED: World Green Building Council, www.worldgbc.org, www.usgbc.org.

BREEAM: BRE Environmental Assessment Method, www.breeam.org.

BEES: Building for Environmental and Economic Sustainability is a software tool for selecting environmentally preferable building materials, www.bfrl.nist.gov.

Daylighting

In principle, daylighting simply involves letting natural light into a building. In practice, it is more complicated, for you want visibility, not glare, and in most commercial buildings, you want light but not heat. Daylighting's most obvious benefit is energy savings – you don't need to turn on the lights. But that is often the least of its benefits.

In an organizational setting, the highest cost associated with a building is not the building itself but the people in it. With that in mind, minor increases in capital costs to incorporate certain green features can at times provide a healthy return on investment. 'The biggest benefit of daylighting is the impact it has on the people in the space. If it weren't for people, we wouldn't be designing interior environments. Your highest overhead walks into the office on two legs every day. The cost of loss of productivity is incredible to a corporation,' says Stefan Graf, principal at Illuminart, based in Ypsilanti, Michigan.

> *Assume the cost to employ a worker is roughly $75,000 per year. If that employee works in approximately 150 square feet of space that originally cost around $15,000 to build, a 20 per cent productivity uptick on a $75,000-per-year worker pays back the entire cost of building construction in the first year ($15,000). 'These productivity benefits are just huge,' emphasizes Loveland, 'and we know that they're most directly correlated to daylight.'* [2]

A 20 per cent increase is not unrealistic. Based on the best research available from Carnegie Mellon University and others, daylighting appears to improve productivity and reduce absenteeism by up to that level. There are benefits beyond the workplace as well. Daylighting improves learning in schools, increases sales in retail environments and helps the elderly in retirement homes sleep better and live longer. In hospitals, people recover faster when they have access to daylight.

Of course, you will still need some lighting systems, but you can choose the most efficient fixtures and use daylight and motion sensors to limit their use. Lighting retrofits can often pay for themselves in just a couple years. Make sure lights can be turned on in sections of the building so that, for example, the entire building doesn't have to be lit when the janitors are in one area.

Site selection

Where you place the building and what direction you point it can be important factors as well. In most cases, you want to choose a site that can easily be accessed by a variety of transportation modes – public transport, bike and car. This makes alternative transportation a viable option. Portland State University intentionally situated its parking farther away than the transit stop so that people who take the light rail or bus only have to walk one-third as far to reach their destination as drivers do.

Industrial ecology involves co-locating properties that make use of one another's waste products. The most widely cited example is Kalundborg, Denmark where waste heat, biomass, water and other resources are exchanged among synergistic operations. This kind of relationship is easier to achieve when planning new sites, but at least consider who your neighbours are and investigate whether they might be dumping something you need.

The orientation of your building can have energy and lighting impact as well. Combining a sun-facing orientation with an engineered overhang enables you to take best advantage of sunlight and heat. Exterior glazing helps you efficiently manage light and heat. It is also wise to have at least part of your roof facing sunward so that you are positioned to make use of photovoltaic technology when it becomes feasible or so that you can easily add solar thermal systems to preheat water for boilers or hot water heaters.

Material selection

Obviously, buildings use a tremendous amount of the world's resources. So it is critical to minimize the impact of construction or remodels for the benefit of both the natural world and the building's users. You can buy low-VOC (volatile organic compound) paint, recycled and recyclable carpet and certified sustainable timber, often at prices competitive with traditional products. You can further avoid unnecessary materials by, for example, leaving rafters or piping exposed or by colouring a concrete floor instead of covering it with underlay and carpet.

In the building shell, give preference to materials with lower embodied energy (the amount of energy necessary to make them) where possible. For example, wood (which you would want to source from certified or well-managed forests) has a relatively frugal embodied energy of 639 kWh/ton. Brick has 4 times as much, concrete 5 times, glass 14 times and steel 24 times.[3]

Consider also how best to use the materials. Deschutes Brewery, a microbrewery in central Oregon, for example, put the insulation on the outside of their concrete building. This put the thermal mass inside the building. At night, they flush in the cool night air, which is then absorbed into the concrete walls and slowly released during the day. Because of their climate, they only need to use refrigeration to keep their cases of beer cold for two months a year.

RESOURCES

'Creating a High Performance Workspace G/Rated Tenant Improvement Guide' by the City of Portland Office of Sustainable Development. There is a chapter on finishes and furnishings. LEED Green Building Rating System for New Construction and Major Renovations.

Mechanical systems

With good design, you may be able to radically reduce or eliminate your HVAC system. The Eastgate office complex in Harare, Zimbabwe requires no air conditioning and almost no heating, despite the fact that the weather oscillates between 35 and 104°F. The architects took a lesson from termites to maintain a comfortable climate inside the building. Termites in Africa build tall, complex structures that must be kept at a narrow temperature range to grow food. They use underground tunnels to draw in cool air from the earth and open and close their 'windows' to create air flow and manage the temperature. Similarly, the Eastgate complex is actually two buildings linked by bridges across a shady, glass-roofed atrium open to the air. Fans suck fresh air in from the atrium, blow it upstairs through hollow spaces under the floors and from there into each office through skinting board (baseboard) vents. As the air rises and warms, it is drawn out through ceiling vents. Finally, it exits through 48 round brick chimneys.

To save energy, plan any system that requires piping carefully. The amount of energy needed to move something through a pipe increases geometrically as the pipe diameter shrinks. Bends in the piping also increase energy requirements. Lay out water pipes, compressed air pipes and the like in as straight a line as possible with the largest pipe size feasible. Then consider variable speed drives that can adjust the fan or pumping speed as needed. At the Collins Company mill in Klamath Falls, Oregon, they installed a back-pressure steam turbine generator to utilize wasted energy in their compressed air system, providing almost half the power needed to run the plant. They figure the annual savings to be around $250,000.

Construction waste

Construction waste is clogging our landfills. But carpet, concrete, studs, steel, plasterboard and other building materials can often be reused or recycled. Setting up the Natural Capital Center in Portland, Oregon involved turning an old warehouse into office space. They were able to reuse or recycle 97 per cent of their construction debris. So before you begin any construction or remodelling project, set stretch goals for the diversion of waste.

RESOURCES

Morton, Steven (2002) 'Business Case for Green Design: Sustainable Design is More than Good Intentions; It's a Way of Reaching Business Goals, www.facilitiesnet.com/bom/Nov02/Nov02environment.shtml.

Yale produces its *Journal of Industrial Ecology,* which is published by the MIT Press, mitpress.mit.edu/catalog/item/default.asp?ttype=4&tid=32.

Graedel, T. E. and B. R. Allenby (1995) *Industrial Ecology.* New Jersey: Prentice Hall.

Allenby, B. R. (1999) *Industrial Ecology – Policy Framework and Implementation.* New Jersey: Prentice Hall.

www.healthybuilding.net provides information on health impacts.

The Northwest Energy Efficiency Alliance has a useful website, www.BetterBricks.com.

Operate the building efficiently

The design of a building will clearly dictate the range of performance you can expect. However, everyday decisions can have a huge impact as well. Some are within your purview as a facilities manager, but you will need to become a behaviour modification expert as well.

Commissioning

It would be funny if it weren't so common: most buildings simply don't function as intended. Parts of the building may be hot while others are cold. The electronic controls may not be set properly. Building commissioning is the process of checking, usually with a third party, if the building is functioning the way it was designed. Aster Publishing in Eugene, Oregon saved more than $40,000 on its annual electricity bill in part by correcting an improper economizer operation and disabled HVAC controls.[4] These services may not be free, but they often pay for themselves in the first year.

Energy management

Probably the biggest operations and maintenance (O&M) cost a facility manager watches is energy. Certain factors are largely within your control: flushing the building with cool evening air to reduce the air conditioning (AC) load the next day; bringing parts of the building on over time so you don't create as much of a spike in energy demand; etc.

The big headache is usually the occupants: whining about being too hot or too cold, twiddling the thermostat, sneaking space heaters under their desks, leaving lights and computers on, etc. There are actions that you can take which will have some success. For example, Tufts University in Massachusetts estimated that if all students turned off their computers for six hours at night, they could save 572 tons of carbon equivalents and $87,000. Comparing current energy use in your buildings with past records can also uncover unnecessary use. But in reality, this will be the hardest part of the job.

Find creative ways to educate and inform occupants about the impacts of their decisions. Tri-Met, the transit authority for Portland, Oregon's metropolitan region, employed at least one elegant tactic – they posted the electricity bill in the lifts. No entreaties. No guilt tripping. Just information. And their energy use dropped by 20 per cent in the next month!

When doing remodels, set up better measurement systems. For example, SERA Architects in Portland, Oregon installed a separate electrical metering system when they remodelled their offices so that each would pay its own energy bills. They immediately switched to green power (at a nominal annual cost of $800 for 9000 square feet) and further divided their metering to separately track lighting, mechanical systems and plug loads. This separate metering enables them to target improvements and monitor energy use.

RESOURCES

Selling Energy Projects, by Loren Snyder, GreenBiz.com, www.greenbiz.com/news/reviews_
third.cfm?NewsID=27384.

Manage waste

The first step in managing waste is to change your thinking. It's not waste, it's a resource. This new mindset has allowed a number of organizations to achieve the goal of zero waste to landfill. Just imagine no dumpsters/skips!

- Interface has eliminated over US$165 million in waste. They have learned how to make new carpet from old carpet, reducing their need for oil. They also have a factory powered in part by solar energy.
- Xerox has saved more than US$2 billion since 1990 and diverted the equivalent of 2 million printers and copiers from the landfill. With their remanufacturing system, they take back old copiers and disassemble them. Parts that pass rigorous testing then get put in new products.
- Hewlett Packard in Roseville, California reduced its waste by 95 per cent and saved $870,564 in 1998. One action that contributed to this was switching from pallets to reusable slip-sheets to transport product.
- In 2000 Epson in Portland, Oregon reduced its waste to landfill to zero and saved $300,000. One of the strategies they used to achieve this was to buy a compactor to compress foam packaging, which was passed on as input to another manufacturer. Excess ink is shipped off as pigment for paints. The final 10 per cent that can't be reused or recycled is sent to a facility to be burned for electricity.

From the above examples, certain appropriate strategies become clear. Do a waste audit to see what is being thrown away. Even better, do a purchasing audit to see what you are buying – for your major purchases, consider their necessity, sourcing, recyclability and longevity. Find markets for whatever 'residual resource' (normally referred to as waste) you

---

RESOURCES

GrassRoots Recycling Network website, www.grrn.org.
Zero Waste Alliance, www.zerowaste.org.
Check with your local college or municipality to see if they offer low-cost waste assessments.

can't prevent through purchasing practices or process changes. Many communities have a waste exchange website that helps connect potential users of various waste streams.

Provide green cleaning and landscaping services

Many facilities contract out their cleaning and landscaping services. Whether you do the work yourself or contract it out, seek out greener, more benign options.

Many traditional cleaning products are loaded with hazardous chemicals and artificial fragrances. These often cause skin irritation and/or respiratory problems for cleaning staff and represent a significant spill risk. Such fragrances can also increase sick days for employees who have respiratory problems such as asthma.

Much of this risk is truly unnecessary. There are effective green cleaning products to serve almost every cleaning need. Instead of using a strong caustic product on every surface, decide when and where the 'big guns' really need to be used.

Most of the same points can be made for landscaping chemicals. If you use native plants appropriate to their location, the need for chemicals drops considerably. If you have any lawn, lower your standards and allow some 'weeds' to interrupt the monotonous carpet of green. Spray and fertilize only when needed, using the most benign product that will do the job. Switch back to raking instead of using noisy, polluting leaf blowers. Replace gasoline- or diesel-powered equipment with ones using cleaner fuels such as biodiesel, compressed natural gas, hydrogen or electricity (if it is sourced from renewables).

In both cases, periodically do a chemical inventory, tallying what you use and rating the products by hazard. Make every effort to eliminate those products that pose the most threat to environmental or human health. Material safety data sheets can help you with these decisions.

When we have done chemical inventories for clients, we find that initiating the inventory often leads to other business benefits. People clean out their shelves of old, unused product

---

RESOURCES

The Unified Green Cleaning Alliance has a recommended list of criteria for sustainable cleaning products, www.zerowaste.org/ugca.htm#final.

Green Seal has a certification system for cleaning products, www.greenseal.org.

Green/Blue is working on several projects related to chemicals, packaging and design for the environment issues, www.greenblue.org/activities.

The Zero Waste Alliance has a Chemical Assessment and Ranking System (CARS) software program that can assess the sustainability of product ingredients, www.zerowaste.org.

King County, WA has done an analysis of a number of commonly used landscape products, rating them on a scale from high concern to low, www.govlink.org/hazwaste/publications/COC_Report.pdf.

so they don't have to count it in the inventory. We often discover that the same organization buys different products from different vendors to serve the same purpose; when they combine purchases, they often get a significant quantity discount. To make the process of doing a chemical inventory easy, require your vendors to provide you with your usage information.

Manage transportation issues

Add up the amount of land – both parking and access roads – that you have devoted to the car. How much more would that property be worth if it were a building site? This is your missed opportunity cost. Now figure out what it cost to build those parking areas and associated swales, landscaping and sewer lines. Add these two numbers and divide by the number of parking spaces. The purpose of this maths problem is to make the point: there really is no such thing as free parking.

Portland State University calculated that they could not accommodate the expected growth in student numbers if they maintained the same student to parking ratio. Their existing 30 per cent public transport use – a level that would be the envy of many institutions – would have to be radically improved. As previously mentioned, they placed what parking they did provide further away from campus than the transit stops. They charge for parking and indicate the *annual* total on the monthly bills to shock people into the recognition of what it costs to own and operate a car; some of the parking revenue is used to subsidize bus passes and bike facilities. They provide a 'Flexcar' (a shared vehicle that can be rented by the hour) for people who do not have parking spaces. All this contributes to managing costs and reducing climate impact.

When it comes to transportation, the *Field of Dreams* movie refrain 'if you build it [near bus stops], they will come [via public transportation]' doesn't work without carrots and sticks. So charge *at least* what it costs you for parking. If you can, subsidize bus passes and help people find alternative ways to get to work. Reserve the best parking spots for car pools. Instead of validating customer parking, consider giving drivers a free bus ticket instead.

Of course, some people will still need to drive. So Quantec LLC, a small 35-person firm in Portland, Oregon, offers its employees a $9000 incentive to purchase a hybrid Toyota Prius ($150 per month over 60 months). They also buy bicycles for people who

---

RESOURCES

The Westside Transportation Alliance advocates balanced transportation choices, www.wta-tma.org.

The US Environmental Protection Agency's Office of Transportation and Air Quality, www.epa.gov/otaq.

prefer to commute that way. In addition to reducing greenhouse gases and air pollution, Quantec found these are effective programmes to recruit and retain good talent.

Conclusion

Because of the potential for cost savings and the relative size of the impacts, many organizations begin their sustainability efforts with a focus on their facilities. While you will find the biggest opportunities when you are first building or selecting a new facility, there are still many measures you can take with an existing structure. Where you are a tenant and don't control many aspects of the management of the facility (eg you don't have a separate electric meter or any influence over cleaning practices), consider your leverage with your landlord or opportunities to unite with other tenants to make requests for different services.

SCORE FACILITIES

See page 31 for how to complete this assessment and page 33 for how to interpret your score.

FACILITIES				
Practice	Pilot *1 point*	Initiative *3 points*	Systemic *9 points*	Points
Energy: Reduce environmental and social impacts associated with energy use through conservation, renewables and production.	At least every 5 years, conduct an energy audit and act on results.	Have in place systems for monitoring and reducing energy use both from equipment and human behaviour.	Purchase or produce at least 50% renewable energy.	
Waste: Move toward a zero waste facility.	Conduct a waste audit and act on results. Have systems in place for waste reduction (eg recycling is more convenient than refuse receptacles, monitoring and feedback systems, signage).	Provide incentives for employees and haulers to divert resources from the waste stream.	Achieve zero waste (at least 90% reduction in solid waste going to the landfill) while directing residual products to the 'next best use' whenever practical.	

FACILITIES				
Practice	Pilot *1 point*	Initiative *3 points*	Systemic *9 points*	Points
Landscaping: Provide landscaping that maximizes ecological benefits.	Conduct chemical assessment of landscape products and eliminate any that qualify as 'high concern' in the Washington State list or equivalent. Use no persistent bioaccumulative toxins (PBTs).	Minimize use of synthetic chemicals. Design landscaping to minimize water and pesticides and maximize ecological value (eg planting low-maintenance and native plants).	Restore or replace natural features of significant ecological value on your property (eg restore a stream, provide habitat on an eco-roof).	
Parking and transportation facilities: Create incentives for alternative transportation.	Provide free parking for car-poolers. Provide bike parking and shower facilities.	Subsidize bus passes and/or provide other incentives for alternative transportation.	Choose sites that permit commuting choices, including convenient alternative transportation.	
New construction and remodels: Use green building principles and practices.	Achieve LEED certified or equivalent. Use life cycle costs, not first costs, as the basis of decision-making.	Achieve LEED silver or equivalent.	Achieve LEED platinum or equivalent.	
Building Operation: Use green building principles and practices in building operation and maintenance.	Achieve LEED EB (existing buildings) or equivalent.	Achieve LEED EB silver or equivalent.	Achieve LEED EB platinum or equivalent.	
Cleaning: Use cleaning and pest control products and methods that minimize toxic substances.	Have 50% or more by volume green cleaning products (Green Seal, Green Cross, UGCA or equivalent). For paper products, source ones with high recycled content.	Have 75% of cleaning products green/sustainable; non-toxic pest control methods. Apply integrated pest management practices.	Have 100% of the cleaning products green/ sustainable; non-toxic pest control methods are used.	

FACILITIES				
Practice	Pilot *1 point*	Initiative *3 points*	Systemic *9 points*	Points
Fleets: Minimize the impacts of the fleet through the selection, maintenance and use of vehicles.	Implement a maintenance programme that minimizes hazardous waste, maximizes recycling and uses bio-based and non-toxic alternatives (eg the EcoLogical certification programme).	Assess the needs of drivers and select vehicles with the best fuel efficiency and emissions that meet these needs. Develop systems to minimize driving distance.	Use alternative fuels (biodiesel, ethanol, hydrogen) for all fleet vehicles.	
Water: Minimize the use of water and reduce rainwater run-off.	Conduct a water audit and act on the results. Eliminate any wasteful uses of water (eg single pass cooling towers).	Have a formal system in place for reducing water use and have methods for capturing and treating some of the rainwater that falls on the property.	Eliminate the need for water other than what falls as precipitation on the property (eg through recycling, water treatment) and keep 90% rainwater run-off on site in normal rain years.	
			Total Score	
			Average	

Human Resources: How to Support the Change Process and Bolster Employee Commitment

While at first sight it may not seem to be the case, human resource professionals are actually in a good position to influence the sustainability of an organization. When taken together, the practices and strategies we are addressing in this book amount to an organizational change initiative not unlike those from the last few decades, particularly Total Quality Management, process improvement, customer satisfaction and participative management. However, human resource (HR) professionals have been slow to pursue sustainability, in large part because they don't understand how much they have to offer.

The authors can identify with this problem. We too come from an organizational development background and when we encountered the concept of sustainability as a business issue in Harvard Business Review in the mid-1990s, we had an epiphany: by showing our clients how to be more productive, in many cases we had also shown them how to deplete the world's resources better, faster, cheaper. This was not the legacy we had in mind! We also experienced a crisis of confidence. There was no going back to the blissful state of ignorance but yet we couldn't see the path forward. What did we know about sustainability? We weren't biologists or chemical engineers? What did we have to offer?

What we've discovered on our journey is that implementing sustainability is a lot like implementing any other corporate change initiative. As an internal consultant, you need to get up to speed on certain concepts and terms, but the most troublesome issues most organizations face are not technical ones (do we use this chemical or that?) but concern organizational change: How does sustainability fit with our corporate strategy? Where should we begin our efforts? Who needs to be involved and how can we engage them? What framing is going to be most helpful? What structures do we need in place to manage the effort? At what point do we 'go public' with our efforts, internally and externally?

It's ironic that while we tiptoed into this field, we have never felt more valued for the contribution we bring. Technical people, including scientists and engineers, the same ones who roll their eyes when you try to engage them in a team-building exercise, have practically begged for our help. As one engineer put it, 'To do this work, you have to bring together a good cross-section of people, all of whom have their own opinions. Pretty soon, someone gets angry and then I don't know what to do.' Many human resource professionals have excellent facilitation and conflict management skills, exactly the skills that others in the sustainability field lack.

WHAT YOU SHOULD KNOW ABOUT SUSTAINABILITY

As we investigated sustainability, we found many organizations making unnecessary implementation mistakes:

Spray-and-pray training. A manufacturer of wood products trained all their employees in The Natural Step framework and then sat back, waiting for miracles to happen. Of course, many people forgot what they were taught since there was no planned way to use the knowledge immediately. Few ideas were suggested until the organization put into place a more structured way to involve staff.

The big black hole. Another company trained all employees on sustainability and asked employees to share ideas about actions the organization could take. These ideas were collected but there was no process to assess them, act on them or give feedback to employees about them. So for about two years, the ideas disappeared into the black hole, leaving employees wondering just how serious the organization was.

A rose by any other name. An organization based in 'Ecotopia' (Oregon) found out the hard way that their employees on the east coast of the US didn't have the same connotations for such terms as 'environmentalist'. Rather than building excitement with their training, they were deepening the resistance to the concept.

If you don't know where you're going... A boss in a property development firm got the sustainability bug and hired someone to lead the effort. However, the top management team had never had a conversation about how sustainability fitted into their business strategy. At this point in time, they have got through two sustainability coordinators, both of whom left in frustration.

Unrequited expectations. The owner of a construction firm got his employees too excited about sustainability. Employees started leaving because they felt the company wasn't changing fast enough.

You should recognize these change management mistakes. They are generic problems. Had these organizations involved an HR professional in their plans, they might have avoided these unnecessary complications.

So don't be intimidated if you don't know the difference between PVC and PBTs. It doesn't matter. Your skills are critical to carrying out sustainability. It's your job to be the generalist, the change consultant, the process designer, the meeting facilitator. These are all things you know how to do. For the technical sustainability topics you don't already have under your belt, take a class, read a book or hire a sustainability expert as a shadow consultant. You'll pick it up quickly.

Sustainability is at its core an issue requiring organizational change and cultural change. Edgar Shein, author of *Leadership and Organizational Culture*, identifies five primary mechanisms that affect culture:

1   what leaders pay attention to, measure and reward;
2   how leaders react to critical incidents;
3   what leaders deliberately role-model;
4   criteria for allocating rewards and status; and
5   criteria for selecting, recruiting, promoting and firing.[1]

Note how many of these mechanisms are the responsibility of human resources, either overtly through HR systems or through management training and coaching. So HR is key to making sustainability 'stick'.

STRATEGIES YOU CAN USE

We see the role of the human resources director and department falling into the following categories:

- **Introduce the concept to top executives**. If your senior managers are not yet well versed in sustainability, assess when the time is right and then find the best way to introduce the topic.
- **Consult on the implementation**. Help put in place a plan that has a high probability of success.
- **Align human resource systems**. Incorporate sustainability into your HR systems (eg orientation/training, hiring, reviews, pay, benefits) to reinforce the organization's efforts.
- **Model appropriate behaviours**. Assess your own impacts and make changes to your meeting management, paper processing and other tasks.
- **Measure the benefits**. Enhance your existing measurement systems to track the return on your sustainability initiatives.

Introduce the concept to top executives

Because the HR department often includes an organizational development function and may facilitate strategic and operational sessions with top management, HR professionals are often in a good position to introduce new trends to senior management. Unfortunately, few in HR are well versed in sustainability. Remember, you don't have to be the expert. Your role may be as simple as pointing out articles about sustainability as a trend and inviting management to explore this as one of many interesting global trends that could affect their business. Here are some ideas to get you thinking:

- Route a reprint of a sustainability-related article from a respected management publication (eg *Harvard Business Review*, *MIT Sloan Management Review* or *Business Week*).

RESOURCES

Here are some of our favourite articles to introduce executives to sustainability:

Senge, Peter and Goran Carstedt (2001) 'Innovating our Way to the Next Industrial Revolution,' *MIT Sloan Management Review*, Winter. This article provides a good explanation of why sustainability is going to be the real 'new economy' (versus the dot-com version of the not-so-new economy). This would be an excellent summary to give to executives unfamiliar with the issue as it includes most of the basic concepts (eg natural capitalism), quotes from big-name executives, differentiates eco-efficiencies from sustainability, and recounts some good profitability stories.

Hall, Jeremy and Harrie Vrendenburg (2003) 'The Challenges of Innovating for Sustainable Development', *MIT Sloan Management Review*, Fall. This article helps to explain why sustainability can be viewed as cutting both ways. 'From a company's perspective, innovation can be a primary source of sustained competitive advantage as well as a significant source of risk, competitive disruption and failure... The additional interacting pressures from social and environmental concerns make SDI [sustainable development initiatives] more complex than conventional market-driven innovation.' Monsanto's GMO debacle is given as an example. The article also explains how Suncor and Transalta have managed that risk successfully.

'Global Sustainability and Creative Destruction of Industries', *MIT Sloan Management Review*, Fall 1999. This article does a good job of distinguishing green strategies from sustainability ones. For example, green strategies focus on incremental improvement in existing products, processes, suppliers and customers, while sustainability involves focusing on emerging technologies, markets, partners and customers – a list which suggests more emphasis on discontinuous creative destruction/restructuring of industries. It also segments the global market into three parts: consumer economy (1 billion people), emerging markets (2 billion people) and survival economy (3 billion people). Depending upon which market you're in, you should be asking different questions and focusing on different results.

The 'Millennium Ecosystem Assessment' study, performed for the UN by scientists from all over the world, summarizes the main issues. The 31-page overview report 'Living Beyond Our Means: Natural Assets and Human Well-being' nicely covers the global challenges we face, www.millenniumassessment.org/en/index.aspx.

- At a management meeting, show a video related to sustainability (eg 'The Next Industrial Revolution') and use it as a discussion starter.
- In preparation for a strategic planning session, suggest to management that sustainability should be one of a handful of emerging trends they should examine.
- Bring in executives from other respected organizations to talk about why they have adopted sustainability as a strategic issue and how they use it to improve their performance.

Consult on the implementation

Many of the mistakes organizations make implementing sustainability are predictable change management blunders. This is hardly surprising given that most of the people implementing sustainability have no change management training. HR professionals can be critical partners in crafting a successful implementation plan to fit their particular organization's circumstances. They understand the importance of involvement; they know how to respond to resistance; they are familiar with reframing techniques to enrol stakeholders; they are in control of many of the communication and educational systems; and they often coach managers in their own performance.

For example, the new executive director of the Oregon Museum of Science and Industry in Portland, Oregon was passionate about sustainability but recognized that in her organization, top-down directives were rarely as long-lived as bottom-up ones. So she hired us to help her develop an implementation strategy. We formed a steering committee of employees and managers whose job it was to study sustainability, catalyse a few pilot projects and, by the end of the year, recommend whether the organization should adopt sustainability as one of its strategic goals. The steering committee developed two broad improvement goals: zero waste and climate change. A task force was formed to work on each issue and they reported their results back to the steering committee. They made reports to all-staff meetings about reducing their solid waste by 40 per cent and encouraging alternative transportation. The steering committee also set up informal lunchtime sessions where people could learn about sustainability. By the end of the year, everyone at the museum was familiar to some extent with sustainability and the steering committee gave the executive director the enthusiastic go-ahead she had hoped would come.

A second role that the HR department can play is to help individual departments map out and improve their processes. Many environmental impact analyses, especially those associated with environmental management systems, are based on a process diagram. Many HR professionals, either through their experience with organizational development or the quality management fields, are well prepared to do this.

RESOURCES

Doppelt, Bob (2003) *Leading Change toward Sustainability*. Sheffield, UK: Greenleaf Publishing.

Align human resource systems

Human resource systems have a powerful influence on employee behaviour, so it's important to ensure that your systems are supporting the behaviour that you want. Companies that touted teamwork and collaboration, for example, soon discovered that their individually focused performance appraisal and reward system undermined the collaboration they were trying to instil. If you don't watch for these types of mismatches you can undermine your own implementation efforts.

Orientation. Many organizations run a blanket training programme when they begin a sustainability effort but then forget about employee turnover. Including sustainability in your new employee orientation will ensure that you don't lose ground.

Selection and job descriptions. Eventually, sustainability becomes embedded in the jobs people do. This should be reflected in job descriptions and selection criteria. Chevron made an understanding of environmental issues a selection criterion for their CEOs.[2] You will also want to reach out to disadvantaged populations. While this may already be part of a strong diversity programme that you pursue for other reasons, sustainability strengthens the case for engaging with this segment of society. In the US at least, sustainability still is predominately an upper-middle-class white phenomenon. As you hire people from disadvantaged or minority communities, you not only extend the concepts of sustainability to new populations, you learn more about what is important to those communities, helping you to reframe sustainability in terms that will resonate with them.

Training. Embed sustainability into your training programmes. In particular include it in supervisory and management training, but you can also include sustainability-related examples in many other classes. Make sure all employees get some basic-level understanding of sustainability concepts and, over time, provide more in-depth training in specialized topics as they are needed. Remember that training doesn't just happen in classrooms. Find ways to embed sustainability into regular staff meetings and other corporate communication vehicles.

Reviews and rewards. Align your pay and reward systems with your sustainability policies. Often, linking a minor portion of pay to sustainability is enough to get action. Norm Thompson, a catalogue retailer, wanted their buyers to use sustainability as part of their decision-making process when they chose products for their catalogue. But just telling them this was not enough to change behaviour because their pay system didn't reward them for the extra work. So HR told them that 10 per cent of their pay would be based on improving the sustainability quotient of their purchases. This got their attention! Instantly, the buyers wanted to know how they could tell if one product was greener than another. This led to the creation of an elaborate scoring system and associated toolkit. The entire toolkit can be downloaded from www.NormThompson.com/Sustainability (under 'Products with a Purpose').

Certainly, you will also want to ensure that you are paying a fair, living wage. Deciding what constitutes a living wage can be a knotty problem, however. Rejuvenation, a small period lighting manufacturer in Portland, Oregon, struggled with how to determine a living wage and how to fund paying it in a world of global competition. They found a regional research study on what constituted 'fair pay' but learned that what is adequate for a single adult living alone is different from that for a dual-income couple or parents with three children. This led them to learn more about their employees' households. They used this information to determine a fair wage and then did what they could afford to provide that for their entry-level employees. Part of their strategy is to accelerate pay increases for the lowest grade positions faster than higher grades to close the gap.

Most organizations link their performance review systems to pay, so find ways to embed sustainability there as well. This can take some effort since the goals are often linked to job tasks. One of the barriers associated with implementing sustainability is that people can't imagine what they should do differently. The solid waste division of the Washington Department of Ecology found that many people said 'I just follow the regulations' while others had no problem envisioning how to incorporate sustainability into their everyday work life.

To solve this problem, we helped them develop a process for guiding employees so they could integrate sustainability into their jobs. The department already had Job Alike Groups (JAGs) that were composed of people from across the state who did the same job. We designed a process similar to 'backcasting' where the JAGs examined their work process, identified their impacts, defined the sustainable future state and then worked backward to identify what they would have to do differently in ten, five and one years as well as things they could change now. We trained people to facilitate these JAG meetings. The management JAG went through a slightly different process to determine how to support these efforts. This included a process linked to their performance review system. Employees were expected to bring ideas about how to change their work practices to the performance review discussion so that these new practices could be reflected in individual performance plans.

Reward programmes. Award/reward programmes and contests can be risky because the psychological effects of rewards on human behaviour are quite complex. (We recommend *Punished by Rewards* by Alfie Kohn for more on this.) Sometimes it's just a matter of making sure there is something in it for the employee. Luper Brothers is an auto repair shop in Lewiston, Idaho. In the office, Luper Brothers' employees recycle aluminium, cardboard, plastics, scrap iron and polystyrene. They realized that nagging wasn't the best way to get employees to recycle. Instead, they developed an incentive programme that enabled employees, on their own time, to recover the more valuable metals and metal parts (copper, aluminium, bearings) from waste components and earn extra income by selling them.

One of the most famous and effective reward programmes was run by Dow Chemical Company back in the 1980s to improve environmental performance. While the example is dated, there is a lot to learn from their success. In 1982, their Louisiana Division created a contest to find energy-saving projects with a high return on investment. In that first year, there were 27 winners, requiring capital investments of $1.7 million and an average return on investment (ROI) of 173 per cent. What was most surprising, violating the commonly held assumptions about diminishing returns, was that each year the employees found better and better projects yielding better ROIs. Many of these projects involved process improvements such that the productivity gains started to exceed the energy and environmental benefits. After ten years the programme was generating ideas that on average returned 300 per cent! What was going on? Why didn't they quickly exhaust the low-hanging fruit? We believe the employees got increasingly sophisticated in their ability to identify improvement opportunities.[3]

Transportation-reduction programmes. Many HR departments operate programmes to reduce commuting impacts. These range from subsidizing bus passes and coordinating car pools to encouraging telework. For service organizations, transportation may be a major source of environmental impact. For example, at SERA Architects in Portland, Oregon, their backcasting process revealed that commuting and travel were by far their biggest impacts, bigger by a factor of two over any other activity. At the time they began investigating travel issues, they were issuing each employee with the cash equivalent of a monthly bus pass. Employees could do what they wanted with the cash, so drivers were using it for parking expenses. The firm didn't feel that the policy really sent a strong enough message. When they crunched the numbers they discovered that 33 per cent of their staff were commuting alone in cars and that the travel subsidy the firm paid out to them came to enough to give every employee an extra two days' paid holiday. SERA decide to revoke the payment to single occupancy commuters and gave every employee the extra two paid days of holiday. Now they ask each employee to submit a quarterly travel report. If an employee can demonstrate that he used alternative transportation to get to work at least 80 per cent of the time, he is paid a quarterly bonus equal to the cost of a three-month bus pass.

In the US you can set up a pre-tax Transportation Savings Account (similar to a health savings account) that allows employees to pay for alternative transportation expenses (eg bus passes) with pre-tax earnings. Japanese auto maker Mazda is paying employees 1500 yen (about US$12.50) a month to walk to work to improve their health and help the environment. Employees must live at least two kilometres away from work and commute by foot at least 15 days a month to qualify. Yamaha has a similar programme. These programmes may pay for themselves in reduced health plan costs.

Historically employers have felt that employee commuting was not their business. But take a bit of time to compute the cost of providing employee parking. What is the cost of that asphalted land? What is the cost in obesity and related health problems to your health plan when you make it easy for employees to limit their exercise.

Portland State University, sited in downtown Portland, Oregon, realized they couldn't possibly increase their student population as their strategic plan directed if all employees needed a parking space. So they did a number of things to encourage alternative transportation. Parking lots are inconveniently located whereas public transit stops are close to the front doors. Monthly parking passes show the annual cost of parking on the receipt to emphasize the true cost of driving. The university also provides 'Flexcar' benefits so that professors and employees can rent a car on an hourly basis when a car really is the best way to get around.

Progressive Investment Management, a socially responsible investment manager, actually charges their employees for the climate impacts of their transportation choices. Employees track both business trips and commuting, and a fee to purchase carbon offsets is deducted from their annual bonus.

Investments and retirement funds. In many organizations, the retirement benefits are part of HR responsibility. Screening investments on social responsibility criteria can send important signals to the marketplace. The huge California public employees' pension programme, CalPERS, has been a leader in this practice.

RESOURCES

Hitchcock, Darcy (2001) *Making Sense of Sustainability: An Employee Guide.* Portland, OR: AXIS Performance Advisors, Inc., www.axisperformance.com/sust_series.html.

Galea, Chris (ed.) (2005) *Teaching Business Sustainability: Volume 1 – From Theory to Practice.* Sheffield, UK: Greenleaf Publishing. NOTE: Volume 2, *Case Studies* was due for publication in 2005 but has not yet been released at the time of writing.

Model appropriate behaviours

Certainly, HR should model sustainable behaviour by implementing the suggestions in the chapter on services and office operations. You should also set the tone for work/life balance. The HR department is also well placed to organize and participate in community projects. Apply environmentally preferable purchasing guidelines when you purchase products and services. When you arrange meetings, use a green caterer who offers locally grown, seasonal produce, buffet-style meals that reduce packaging, and reusable flatware and glasses.

Use your influence and your contacts across the organization to align actions with words. Encourage your legal staff to print contracts on both sides and to allow electronic signatures. Encourage purchasing to implement environmentally preferable purchasing policies and work with facilities to improve the comfort of and air quality in the building.

Measure the benefits

Learn how all the various parts of the business affect human health, employee satisfaction and productivity. Did you know that green cleaning products can reduce absenteeism related to asthma and other lung- and skin-related sensitivities? Did you know that daylighting and other green building practices can improve productivity? Have you thought about how sustainability can bring meaning to work and help you attract and retain employees? So talk to your facilities manager about the cleaning arrangements and get involved if there is a remodel planned. Work with top management to maximize the benefits of their sustainability initiative so that it inspires both applicants and employees.

You can help make the business case for sustainability by measuring your own improvements and also helping others gather quantitative and qualitative data. The following list should help you see opportunities:

- Measure productivity before and after a remodel in which green building techniques are used.
- Track absenteeism before and after the cleaning staff switch to green cleaning products. Compute both the labour costs and the avoided medical costs.
- Ask job applicants if they are familiar with your sustainability initiative and see how many say they approached you because of your commitment to it. Track the percentages over time to show top management the trend line.
- Compare your retention rates with similar organizations that have not adopted sustainability. Compute the cost savings by factoring in the cost of advertising for, screening, hiring and training new employees.

SCORE HUMAN RESOURCES

See page 31 for how to complete this assessment and page 33 for how to interpret your score.

HUMAN RESOURCES				
Practice	Pilot *1 point*	Initiative *3 points*	Systemic *9 points*	Points
Executive education: Provide executives with education on sustainability.	Expose executives to sustainability through articles, speakers and other methods.	Provide executives with formal training on sustainability and incorporate discussions of its relevance in planning meetings.	Make sustainability knowledge and commitment a selection and performance criterion for executives.	
Implementation strategy: Develop a plan to support implementation of leadership vision and strategy.	Launch a sustainability pilot initiative.	Help to manage a formal, organization-wide sustainability initiative.	Help the organization embed sustainability into all business systems (planning, budgeting, reviews, rewards, etc.)	
Culture: Make sustainability 'how we do things here'.	Develop an empowered culture where employees routinely come up with ways to improve performance; sustainability is one of the areas employees focus on.	Have a formal system for recognizing employee contributions to sustainability.	Demonstrate through word and action that sustainability is a core value of the organization.	
Employee Orientation and Training: Provide ongoing sustainability education for all employees.	Provide training to employees involved with sustainability efforts.	Train the entire staff on sustainability concepts and appropriate frameworks.	Routinely offer training on advanced sustainability practices.	

HUMAN RESOURCES				
Practice	Pilot *1 point*	Initiative *3 points*	Systemic *9 points*	Points
Performance systems: Embed sustainability into job descriptions, selection criteria, and performance reviews.	Have a formal process to help employees discover how to apply sustainability into their everyday work.	Rewrite job descriptions and selection criteria to include sustainability for all appropriate employees.	Incorporate sustainability into performance evaluations	
Pay: Link rewards and pay to sustainability performance.	Provide a fair, living wage to all employees.	Provide an award or reward programme to encourage sustainability innovations.	Maintain a fair ratio between the highest and lowest paid employee.	
Organizational climate: Provide a respectful and productive workplace.	Conduct an employee survey at least every 2 years and act on the results (including such elements as employee involvement, diversity, work/life balance and living-wage jobs).	Actively recruit from and provide jobs for people from disadvantaged populations (eg people with disabilities, minorities, at-risk young people).	Be listed as one of the best places to work in the region or country.	
Commuting: Provide effective incentives to encourage the use of alternative transportation and/or reduce the need to commute.	Do not provide paid parking except for car-poolers. Promote the use of alternative transportation. Site the office such that it can be easily accessed by at least one alternative transportation method.	Provide assistance for alternative commuting including subsidized bus passes, bike facilities, showers, etc.	Provide financial incentives to encourage alternative transportation including bonuses, carbon offsets, etc., and/or provide financial assistance for employees to purchase the most environmentally responsible car models available.	

HUMAN RESOURCES				
Practice	Pilot *1 point*	Initiative *3 points*	Systemic *9 points*	Points
Volunteering and charities: Support the communities in which you operate or which you affect.	Have systems that encourage employees to donate to charities and to volunteer.	Allow employees to volunteer during paid work time.	Select certain charities or social/ environmental issues that are strategic to your organization and provide at least 40 hours per person of pro bono services per year.	
			Total Score	
			Average	

Purchasing: How to Determine What to Buy and How to Work with Suppliers

Over the last decade, purchasing has transformed from an administrative function to a strategic one. It's no longer enough to get the product on time and at the cheapest possible price. Now purchasing has become integral to managing waste, protecting product claims and managing the entire supply chain. Just-in-time manufacturing requires more intimate relationships with a smaller number of suppliers. Customer requirements are driving the need to know what is in the product. Public and shareholder expectations drive buyers to investigate the labour and human rights practices of their vendors. So purchasing today is key to efficiency, competitiveness and image. This chapter explores how these drivers relate to sustainability in more depth.

WHAT YOU SHOULD KNOW ABOUT SUSTAINABILITY

The purchasing corollary to the old adage 'what goes up must come down' is 'what comes in must go out', meaning either as product or waste. One study of 'material throughput' in US manufacturing discovered that only 6 per cent of the inputs ended up in the product![1] We are purchasing huge quantities of stuff that doesn't get translated into sales. And much of what's left must be paid for *again*, in tipping fees or emissions permits. Getting control over your purchasing choices can not only reduce your environmental and social impacts, it can also save you costs relating to material input *and* output.

Companies increasingly have to substantiate environmental claims about their products. Many governments and companies are issuing environmentally preferable purchasing policies, in some situations publishing grey lists and black lists of chemicals they want to see less of or have phased out entirely. This requires you to know what is in the sub-assemblies, components and additives that go into your product. In 2001, just in time for the holiday season, The Netherlands banned Sony Playstations because the cables contained too much cadmium, causing a media uproar and earning Sony a hefty fine.

Through surveys and other methods, purchasing agents must understand what is in the products they buy.

Several years ago, Nike was surprised to discover that the public held them responsible for the labour practices of their suppliers. Nike doesn't manufacture anything; they use suppliers, mostly in Asia, to manufacture their shoes and clothing. After stories about worker abuses and low wages hit the papers, Nike's image took a dive. If the public makes no distinction between the practices of a company and those of its major suppliers, then it is prudent to know all you can about the social, ethical and environmental practices of your vendors.

Just-in-time manufacturing has led to sole-sourcing or reducing the number of suppliers. With this comes a level of risk. What happens if your only supplier of a key component has a significant problem – their plant blows up, the department of environmental quality shuts them down or one of their critical raw materials is suddenly classified as a hazardous material? Instantly your entire supply chain can be disrupted. To manage that risk, many purchasing departments require suppliers to have an environmental management system or to be ISO 14000 certified.

The world is so interconnected, one mishap can lead to a host of problems. For example, when a fire destroyed Philip's semiconductor plant in Albuquerque, New Mexico, the supply of radio frequency chips used in cell phones was cut off to both Nokia and Ericsson. While the fire was caused by lightning, not human error, it demonstrates the importance of having strong supply chain management systems. When the fire prevented Philips from shipping their product, the resulting shortage devastated Ericsson as they did not have supplier redundancy built into their system. Nokia, on the other hand, met its production targets and took market-share away from Ericsson, who ended up by missing their production targets and posting a US$1.7 billion loss in their handset division that year.[2]

Determining whether product A is more sustainable than product B can be a daunting task, much more complicated that it would first seem. Yet purchasing departments are now being asked to make these assessments. Often they turn to product certification schemes (Green Seal, Energy Star, Food Alliance, Forest Stewardship Council, etc.), which are audited by a third party. However, this is only a partial solution as there are often competing certification schemes making different claims for the same product. Purchasing must then assess whether certification A is better than certification B!

Some organizations have used purchasing as a way to move an industry toward sustainability. A number of clothing manufacturers, under the umbrella of Business for Social Responsibility, tackle sweatshops and other international labour issues. Nike and Patagonia have joined forces with others to create a reliable market for organic cotton (since a quarter of the world's herbicides are used on this crop).

STRATEGIES YOU CAN USE

As you can see, purchasing is not just paper-pushing anymore. So what are the strategies progressive purchasing departments are using to help their organizations become more sustainable? We've organized the most common strategies into two loose categories:

1 **purchasing practices** – the systems, policies, and procedures that support sustainability; and
2 **purchasing projects** – typical ad hoc tasks that are undertaken to solve a particular problem.

Purchasing practices

Purchasing practices includes those policies, procedures and systems that support or encourage sustainable choices. This section looks at some of the more common best practices.

Adopt sustainable or environmentally preferable purchasing (EPP) policies

Many organizations, especially governmental agencies, are establishing EPP guidelines. Forty-seven US states have some form of buy-recycled policies, and many local and state agencies go far beyond this.[3] The city of San Francisco, for example, has just become the first city in the US to enact a law that requires all city purchases to take public health and environmental stewardship into consideration. The law affects everything from toilet paper to computers and covers the $600 million per year the city spends on products.[4] These policies send important market signals, rewarding those with more sustainable products and services while hanging a carrot out for those who don't. As the name implies, most EPP policies focus only on environmental attributes (often including human health), leaving out the socio-economic elements that are equally important to sustainability; but at least they are a start. You can incorporate socio-economic elements into a sustainable purchasing policy by adding other criteria such as labour practices, diversity and community contributions.

Depending on the culture of the organization, these EPP programmes may take the form of formal policies and guidelines or simply accepted practice. Don't reinvent the wheel; many of them are available on the internet, so borrow freely.

You can also use eco-labels as a proxy for doing all your own investigation. Appendix B lists some of the labelling and certification programmes available. Note that choosing to use these certifications may disadvantage small businesses, so you may want to provide a way to offset this.

RESOURCES

The Center for a New American Dream's website includes a host of examples, www.newdream.org.

For information about eco-labels used in the US go to www.ecolabels.com.

The US Environmental Protection Agency has created environmentally preferable guidelines for computers; go to www.epa.gov/oppt/epp/electronics.htm.

Embed EPP or sustainable choices into online systems

In a decentralized purchasing environment, one of the most effective ways to encourage people to choose EPP products is to make them easiest to find and procure. When someone searches for notepads, for example, the ones made from recycled content should show up first. Make chlorine-free copy paper pop up first on your online purchasing system. If an employee needs a less sustainable product, make them dig for it.

TriMet, the transit authority for the Portland, Oregon metropolitan region, worked with Office Depot to further develop internal green purchases. They examined their top 20 purchases (this included file folders, paper, post-it pads, pens, pencils, pads, etc.) and then worked with both Office Depot and Boise Cascade to identify recycled options to make them the first items employees see when they go online to make purchases. As environmental engineer Kevin Considine explains, 'Their product lines are limited to what I would call more conventional choices – no options for 100 per cent post-consumer chlorine-free kenaf paper or anything like that.' He acknowledges that the greener options have cost them more at times, but says that these prices are coming down because of the increasing green market they are helping to create. 'It was relatively easy [to set this up] and more options are being added to their product line each year that meet performance needs and are at least a greener option.'

Embed sustainability language into RFPs and contracts

Sustainability brings together strange bedfellows at times. We once had someone approach us to bid with them on a wastewater treatment job. We admitted to knowing nothing about wastewater treatment. No matter; they wanted us on the team anyway because we understood sustainability and the request for proposal (RFP) made mention of it. In the process of writing the proposal, we were able to impart a lot about sustainability. (Mercifully, we didn't get the job.)

Never underestimate the power of including mention of sustainability or related terms in an RFP. It definitely gets attention and it helps to pre-empt the nay-sayers who claim that customers aren't asking for sustainability. You don't even need to rate it particularly highly in your evaluation criteria. But doing so will stimulate creative thinking and innovative proposals.

Similarly, write sustainability language into your contracts. Cleaning contractors can be asked to use Green Seal or equivalent products. Require your landscaping firm to use integrated pest management with synthetic pesticides used only as a last resort. Building contractors can be expected to recycle or reuse 90 per cent or more of construction debris. Professional service firms can publish reports on chlorine-free, 30+ per cent post-consumer recycled paper and bind reports without plastic covers or vinyl binders. Arm-twist your lawyers into printing contracts double-sided. Maybe use existing eco-labels, third-party certification schemes and standards as additional criteria.

Writing contract language is another place where you'll want to leverage what others have done. Use the resources below to fast-forward your process. Also check out the appropriate third-party certification programmes.

RESOURCES

EPA's environmentally preferable purchasing contracts database, www.epa.gov/oppt/epp/database.htm.

EPPNet www.nerc.org/eppnet.html.

Government websites, especially King County, Washington and Santa Monica, California; Massachusetts and Minnesota.

For information about eco-labels used in the US go to www.ecolabels.com. See also a listing of common eco-labels used internationally in Appendix B.

The Unified Green Cleaning Alliance website has standards for sustainable cleaning products, www.ugca.org.

Use service contracts to align the interests of your vendors with your own

Sometimes the solution is to change the incentives in a contract so that the vendor's interests are aligned with yours. Often this takes the form of service contracts that convert products into services. Instead of buying paint, you purchase the service of painting widgets. Now the vendor doesn't want to sell you the maximum amount of this toxic product but instead benefits from reducing the product's use and reducing its toxicity.

These service contracts are used most commonly for chemicals and resource management issues. For example, Portland State University's waste hauler used to be paid for each ton of garbage that was hauled way, creating a negative incentive for recycling. The more that was recycled, the less waste they could haul away and get paid for. As a result, the hauler did not have any reason to help Portland State reduce waste or increase recycling. So the university set out to craft new contract language whereby both parties shared in the benefits of increasing the recycling rate by compensating the hauler for helping to reduce waste and process recyclables. 'It's great,' says Michele Crim, their sustainability coordinator, 'Now they are setting up site visits for our recycling coordinators to show them an effective collection process from beginning to end.'

Implement a supply chain environmental management system

Supply chains have become increasingly critical to business, requiring collaboration across organizations. Outsourcing, just-in-time manufacturing and cradle-to-grave legal risks all imply that you must manage beyond the walls of your own operation.

The most common approaches to greening the supply chain are summarized in the table below:[5]

Table 9.1 *Options for working with suppliers*

Approach	Use when...
Choose greener products	You know what is 'greener' and where to get it.
	Example: Switch from a petroleum-based solvent to a water-based one.
Notify vendors	You know what is 'greener' and your current vendors don't offer this to you now.
	You want to keep using the same vendors.
	Example: Send a letter to your contractors to inform them that when you renew their contract, you will require they use Green Seal or equivalent products.
Survey suppliers	You need to know what is in your product.
	You want to influence your suppliers' business strategy.
	Example: Send a survey to your supplier of cabinets to enquire about formaldehyde.
Create a coalition	You are a small customer for your supplier and don't have enough clout to get their cooperation.
	Cooperating with other companies will not undermine your competitive advantage.
	You want to create a reliable market for a product.
	Example: You want to get 100% post-consumer recycled paper but it costs more so you form a coalition of other firms in your office building to purchase larger quantities, reducing the cost to that of 30% recycled content reams.

Table 9.1 *Options for working with suppliers* (cont'd)

Approach	Use when...
Host a supplier workshop	You need to improve your process, product or business relationship with your suppliers.
	You plan to continue using the same suppliers.
	Example: Invite one of your first-tier suppliers to a workshop to explore how to improve the quality, cost and environmental performance of your processes.
Partner with an NGO	You need the credibility of the non-governmental organization (NGO) (eg to avoid accusations of 'green-washing').
	The NGO has existing relationships with other suppliers who provide a more environmentally friendly product.
	You need a respected, neutral party to convene your competitors.
	Example: As a coffee shop, you want to develop a market for free-trade, shade-grown coffee. You need an NGO with connections to coffee growers to set up long-term contracts and to certify that your coffee meets these claims.

Ben Packard, director of environmental affairs at Starbucks, emphasizes:

It's a mistake to isolate 'greening the supply chain' as something completely different. It should be presented and received as one of many customer expectations (in addition to price, performance, quality, etc.). If you treat it as a new and separate conversation, it may look more difficult than it needs to be. Given the natural tendency to resist change, there is no need to make this any larger than it needs to be as long as you are able to get the performance improvements you are after.[6]

RESOURCES

Hitchcock, Darcy (2001) *Greening the Supply Chain*. One of the booklets in the Sustainability Series™, www.axisperformance.com/sust_series.html.

Willard, Marsha and Chris James (2001) *Choosing Greener Products*. Part of the Sustainability Series™, www.axisperformance.com/publications.html.

Hitchcock, Darcy (2004) *Partnering with Vendors: Supplier Workshops for Mutual Gain*. Part of the Sustainability Series™, www.axisperformance.com/publications.html.

National Environmental Education and Training Foundation (2001) *Going Green ... Upstream: The Promise of Supplier Environmental Management*. Washington DC: The National Environmental Education and Training Foundation.

To figure out which of these options you should pursue at any one time requires some up-front planning. That's where a supply chain environmental management (SCEM) system can be helpful. As with any management system, you need a way to set policy and priorities, plan, monitor the implementation and review the results.

Buy green power

No discussion of buying greener would be complete without considering the source of your power. Many utilities are now offering 'green power' options. When considered collectively the impacts of the power-generating industry are not trivial. According to the US Environment Protection Agency (EPA), the US electric power industry produced 1.1 billion pounds of toxic emissions in 1998, or 15 per cent of all US toxic emissions. In addition to toxicity concerns, many electricity sources produce greenhouse gas emissions, which have potentially adverse impacts on the global climate. In 1994, for example, 36 per cent of US carbon dioxide emissions were attributed to the utility industry against 30 per cent for transportation, 23 per cent for industrial facilities, 7 per cent for residential households and 4 per cent for commercial operations.[7]

This does not have to be an all-or-nothing decision. You can decide to increase the percentage of your energy that comes from renewable sources by, for example, 10 per cent a year. Use energy efficiency measures to offset the additional cost. Since the fuel cost for renewables (eg wind and solar) is both stable and free, you may be able to set up long-term green power contracts that sidestep the volatile prices for fossil fuels, coming out ahead in the long run.

Create incentives and checklists for making more sustainable choices

Most of the strategies discussed above require someone to stop and think about what they are buying. And in this busy world, only a small proportion of people will be passionate enough to make the effort without some assistance and nudging. Such was the case at Norm Thompson, a catalogue retailer. The owners were passionate about sustainability and had trained practically everyone in the company. Having won over their employees they set their sights on transforming the catalogue industry by convincing their competitors to use 10 per cent recycled content paper (currently most catalogues are printed on 100 per cent virgin-fibre paper).

Despite all the hoopla and executive support, the buyers who sourced products for the catalogues had a difficult time understanding how to make better choices for product materials and, consequently, were struggling to make progress towards sustainable merchandise. Faced with this problem, corporate sustainability manager Derek Smith did two things. First, he produced a simple scoring system for the buyers to use when evaluating the products they were considering (see Table 9.2). And second, the company

Table 9.2 *Environmental score sheet*

Product choices/ characteristics	Option 1	Option 2	Option 3	Option 4
Durable				
Repairable				
Reusable				
Low maintenance				
Post-consumer recycled content				
No/low toxicity				
Organic				
Maintains biodiversity				
Recyclable				
Biodegradable				
Packaging efficiency				
Energy efficiency				
Other vendor activities (eg zero waste, green building)				

tied 10 per cent of the buyers' commission to improving their score over time. Even this small percentage was enough to capture the attention of the buyers.

The worksheet is adapted from Norm Thompson's 'How to Evaluate the Environmental Value of Products' and is reprinted with their permission. Use it to evaluate product options. You can use checkmarks or give the items scores. If certain characteristics are more important to you than others, you can give a multiplier or weighting to each characteristic.

RESOURCES

Norm Thompson Sustainability Toolkit, www.bsr.org/CSRResources/Environment/ NormThompson_Sustainability_Toolkit.pdf.

Work with disadvantaged businesses and people as an economic development strategy
The social side of sustainability often gets lost since the environmental side is easier to address. Purchasing agreements, though, offer opportunities to also address social

considerations. Stop to ask the question, 'How can we maximize the benefits to both ourselves and society?'

Ben & Jerry's has long been recognized for its interest in socially responsible business practices. When they needed an additional source of brownies for their ice-cream, they signed a contract with the Greystone Bakery in Yonkers, New York, a non-profit organization that hires and trains people who are hard to employ, and uses its profits to house the homeless.

Non-profit organizations can also expand their positive impacts by designing their services for maximum impact. The Prison Pet Partnership Program takes dogs from shelters and gives them to women prison inmates to train the dogs as service animals. The dogs' lives are spared, and the prisoners are taught skills in grooming and dog training. The dogs provide low-cost services for people with a host of different disabilities, and society benefits because the recidivism of the prisoners involved in the programme is significantly less than the average. The charity could have made different decisions that would have resulted in fewer benefits: they might have used pure-bred dogs from breeders, not used inmates to train them or only prepared the dogs to be good house pets. The decisions you make about vendors, suppliers and contractors can make a difference, big or small, to the well-being of our society. It's your choice.

Life cycle assessment and life cycle costing
Life cycle assessment (LCA) is a process of examining the impacts of a product over its entire lifetime: Where do the raw materials come from? How are they transported? How is the product manufactured? How is the product transported and sold to a customer? How does the customer use the product? What happens at the end of its useful life? LCA quantifies the environmental impacts at each step in this life cycle and can be used to select products that have the lowest negative environmental and social impacts.

As a purchaser, you can request life cycle assessment data from your vendors. However, because LCA results depend entirely on the assumptions upon which they are based, it's important to assess whether the assumptions used are unbiased and fit your situation. ISO standards require an external review of LCAs to mitigate this problem.

Related to LCA is life cycle costing (LCC), examining the costs (as opposed to the environmental impacts) over the life cycle of a product, from research and development and manufacturing to maintenance and disposal. Similar to activity-based costing, LCC helps you get a clearer picture of the true costs of several product options – it often becomes clear that the cheapest first cost is often not the cheapest in the long term. LCC allows you to take into account such factors as the longevity of the product, associated safety precautions and disposal costs.

For example, vinyl flooring is usually one of the cheapest first-cost flooring options. However, many other flooring options last longer, avoiding additional replacement and installation costs. So over the lifetime of the floor, vinyl is often not the best choice.

LCC can help you determine the best overall return between options in capital projects. For example, most of the cost of a building is in its operation, not its construction, so LCC can help you determine which environmental features pencil out over the long term, even if they add up-front costs. Once you factor in training, safety equipment, hazardous waste permits and disposal costs, a product you thought was the most cost-effective might turn out not to be.

RESOURCES

LCA for Mere Mortals by Rita Schenck, published by the Institute for Environmental Research and Education, www.iere.org/mortals.html.

BEES is software that helps you select more sustainable building supplies, www.epa.gov/oppt/epp/tools/bees.htm and www.bfrl.nist.gov/oae/software/bees.html.

Eco-indicator 99 is an LCA impact assessment method developed with the need for a practical eco-design tool in mind, www.pre.nl/eco-indicator99/default.htm.

Sustainable Products Purchasing Coalition, www.sppcoalition.org.

ISO 14040, www.iso.org.

US EPA website for LCA, www.epa.gov/ordntrnt/ORD/NRMRL/std/sab/lca/index.html.

Purchasing projects

In addition to setting up policies and systems, purchasing departments also undertake specific improvement projects, often in collaboration with other departments or groups. Some of the more common initiatives are described below.

Conduct a waste or purchasing audit

Trawling through dumpsters/skips is not just a way for the poorest members of our society to make ends meet; it's also a great way to learn about where your money is going. Of course, if you're smart, you divert the waste before it ends up in the dumpster and do a representative sampling, but it's still a messy process. However, as you sort the detritus into categories – food, paper, recyclable metals, glass, etc. – you will gain some interesting insights.

At the Oregon Museum of Science and Industry, a waste audit uncovered that almost 40 per cent of their waste was food, of which a third was liquids (watery soft drinks and ice). Why, they wondered, are we paying to haul water away when we could just pour it down the drain? As a stop-gap solution, they marked one of their bins 'liquids only', which instantly reduced their waste by 5 per cent. Then they started to think about their outdoor bins. Portland is famous for its rain, yet the bins were designed in such a way that rainwater got into them. So they were also hauling off rainwater.

This analysis led them to make more far-reaching changes. They now divert 3–4 tons of food waste into a worm bin that doubles as an exhibit to teach visitors how to follow their example. The exhibit designers are also focusing on reducing the waste associated with exhibit construction. The goal is for 80 per cent of each exhibit to be either made from recycled materials or be recyclable/reusable. They have discovered three main ways to make an exhibit sustainable:

1   Design exhibit components so that they are easily updated – content can be changed without changing structure.
2   Make exhibit components standard, allowing interchangeability of parts.
3   Choose construction methods and materials that can be recycled at the end of life of the exhibit.

The focus of the design will be on the end of life of the exhibit. The question of construction methods is relatively simple to address – bolting bits together makes it easier to take them apart at the end of the exhibit's life than gluing them. Material choices will be made based on composition, durability and how the manufacture's factory profile rates with regard to environmentally friendly practices.

Usually, doing a waste audit is a task for the facilities department (you'll be relieved to know), but a purchasing employee should also participate. It's at that point that you'll get a sense of how much of what you are buying is going straight into the skip. At Portland State University, they worked out that they were buying and throwing out 1400 paper cups a day. Doing a purchasing audit in conjunction with a waste audit can be revealing.

RESOURCES

Hitchcock, Darcy and Larry Chalfan (2001) *Approaching Zero Waste*. Portland, OR: AXIS Performance Advisors. Part of the Sustainability Series™, www.axisperformance.com/sust_series.html.

US Environmental Protection Agency resources on zero waste:

- JTRnet Archives – Zero Waste Case Studies. This EPA webpage provides information on companies who have achieved greater than 90 per cent recycling, www.epa.gov/jtr/jtrnet/zerocase.htm.
- JTRnet Archives – Zero Waste Contacts. Information about zero waste contacts, www.epa.gov/jtr/jtrnet/highrate.htm.
- JTRnet Archives – Zero Waste Definitions. Discussion on defining zero waste, www.epa.gov/jtr/jtrnet/zerodef.htm.
- JTRnet Archives – Zero Waste. Information on zero waste efforts, www.epa.gov/jtr/jtrnet/zerowast.htm.

Create a reliable market for a targeted product

Sometimes the materials you would prefer to use aren't available in reliable quantities (eg organic cotton or organic hops) or production is at such a low level that the costs are prohibitively expensive (eg kenaf paper). In these situations, the industrial infrastructure is not yet there to track chain of custody. The only way to solve this problem is to partner those in the industry; roll up your sleeves and figure it out collaboratively. Long-term purchasing commitments build confidence in potential suppliers that making sustainable investments pays off.

Government plays a particularly important role in using purchasing as a market driver. Short-term incentives (tax credits, deductions, rebates, etc.) can offset the additional cost of innovative new products until the market is large enough to create production efficiencies. For example, the Northwest Energy Efficiency Alliance set up a system of rebates for buyers and dealers to offset the cost of front-loading washing machines, which used a fraction of the water and energy of traditional models. Initially these front-loaders sold at a premium over traditional, inefficient ones, in part because there were no US manufacturing plants making them. By offsetting that cost premium, it made it easy for customers to choose the greener option. 'The market share of these machines has increased from a few percentage points at the beginning of the programme to over 12 per cent after the first 18 months,' said Margaret Gardner, executive director of the Alliance. 'Our consumer and dealer surveys have also demonstrated acceptance of these machines by the market.' In the past, the lack of domestically produced front-loaders held back consumer purchases of the more efficient machines. Within two years, several major manufacturers including Frigidaire, Maytag and Amana introduced resource-saving models, making it possible to phase out the incentives.[8]

Nike and Patagonia teamed up to create a market for organic cotton. Cotton is responsible for about a quarter of the world's use of herbicides, which pollute streams and make workers sick. The problem for Nike was that there was an insufficient supply of the organic alternative – they could buy up the entire global harvest and still not have enough for their T-shirts and other clothing – so they instead made long-term commitments to increase the percentage of organic cotton in their clothing over time. They are now the largest US buyer of organic cotton – in 2000 $182 million or 20.9 per cent of Nike's US net revenues of $868 million were generated by sales of organic cotton-blended products (T-shirts, sweatshirts and fleece) sold in the US. Currently these products are 5.7 per cent organic cotton, according to Heidi Holt, global environmental director for Nike's clothing division, and the company has a goal of a minimum of 3 per cent organic cotton in all of its cotton clothing by 2010 and plans to launch a 100 per cent organic cotton women's line in the US.[9]

Creating a market for environmentally or socially preferable products doesn't always have to cost more, at least not for long. Portland, Oregon architectural firm Yost Gruba Hall made a commitment to pay more for recycled paper; within a year their vendor was able to lower the price to that of traditional products, at least in part because YGH helped to establish the demand.

Research sustainable alternatives for a specific function or product

Unfortunately, in the real world, what is better is not always obvious. Rarely is there a perfect answer. So deciding whether to choose product A or B is often a matter of weighing priorities. One product comes from farther away but provides employment to indigent women in Bangladesh. One flooring material is filled with recycled plastic but is not recyclable at the end of its useful life while the alternative is wood but not from a sustainable source. The #5 plastic container is not easily recycled but is lighter so it saves on fuel. How do you wade through these confusing variables?

One solution is to do an LCA, but in reality there will never be enough time to do one on all your options and you often can't rely on LCAs done by others because they may be skewed by bias (as in the case of a manufacturer picking assumptions that favour their product) or they may be based on assumptions that don't apply in your situation (eg an LCA that was done for France, so the transportation and energy mix assumptions don't represent the situation in the US).

So the practical response is usually to determine your own priorities and then assess your options against those criteria. This may seem obvious, but cost is always on the list. A sample of environmental and social criteria is given in the example below. A weighted criteria chart helps you manage multiple variables where the importance of each variable is different. If the criteria are all of equal importance to you, you can simply score each option without the weighting or check the option that best meets each criterion and compare the number of checks each option earned.

The two weighted criteria charts overleaf provide examples of criteria you may find important when making purchasing decisions. Once you have listed all the relevant criteria, weight each one on a 1–10 scale, with 10 being very good or high. Grade each option against each criterion, again from 1–10 and put the result in the grey box. Multiply the weight by the grade to produce a score and insert that in the white box beneath the grey one. Add all the scores in each column to see which option fared the best. The first of the two charts has been completed as an example.

One note about cost: don't just assume that the sustainable product will cost more, even if it appears to. Compare actual usage. For example, Nike found that even though a water-based solvent cost more per gallon, it didn't evaporate as fast as the petroleum-based equivalent. It stayed in the bath, instead of exposing workers, and thus cost less per shoe to use. So before you settle for the less-sustainable option based on cost, ask yourself whether you will avoid any costs (disposal costs, sick days and medical costs, training in the use of hazardous materials, protective gear, legal liabilities, insurance costs, etc.) by choosing the more sustainable option.

Table 9.3 *Sustainable products checklist*

Environmental Characteristics			
Criterion	Weight	Option A	Option B
Reusable	10	3	5
		30	50
Recyclable	8	5	4
		40	32
Bio-based	3	1	10
		3	30
Biodegradable (in a reasonable time frame)	5	1	10
		5	50
Energy efficient	10	5	8
		50	80
Water conserving	7	5	5
		35	35
Non-toxic	8	6	8
		48	64
Harvested in a sustainable manner	5	3	2
		15	10
Cruelty-free	4	10	8
		40	32
Minimally packaged	7	7	4
		49	28
Locally available	5	8	3
		40	15
TOTAL		355	426

Table 9.3 *Sustainable products checklist* (cont'd)

Social Characteristics			
Criterion	Weight	Option A	Option B
Provides living-wage jobs			
Helps disadvantaged people or groups			
Encourages a work/life balance			
Develops people within the organization			
Promotes diversity			
Provides gay/lesbian couples with the same benefits as straight couples			
Demonstrates safe work practices			
Protects rights of indigenous people			
Promotes human rights			
Donates time and money to community needs			
TOTAL			

Be sure also to test out the new product to make sure it works as well or better than the old one, following the directions carefully. Sometimes green products need to be applied differently than traditional ones. For example, with cleaning products it can make a difference whether you spray the cleaner on a rag or on the surface. It may be necessary to leave it on the surface for a few minutes before wiping.

Partner an NGO

Sometimes you might not be able to successfully complete your project without the help of others. NGOs can bring credibility, contacts and expertise to your sustainability effort. For example, Dow has collaborated with the National Resources Defense Council to find ways to reduce the environmental impacts of their manufacturing process. Norm Thompson has used the Alliance for Environmental Innovation (affiliated with Environmental Defense) to encourage the catalogue industry to use recycled paper, and Starbucks has worked with Conservation International to support efforts to grow coffee in a more responsible manner.

Ben Packard, director of environmental affairs at Starbucks, warns:

> It's critical that your interests and those of the NGO overlap because the organizations can be so different. It's not enough for them to be a great organization addressing an important issue. The issue [that the two of you are going to work on] must be centrally relevant to both you and the NGO. For example, we worked with Conservation International on shade-grown coffee where they were trying to protect biodiversity and local economies and we could provide a market for their product.[10]

Conclusion

We've made the case in this chapter that purchasing is key not only to competitiveness but also to your environmental and social impacts. As a corollary to the Butterfly Effect, wave money around in the US and you may create storms elsewhere. Changing purchasing policies and procedures will go a long way to improving the sustainability of your operation. We've also provided examples of the kinds of individual sustainability-related projects you might initiate. The SCORE section overleaf contains ideas for what you might do next.

SCORE PURCHASING

See page 31 for how to complete this assessment and page 33 for how to interpret your score.

PURCHASING				
Practice	Pilot *1 point*	Initiative *3 points*	Systemic *9 points*	Points
Policy: Have a purchasing policy related to sustainability.	As a matter of practice, evaluate major purchases based on sustainability and other criteria but have no formal policy for doing so.	Have a formal sustainable or environmentally preferable purchasing policy and promote waste reduction. Shun suppliers that contribute to human misery, war or environmental degradation.	Have a formal policy and have systems to measure progress toward sustainable purchasing.	
Audits: Conduct purchasing audits against goals to assess the impacts (including social) of your purchases, including items with a short life span and toxic materials.	At least every 5 years, conduct an assessment against sustainable criteria on the largest categories of purchases and act on the results.	Conduct an assessment on most or all purchases and routinely seek out more sustainable options.	Use life cycle assessments or life cycle thinking to determine the impacts of major categories of purchases.	
Supplier influence: Choose suppliers based in part on their sustainability performance.	Send out letters and/or surveys to suppliers to express your commitment to sustainability and your intent to give preference to sustainable suppliers.	Actively work with suppliers to develop most sustainable solutions.	Engage in processes to transform the industry.	
Contracting: Include sustainability criteria in the selection of contract services.	Include sustainability criteria and language in RFPs. Make sustainability a minor selection criterion (eg, worth less than 15%).	Include in contracts requirements to perform sustainability-related functions or tasks (eg construction waste recycling, green cleaning products).	Transform your relationship with major suppliers to provide incentives for sustainable performance.	

PURCHASING				
Practice	Pilot *1 point*	Initiative *3 points*	Systemic *9 points*	Points
Reinforcement: Have meaningful systems for assessing progress toward sustainable purchasing.	Have purchasing systems that automatically give preference to more sustainable options (eg the first choice presented in your online purchasing system is the preferred one) but do not prevent people from purchasing less sustainable options. No feedback is provided on purchasing choices.	Measure and report progress toward goals and targets on major categories of purchases, broken down by individual or group so as to provide meaningful comparisons.	Provide employee incentives (via compensation, performance appraisals or other formal means) to encourage purchasers to seek out sustainable options.	
			Total Score	
			Average	

Environmental Affairs: How to Support the Move Beyond Compliance and Eco-efficiencies to Sustainability

In many organizations there is a person or department whose job it is to attend to environmental issues and/or employee health and safety (EH&S). In large operations, especially in manufacturing, there may be a separate EH&S department. Some governmental agencies, such as departments of environmental quality or those responsible for solid waste and wastewater, have this environmental focus embedded in their mission. Other organizations may have a pollution prevention coordinator for whom this is only one role. Some organizations have product stewardship groups. Practically every organization has someone responsible for workplace safety, if only to coordinate cardiopulmonary resuscitation training and to maintain the first aid kit. Even service companies may have an environmental affairs department. In small businesses, sometimes it's just the person everyone knows is passionate about the environment.

Regardless of what they are called, these are the people organizations often turn to when they first decide to pursue sustainability; indeed it's not uncommon for sustainability initiatives to spring from these groups. And while they are often undervalued in an organization, viewed as a necessary evil instead of a strategic part of the operation, sustainability can provide them with an opportunity to elevate their status and make a greater difference in their organizations.

WHAT YOU SHOULD KNOW ABOUT SUSTAINABILITY

EH&S professionals and pollution prevention coordinators have useful technical knowledge that can help an organization in their sustainability efforts. They are likely to be familiar with toxic chemicals, be knowledgeable about climate change and other environmental challenges, and keep important organizational data about environmental performance. They are also in an excellent position to advise management on and educate staff about sustainability. They can, for example, help top management select the frameworks and tools that are most relevant to the organization. (See Appendix A for more information on frameworks.) These technical professionals do, however, have several hurdles to get over; some of the more common ones are explored below.

Beyond compliance. One of the first concepts that EH&S professionals and their organizations must understand is how sustainability differs from business as usual. Many unenlightened executives may assume that if their organization is in compliance with the law, they have done enough. Others may be aware of the benefits of pollution prevention and eco-efficiencies only since such practices often focus on saving money as well as other resources. And even pollution prevention and eco-efficiencies, with their focus on doing better, being greener, don't begin with an understanding of the end-point or with what we must do to be sustainable. In order to convince management to go beyond eco-efficiencies will require a strong, strategic business case.

Technical jargon. The field is littered with intimidating terms with so many syllables that they are commonly reduced to acronyms, making them even more obscure. One of the big-name sustainability gurus repeatedly strings together in his speeches such terms as endocrine disruptor, teratogen and mutagen as if these were everyday conversational English. To be effective, environmental workers have to pull themselves out of their jargon to talk in everyday business language: return on investment, insurance costs, business risks, cost per product, absenteeism, health insurance premiums, and so on.

Feel-good activities. Many organizations launch voluntary green teams or pollution prevention teams to examine environmental or sustainability opportunities. Too often these teams end up focusing on feel-good activities that have no link to the strategic needs of the business. Switching from polystyrene coffee cups to reusable mugs is a good thing to do but won't win you the attention of top management.

Voices of doom. Environmentalists have a reputation for painting gloomy pictures of the future. They are often not the most popular people at parties. Passion is commendable but should be tempered so as not to drive others away. Most people in our society know that we are doing damage to the planet but feel powerless to do much about it; unless you can give them something meaningful to do, rubbing their noses in the problems will only force them further into denial. As James Speth so eloquently points out in *Red Sky at Morning*, 'Apathy is a shield people use to protect themselves against despair and powerlessness.'[1]

Getting overwhelmed. One of the enduring challenges of working in the sustainability field is reconciling all the huge, global sustainability problems with our own tiny span of influence. There is a tendency to want to change everything now; perhaps indeed we should, but that is simply unrealistic. Start with a clear sense of priorities. What will make the biggest difference at this time? Start with projects that show a healthy rate of return and a high probability of success. Patiently gather data that will help you build a business case for stronger organizational commitment. For example, at the large international engineering firm CH2M Hill, one person kept a record of all the times requests for proposals asked for evidence of an environmental management system. After a period of time, this individual had an impressive list, which led CH2M Hill to develop one.

Forgetting the social side of sustainability. When organizations begin to work on sustainability, they often focus on the environmental aspect, and it is easy for EH&S or pollution prevention people to fall into this narrow definition. Remember, though, that sustainability has a social and economic component to it.

Owning the sustainability initiative. Probably the most insidious problem is the tendency of leadership to delegate sustainability to the 'environmental people' (and then wash their hands of it). The EH&S or pollution prevention staff may be excited to get this responsibility, but in the long term this is not the right place to leave things. At some point, sustainability has to become integrated into the entire organization. If you have an environmental management system, you can use it to drive sustainability into other portions of the organization. Try to get it included into strategic planning so that it is overseen by management, not just your own department. Steering committees and other involvement mechanisms can help as well. See the Human Resources chapter for change management suggestions.

STRATEGIES YOU CAN USE

EH&S and pollution prevention groups have powerful tools and knowledge to help in the implementation of sustainability. Often you can be most effective by embedding sustainability principles into what you already do.

Environmental management systems

Many organizations, both manufacturing businesses and some governmental agencies, already have an environmental management system (EMS). Whether or not your EMS is ISO certified, it can provide a powerful engine for sustainability. Such was the case at the Fort Lewis Army Base in Washington State. They had implemented an EMS to save money and reduce environmental impacts. When Paul Steucke then learned about sustainability, he at first thought that sustainability could help their EMS. 'But I had it all wrong,' comments Steucke, 'Our EMS helped our sustainability initiative.' The EMS provided the process and sustainability provided the vision, ie where they were headed.

There are a number of points in an EMS where sustainability can be incorporated:

Vision statement. Here the organizational leaders commit to sustainability as a principle; in some cases, a specific framework such as The Natural Step can be referenced.

Aspects and impacts analysis. In examining the environmental impacts of your organizational activities, you can employ a sustainability framework as the structure. Doing this is likely to change your priorities. For example, a traditional EMS may rate impacts based on energy use whereas a sustainability management system might evaluate climate impacts. While energy and climate are related, this switch can result in different priorities. For example, if you happen to use one of the obscure gases with a high climate impact (for example sulphur hexafluoride), this might become more of a priority than something else that might reduce energy use.

Targets. Sustainability, at least the environmental part of it, provides what some call non-negotiable targets for human activity. We can't negotiate with nature to tolerate more mercury in living tissues so that we can burn more coal. With a sustainability management system, these long-term targets often spur innovative thinking. As one architect put it, 'Ask me to design a building so that it saves 10 per cent more energy than an equivalent building, it'll cost you more. Ask me to design a building that saves 50 per cent, and I'm forced to rethink the entire design and it may cost less.' In the case of the Fort Lewis army base, their 25-year goals set ambitious targets rooted in an understanding of a sustainable end-point. These included achieving zero waste, reducing the base's drinking water use by 75 per cent, rehabilitating all endangered species in the South Puget Sound region, having zero discharge of wastewater to Puget Sound and using renewable energy for all their base-generated energy needs.

RESOURCES

ISO 14000 is a globally accepted set of standards to guide the development and certification of an EMS, www.iso14000.com.

Zero Waste Alliance, www.zerowaste.org.

Developing Effective Systems for Managing Sustainability and *Embedding Sustainability into your EMS* are two booklets in the Sustainability Series™ that provide an overview in lay terms, avoiding the terminology of ISO 14001, www.axisperformance.com/sust_series.html.

Chemical management systems

Organizations often have a host of different toxic chemicals on site: paints, pesticides, cleaning products, solvents, air fresheners, adhesives, etc. Typically, different people in the organization purchase different products, products pass their use-by dates and all too often material safety data sheets are missing or out of date. Until you pull all this data into a chemical inventory and establish a chemical management system, it is hard to evaluate your risk and to identify what you should work on next.

When we conducted such an inventory for one of our clients, we discovered that in addition to all the problems above, they were missing opportunities to save a significant sum of money by consolidating their purchases. Since the inventory combined both a toxicity rating and annual volume data, it provided the client a clear sense of priorities with regard to products for which they wanted to find less toxic alternatives.

Part of an effective chemical management system involves controls on purchasing. Some organizations have implemented a chemical pharmacy approach where there is a single location where chemicals are purchased and stored. These are dispensed in small quantities as needed and left-over supplies are returned to the pharmacy. This approach can be particularly useful in universities, where without such a system odd containers of chemicals may be spread out in departments all over the campus.

Resources

The Stockholm Convention on Persistent Organic Pollutants (POPs) lists the 'dirty dozen' chemicals of greatest concern, www.unido.org/doc/29428.

The Chemical Assessment Ranking System or CARS is a database managed by the Zero Waste Alliance. It provides a much more thorough way of rating products than the method explained above and incorporates data from reputable sources regarding greenhouse gases, carcinogens and the like, www.zerowaste.org.

King County, Washington produced a listing of chemicals by use and ranked them from highest concern to lowest, www.govlink.org/hazwaste/publications/COC_Report.pdf.

The Unified Green Cleaning Alliance developed standards for sustainable cleaning products (beyond the 'green' standard that is commonly in use), www.zerowaste.org/ugca.htm.

The REACH Directive is an important piece of European legislation related to toxic reduction.

Chemical substitution

Once you have an up-to-date chemical inventory, you can evaluate products for replacement. Often this is just a matter of asking vendors about less toxic options. In many fields, there are already green product lines. In other cases, you may need to secure the services of a green chemist to investigate options.

For example, the Port of Portland, in Oregon, wanted to switch to greener cleaning products. Their existing vendor didn't have a line of green cleaning products at the time, but rather than seeking a different cleaning firm, the Port used their influence to get the vendor to investigate different, safer chemicals. The cleaning company discovered that their supplier, the distributor, also didn't have a line of green products, so they involved the formulator. The Port worked with the whole supply chain to develop a line of green cleaning products so that everyone benefited: the formulator and distributor now had a product that provided a competitive advantage and the Port reaped the benefits associated with reducing toxics on site.

RESOURCES

King County, Washington produced a listing of chemicals by use (eg pesticides, cleaning products) and ranked them from highest concern to lowest, www.govlink.org/hazwaste/publications/COC_Report.pdf.

The Unified Green Cleaning Alliance developed standards for sustainable cleaning products (beyond the 'green' standard that is commonly in use, www.zerowaste.org/ugca.htm.

The Northwest Coalition for Alternatives to Pesticides (NCAP) has a lot of information about alternatives to pesticides, www.pesticide.org.

Green chemistry

Green chemistry is an emerging field that seeks the most benign ways to make chemical products. It considers the toxicity of by-products as well as that of the product, and the efficiency of the process. This technique can be helpful if you need to research alternative production methods. For example, BHC, in Bishop, Texas applied green chemistry principles to the manufacture of ibuprofen, a common painkiller. The old 'stoichiometric' process took six steps and roughly 60 per cent of what was created was by-product, not ibuprofen. They switched to a process using a catalyst that can be recovered and reused after the chemical reactions. This green chemistry process took only three steps (versus six) and 99 per cent of what was created was either product (80 per cent, twice as much as

---

RESOURCES

The University of Oregon specializes in green chemistry, www.uoregon.edu/~hutchlab/greenchem.

Green Chemistry Institute, www.lanl.gov/greenchemistry.

US Environmental Protection Agency (EPA) website, www.epa.gov/opptintr/greenchemistry.

The Toxics Network has information on various chemicals, www.oztoxics.org.

before), the recovered catalyst (which can be used again to make more ibuprofen) or the by-product, acetic acid (the main ingredient in vinegar).[2]

Conclusion

EH&S and pollution prevention professionals all have an important role to play in sustainability. They can act as a technical resource and they may control an EMS that can embed sustainability into the fabric of the organization. However, they should be careful not to take on too much responsibility. In the long term, this is not the right place for sustainability to reside – you don't want it to be the responsibility of just one department. As applies to the total quality movement, you want sustainability to become institutionalized throughout the organization. EH&S and pollution prevention professionals' expertise is probably best used first as a catalyst for change and then later as a source of technical knowledge and data.

SCORE ENVIRONMENTAL AFFAIRS

See page 31 for how to complete this assessment and page 33 for how to interpret your score.

Environmental Affairs				
Practice	Pilot *1 point*	Initiative *3 points*	Systemic *9 points*	Points
Sustainability management systems: Convert your existing environmental management system (EMS) into a sustainability management system (SMS). (Note: If you don't have an EMS, see Sustainability Management System under Sr. Mgmt.)	Have an ISO 14001-conformant EMS.	Actively promote industry-wide practices and standards that protect public health and the environment. Sustainability clearly shows up in the policy and targets. A long-term plan is in place to reach sustainable levels of all significant impacts. The SMS includes goals associated with customer and supplier impacts.	The SMS has become part of the overall management of the organization and is no longer a discrete, separate system. The SMS takes responsibility for the full life cycle of your product or service.	

Environmental Affairs				
Practice	Pilot *1 point*	Initiative *3 points*	Systemic *9 points*	Points
Chemicals and toxics: Eliminate exposure and emissions of chemicals that adversely impact human health and the environment.	Complete a chemical inventory. Eliminate all use of persistent bioaccumulative toxins (PBTs).	Reduce use of hazardous materials to below the level needed for permits. Complete grey and black lists of chemicals to eliminate from the workplace and your products. If appropriate, create a chemical pharmacy.	Use the precautionary principle for purchasing, processing and products. Have phased out all grey and black listed chemicals. Have implemented a cradle-to-cradle system for technical and biological nutrients.	
Water quality and conservation: Minimize the use of water, keep water on site, and treat outflows.	Assess water outflows and develop a conservation plan.	Provide on-site water treatment of most rainwater.	Water discharged is as clean or cleaner than source; no discharge of rainwater from the site.	
Natural resources: Protect natural resources on company properties.	Conduct an assessment of natural resources and act on the results.	Consider natural resource impacts in decision-making.	Restore habitat to replace natural resources lost by development.	
Air quality: Protect the air inside and outside your facilities.	Have conducted air quality testing in all work areas and taken appropriate action to comply with all government regulations.	Have switched to low-VOC (volatile organic compounds) products for all coatings, solvents, paints, adhesives, etc.	Have switched to benign alternatives (eg plant-based, biodegradable).	

Environmental Affairs				
Practice	Pilot *1 point*	Initiative *3 points*	Systemic *9 points*	Points
Emergency response: Have effective plans in place for all serious contingencies.	Have effective crisis response plans for any foreseeable problem. Give higher priority to protecting public health and the environment than protecting your short-term financial interests and image.	Actively engage stakeholders in identifying ways to prevent and deal with foreseeable crises.	Actively promote industry-wide practices and standards that protect public health and the environment.	
Role: Redistribute responsibility for environmental affairs and sustainability across the organization.	Sustainability coordinator and/or environmental affairs is the main source of sustainability leadership.	Sustainability leadership is fully integrated into management.	Role has evolved to one of disseminating sustainability outside the organization (eg lectures, supplier workshops).	
Hazardous waste: Manage hazardous waste to protect human health and the environment.	Have an inventory plan that is fully compliant with all government regulations and OHSAS 18000.	Systematically find replacements for hazardous chemicals.	Eliminate all hazardous chemicals on site.	
			Total Score	
			Average	

Marketing/Public Relations: Whether and How to Promote Your Sustainability Efforts

Most organizations are concerned about their image and their brand, and many organizations are finding that sustainability can enhance both. Marketing and public relations professionals have an important role in this. They can help an organization understand how its market segments feel about such things as corporate social responsibility and the environment, and they can help an organization develop a coherent and compelling message. These issues are ultimately senior management decisions but, as with all marketing, it is best when sustainability is embedded in the entire design and delivery process than added as an after-thought at the end of the process. In this chapter we cover issues that marketing and public relations directors should discuss with top management.

If you know what to look for, you'll find that sustainability is a growth industry. In many sectors, the more sustainable options are experiencing double-digit growth: organic produce, wind power, green buildings, socially responsible investments, to name but a few. Granted, these still represent a small percentage of the entire sectors in which they operate, but at these growth rates they also represent a sweet business opportunity.

Sustainability can help you protect and enhance your brand. Coca Cola, considered the world's best brand name, is pursuing sustainability after being sued in Kerala, India for allegedly causing local wells to run dry. These days incidents like this can quickly become public knowledge around the world. And whether or not the individual case has merit, the public relations damage is done. So after some soul searching, Coca Cola, with the involvement of The Future 500, has now developed an elaborate corporate evaluation tool. 'We want to develop a virtuous, sustainable business cycle,' says Perry Cutshall, director of operations, global public affairs, 'Because of our resources, scope and reach, we can then address broader needs of society in alignment with our mission as a private company.'[1]

Sometimes sustainability can turn around a languishing business through product differentiation. Such was the case with Scandic Hotels in Sweden, who were a run-of-the-mill hotel chain with weakening financial returns and nothing to distinguish themselves until they learned about The Natural Step framework and used it to transform their practices and their image. Not only did this turn around their financial situation, sustainability also helped them create many innovative changes to their operation that have saved time and money.

Consider also the so-called first-mover advantage. By being the first oil company to acknowledge the threat of global warming, BP (formerly British Petroleum) captured the world's attention. It's always riveting when an insider breaks rank. Many of the other energy companies whine that they are doing as much or more regarding sustainability, but they haven't been able to surpass BP's reputation in this regard.

The positive press you can generate by being the first to market with an innovative product can be tremendous. Gerding/Edlen, a small property development firm based in Portland, Oregon, has been nationally recognized in print, on television and on radio for their green building practices. Dennis Wilde commented, 'We couldn't have bought all the PR that this has brought us. We've had one or two articles published about us or our projects every week for the past two years.'[2]

However, communicating about sustainability is a tricky business. You don't want to make your customers feel guilty, either about themselves or about your other products. Sustainability is a complex field so it can be very difficult to frame messages so they don't just confuse people. You certainly don't want to set your organization up for accusations of greenwashing, ie of just using sustainability as a public relations ploy without any action to back it up.

According to Steve Kokes, head of the Coates Kokes marketing firm, marketing professionals need to learn about sustainability and then apply to it what they already know about marketing. He believes that as customers become more aware of environmental issues, they will demand better options. Only a small percentage will pay more or go out of their way to get green products, but, all things being equal, most people would choose the environmental option.

Furthermore, many countries are now increasing their environmental standards, blocking products which contain certain chemicals or which lack a certain certification. You will want to stay ahead of these trends or risk embarrassing media fiascos. Sony, for example, received lots of unwelcome media attention when, just in time for the holiday season, The Netherlands banned Sony Playstations because their cables contained too much cadmium. The European Union in particular is passing more and more legislation about toxics in products. (See, for example, the 'Restriction of Hazardous Substances' (RoHS) Directive and the REACH (Registration, Evaluation and Authorisation of Chemicals) Directive, which switches the burden of proof for a chemical's safety on to the manufacturer.)

From a public relations perspective, you'll want to enhance your organization's reputation and protect your organization from other forms of negative attention. The number of shareholder resolutions in the US has experienced a meteoric rise. Few organizations want to spar publicly with the Investor Relations Research Center, whose long-term members include the Adrian Dominican Sisters and other religious groups as well as pension funds and foundations. Similarly, NGOs like to target the biggest companies in a sector for boycotts and attention-grabbing media campaigns. There are also websites panning various organizations such as Wal-Mart, Nike and the World Trade Organization. Pursuing sustainability, if handled artfully, can be an insurance policy against bad press. Type your company name into Google and you may be surprised to find other sites blasting you.

Sometimes you have to go beyond what your customers are asking for. Toyota and Honda weren't just doing what their customers were asking for when they developed their hybrids; instead they had looked into the future and saw that they needed to redesign the car from the ground up. They bet on a stepping-stone model, rather than deciding, as did General Motors, to go directly to research on hydrogen fuel-cell vehicles. While the American car makers kept saying that the additional cost of a hybrid didn't pay for itself in gasoline, they completely missed the point. Buying is never a completely rational experience. Did they think Hummer owners were going to cover the additional cost with fuel efficiency? Toyota knew that there would be enough people for whom the Prius would have an emotional appeal, people who would see the Prius as an expression of their values. And now, with record petrol prices, a predictable result of peaking oil supplies and other sustainability issues, Toyota can't keep up with demand.

Remember, too, that it's not just about green or environmental marketing; there is also a social component to work with as well. Nike, for example, learned that the hard way. Nike management had assumed they were not responsible for the policies and practices of their contract manufacturers but the public saw the issue differently and the issue was debated at length in the media. Nike is still trying to rebuild its image. On the positive side, many organizations are aligning themselves with non-profit organizations to solve thorny social issues such as hunger, domestic abuse and AIDS. Starbucks recently ran a marketing campaign to sell Ethos bottled water to raise money for safe drinking water projects around the world.

Finally, recognize that you have an internal audience as well. Sustainability can fire up employees and attract talent. Hot Lips Pizza in Portland, Oregon is one of many employers that report that they attract and retain a much higher quality employee because of their sustainability commitment. So use your marketing and public relations know-how to help management craft meaningful communication strategies for internal use as well.

WHAT YOU SHOULD KNOW ABOUT SUSTAINABILITY

Marketing sustainability is fraught with challenges. The field is littered with poorly executed marketing plans that did more damage than good. There are a number of strategic issues you will need to navigate so as to avoid the biggest pitfalls.

Is there such a thing as green or sustainable marketing? 'People talk about the green market, but I don't believe there is one,' says Harvey Hartman, president and founder of the Hartman Group in Bellevue, Washington. His research and consulting firm specializes in environmental strategies:

> We've gotten on an emotional bandwagon with this subject. We've developed a sense that the environment is more important in most people's daily lives than it really is. This doesn't mean there's no market out there. It means that the approach has to adapt to the changing moods of consumers.[3]

Hartman's point is well taken. For the vast majority of people, environmental issues are secondary to their immediate needs. Green marketing won't make up for a detergent that doesn't get the dirt out, or a car that can't go the distance.

The other problem with the concept of green marketing is that it can be devilishly hard to target that market segment. According to Paul Ray's research (at least in the US), most demographic distinctions used by marketers (geography, political affiliations, religious affiliations, etc.) are useless. These do not differentiate the segment most likely to be attracted to environmentally preferable products, a segment Ray calls the Cultural Creatives. So you run the risk of turning off as many people as you entice. Interestingly, the only demographic that Ray found was predictive of environmental values was gender – women were far more likely to care than men.

This implies you are better off thinking about sustainability as just being part of your marketing and public relations messages, not a different way of approaching the world.

Will you (or when will you) go public with your sustainability efforts? It can also be tricky to decide if you should promote your sustainability efforts. Many organizations keep it quiet for a long time until they have significant results to report. Household name companies are at the greatest risk of accusations of greenwashing. The public is suspicious of corporate motives and wary of self-aggrandizement.

Furthermore, unless your organization has already branded itself as the environmental choice, you may run the risk of alienating those for whom environmentalist is a dirty word. Home Depot, a giant retailer of building products, adopted sustainability after being targeted by a Rainforest Action Network campaign. They have researched the source for all or almost all their wood products, from timber to hammer handles, and slowly, quietly, removed products from questionable sources. They don't give customers the choice of a green door or a non-green door. Their sales staff are surprisingly ignorant about the Forest Stewardship Council certification labels on some of their products. We assume this laudable but clandestine approach has to do with not wanting to offend or confuse Home Depot's customer base. The company doesn't just operate in the Pacific northwest (once dubbed 'Ecotopia') – they have outlets in areas where the local community still doesn't have a decent recycling system. They want to be known as one of the biggest suppliers of building products, not as a green supplier of building products. Yet they want to do the right thing and now see their organizational interest in becoming more sustainable.

Do you attach the green or sustainable label to one product or to all products? If you do decide to promote your sustainability efforts and features of your products, you will need to decide if this applies to all your products or just some of them. Toyota, for example, has caught all the US car makers flat-footed with their hybrid Prius. Here they have made the sustainable choice an option. Since most of their vehicles get good mileage compared to other vehicles in their class, they aren't at great risk of making their other products look bad in comparison.

The other option is to move your entire line toward sustainability. IKEA, the European furniture retailer, realized that by offering an Eco-Plus line of products, their efforts could make their other products look bad in comparison. They also realized that selling a green line would do less for the environment than would transforming all their products. So they decided to begin 'greening' their entire line.[4]

Do you sell to one market segment or entice everyone to choose the sustainable option? In the US the Roper Green Gauge tracks environmental views. They have identified five different market segments:

1   The True Blue Greens, a 10 per cent segment, are ardent environmentalists. They take time to investigate options and claims and try to affect other people's beliefs and actions. They are much more likely to donate to environmental groups or be politically active. They are willing to make lifestyle changes to live their values.
2   The Greenbacks, a 5 per cent segment, are willing to pay a little more or go to a little more trouble to get an environmentally preferable product. They claim they will pay up to 22 per cent more, although behavioural studies refute this. They are too busy with their lives to make major lifestyle changes but routinely use their purchasing power to reinforce their environmental beliefs.
3   The Sprouts, making up about a third of the US population, are willing to engage in environmental activities or buy green products, but only if it requires little extra effort. Curb-side recycling or taking plastic bags back to the grocery are examples of programmes they support.
4   Grousers, a 15 per cent segment, do not feel that individuals can make much of a difference. They think it's someone else's job – government or corporations. They will do what is required but very little more, unless there is an incentive (such as a deposit they get back for returning bottles).
5   Basic Browns, the remaining 37 per cent, are not at all convinced that environmental problems are serious. They are not tuned in. It's just not a priority. It's not as if they wake up wondering how to trash the environment. They just don't think about the impact of their actions and inactions.[5]

Faced with these or similar demographics, you have to decide if you want to just appeal to the most ardently green citizenss, whose identity is dependent upon owning and not owning certain products. Or do you want to appeal to the majority of the population, who care about the environment but to varying degrees? Or do you want to make your product appeal to even the Basic Browns? This is a product positioning decision that will affect where you sell your product, how it's packaged and how much you can charge.

If you choose to focus your marketing, you might investigate the market segment that is becoming known as LOHAS, people seeking a Lifestyle of Health and Sustainability. This market segment combines several groups – people interested in sustainable economics, healthy lifestyles, personal development, alternative healthcare and ecological lifestyles. Together, worldwide, this market is estimated to represent US$546 billion.[6]

It has been common to link green or sustainable features with premium pricing. This tactic, however, can cut both ways – it encourages farmers to produce organic fruits and vegetables because they can get a higher price, but by charging a premium you reinforce the notion that doing the right thing costs more and you eliminate much of the market.

However, the sustainable option doesn't have to cost more and some are actually earning higher margins on cheap products sold to the poorest people on Earth. If your company is selling to industrial nations, you only have a sixth of the world's population as potential customers. But if you can find a way to meet the needs of the most needy, you have a marketplace three times as large. The food and personal care products giant Unilever markets laundry detergent to the poorest in India. The small, inexpensive packages meet the needs of the people there, yet the company is earning a higher margin than on their regular boxed soaps. A doctor in India started and runs several health clinics performing eye operations. Even though most of their patients get the services for free, they have improved their productivity to such an extent that their hospital has a gross profit margin of 40 per cent without taking charitable donations or government grants.[7]

Sustainability can also spur innovations that lead to new products. Hewlett Packard, for example, sponsored an electronic inclusion programme, bringing technology to villages around the world. Walt Rosenberg, vice president of corporate and social responsibility said:

> After developing that product [a solar powered printer to make photo ID cards in rural India], we started thinking more clearly about how to serve markets where there is little reliable or even no electricity, and no local power systems. That got us into working on solar power, and other local power plants, which can enable people who live in rural areas to gain access to our technology.[8]

In 2005 the MIT Media Lab unveiled a US$100 laptop computer in the hopes that every child in the world could afford one. Using existing technologies in new ways, it may transform the personal computer industry. It gets energy from a hand-crank, uses open-source software and saves data on a flash memory instead of a hard drive. Once again, a desire to help the world's poor unleashed creative new solutions.

How do you frame the message? Once you've determined whom you are targeting, you have to formulate a message that will resonate with that segment. Since this is the life-blood of marketing, we won't labour the issue other than to share some insights about doing this in the context of sustainability:

- You *can* sell green products to the Basic Browns, you just have to find the right hook. Let's say you are a utility wanting everyone, not just environmentalists, to buy green power. Consider what might entice the Basic Browns. Price predictability would be a selling point for commercial and industrial customers. Since the fuel source for renewables (wind, sun, gravity) is free, renewable power shouldn't be as subject to price fluctuations as fossil-fuel based energy. It could be possible to sign long term contracts where the customers paid a little extra now but guaranteed a price in the long term.
- For a vast majority of the population, you must keep the message simple. The dolphin-safe tuna campaign worked, using its emblem of the charismatic mammal with a smile on the side of every approved tin of tuna. At the same time, your claims must be squeaky-clean and accurate or you will be attacked by those who know the difference. The so-called biodegradable plastic rubbish bags that just broke apart, not down, is an example of a marketing fiasco that reinforced the public's cynicism about corporate claims.

RESOURCES

Ottman, Jacquelyn (1998) *Green Marketing: Opportunities for Innovation.* New York: J. Ottman Consulting/Book Surge.

Hart, Stuart L. and Mark B. Milstein (1999) 'Global Sustainability and Creative Destruction of Industries', *MIT Sloan Management Review*, Fall 1999.

Hall, Jeremy and Harrie Vrendenburg (2003) 'The Challenges of Innovating for Sustainable Development', *MIT Sloan Management Review*, Fall 2003.

Ray, Paul and Sherry Ruth Andersen (2000) *The Cultural Creatives: How 50 Million People are Changing the World.* NY: Harmony Books.

Lakoff, George (2002) *Moral Politics: How Liberals and Conservatives Think.* Chicago, IL: University of Chicago Press.

US Federal Trade Commission, Guides for the Use of Environmental Marketing Claims, www.ftc.gov/bcp/grnrule/guides980427.htm.

McKenzie-Mohr, D., Nemiroff, LS, Beers, L., & Desmarais, S. (1995) 'Determinants of Responsible Environmental Behaviour', *Journal of Social Issues*, Vol 51, No 4, Winter 1995.

Word of Mouth Marketing Association has published the 'Word of Mouth 101: An Introduction to Word of Mouth Marketing', www.wordofmouth.org/wordofmouth101.htm.

- Use the credibility of others to vouch for your products where possible. This may take the form of third-party certifications, independently verified labels, NGO partnerships or award programmes.
- Make green features secondary to personal benefits. Philips Microelectronics, a European manufacturing firm known for their design for environment programme, discovered that they should emphasize personal benefits first and environmental benefits second. For example, the energy saver button on their televisions reduces eye-strain.
- Finally, it's important to make sure your own marketing and public relations materials reinforce rather than violate your sustainability message. Are you handing out throw-away plastic trinkets at trade fairs? Or have you converted your materials to the web and started to send postcards as prompts?

STRATEGIES YOU CAN USE

Community-based social marketing

Community-based social marketing is a method for changing behaviour. It takes into account social norms and other social factors to encourage these changes. It usually includes three steps: a request for commitment, prompting/reminder to follow up on the commitment and reinforcing new social norms. Some of the insights associated with social marketing include:

- Explaining what people are losing now is more effective than telling them what they can gain by changing a behaviour (eg how much money you're wasting each month in energy bills versus how much money you could save by insulating).
- Making a small commitment (such as signing a petition or wearing a pin) increases the likelihood that a person will make much larger changes in their behaviour.
- Public recognition can backfire as a way to motivate organizational changes. Some people don't appreciate being paraded in front of their peers and others may feel slighted.
- Seeking commitments in cohesive groups improves the likelihood of follow-through. If you promise your friends you're going to do something, you are more likely to do it.
- Involving people in assessments (eg energy audits) makes it more likely they will follow through with the recommended actions.

Peter Cooke at the Department of Environmental Quality in Maine decided to use social marketing techniques to encourage employees to do such things at home as checking tyre pressure to improve fuel economy, installing compact fluorescent bulbs and purchasing green power from their utility. He also used this method to encourage changes in behaviour at work, including setting printers to double-sided printing:

> *Each campaign consisted of three emails sent to employees. The first email was a stand alone 'article' in the institution's electronic newsletter. For example, the article on double-sided printing raised awareness about the financial cost to organizations and the environmental cost of unnecessary use of paper. Several days later, Peter, the organization's pollution prevention coordinator, sent all employees a listserv message that referred to the newsletter article and provided step-by-step instructions on how to set double-sided printing as the default for office printers or, alternatively, how to select double-sided printing for single print jobs. The email then asked employees to make a formal commitment to use double-sided printing. Individuals could indicate whether or not they would make a commitment by using pre-designated reply buttons (an MSN Outlook feature). Three days later, the employees who made a commitment to double-sided printing were asked to indicate if they had actually begun using double-sided printing.*[9]

Using Outlook to compile responses, Peter was able to quantify the results of each campaign. Interestingly, the results varied significantly between campaigns. Not surprisingly, the campaign for green power (which would cost employees more on their household utility bills) was much less successful than the others. Duplex printing, an easy work-related change, resulted in some of the best results. Of the 420 employees, about 37 per cent responded to the initial email to make a commitment. Of those, almost 38 per cent said they already did this and an additional 59 per cent made a commitment to do so. Close to 80 per cent of those who made the commitment followed through and only about 20 per cent said they had not done so yet.

RESOURCES

McKenzie-Mohr, Doug and William Smith (1999) *Fostering Sustainable Behavior*. New Society Publishers.

Cause-related marketing

Cause-related marketing is often more associated with social than environmental issues. It comes about usually through a partnership of a for-profit organization and non-profit organization, with the company promoting their product to raise money for the non-profit organization's efforts. The term was first coined by American Express in 1983 when they raised money to restore the Statue of Liberty. Levi Straus took on AIDS when it was ravaging their home city of San Francisco. Recently, as mentioned before, Starbucks launched its Ethos bottled water to fund safe drinking water projects around the world.

Cause-related marketing can get you great public relations opportunities. Liz Claiborne worked to reverse domestic violence and as a result their representatives ended up on many TV talk shows and in many fashion magazines. Their former CEO was also invited to the White House to celebrate the signing of relevant crime legislation.

See if there is a cause that fits with your brand, your customers and your mission.

RESOURCES

Adkins, Sue (2000) *Cause Related Marketing: Who Cares Wins.* Wobern, MA: Butterworth-Heinemann.

Labelling, certification and standards

Labels can be particularly helpful for consumer products and there are a host of labelling systems that already exist. If none exists in your sector, you will need to engage a multi-stakeholder group to determine standards. Since most people are familiar with product labelling, we'll only list some of the more common sustainability-related labels below. Labelling is most effective if the label is simple, clear and respected. Coffee is a product where labelling has gone berserk – you have to choose between fair trade, shade grown, bird friendly and organic. It leaves the customer having to decide who gets hurt: the bugs, the birds or the bean-pickers.

Many labelling schemes require third-party certification. These can be expensive but are often necessary to access markets. Certain governments use certification as a selection criterion for purchases. (See Appendix B for common labelling and certification schemes.)

Stakeholder involvement

Stakeholder involvement and transparency are important tenets of sustainability, and public relations people may participate in planning or running associated tasks. Since just about anyone can be considered a stakeholder, you'll need a way to narrow the field. You want to be sure to include people or representatives with a strong vested interest so you don't get blind-sided. On the other hand, you can't involve everyone. A chart like the one in Figure 11.1 can be a helpful way to organize your thinking.

Place the people or groups into the appropriate quadrants. There may be some who are concerned but have little influence and others who have a lot of influence but are fine

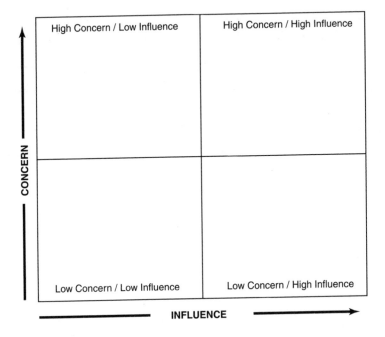

Figure 11.1 *Concern versus influence*

with what is happening. You want to focus on people or groups that have both high concern about what you are doing and are highly influential.

We covered stakeholder involvement in some detail in the Senior Management chapter.

Sustainability reporting

Similarly, public relations is often involved with stockholder reports and other non-financial reports, including sustainability reports. A PricewaterhouseCoopers survey of 1300 CEOs from 43 different countries discovered that 66 per cent included sustainability in their annual reports while 37 per cent drew up a separate sustainability report. Clearly this trend towards a more complete sustainability report is growing – an additional 16 per cent planned to move in this direction in the near future.[10] (See the Finance and Accounting chapter for more information.)

Market transformation

Governmental agencies and non-profit organizations are usually less interested in marketing what they are doing and more interested in creating markets for more sustainable products. They want to transform the entire sector, raising the bar for all. For example, in 1993, in the US, 25 electricity companies, representing one-quarter of the nation's electricity usage, wanted to dramatically improve the efficiency of refrigerators, so they offered the 'Golden Carrot'. Rather than offsetting the cost of research and development, they offered an incentive of $30.7 million to the manufacturer that could design, build and distribute refrigerators that were 25–50 per cent more energy efficient than comparable models. This incentive got the attention of the entire industry. Today's refrigerators are 30 per cent more energy efficient than they were prior to the Golden Carrot.

Organizations have used a host of different strategies to transform the marketplace. In addition to using their purchasing power, they have:

- designed informational labelling (such as the Energy Star labels on appliances);
- created standards and certifications (eg the LEED green building system);
- offered incentives (eg 'feebates', where a fee on less sustainable models is used to provide a rebate on more sustainable models);
- offered technical assistance;
- provided grant funding;
- used tax credits and deductions (eg in the US, Oregon's energy tax credits have been particularly effective in changing behaviour);
- worked through trade associations;
- threatened or implemented new regulations (eg in September 2004 a European Union ruling went into effect banning hundreds of carcinogens and reproductive toxins from all personal-care products on the European market);
- created cap-and-trade market mechanisms; and
- set up third-party organizations (eg to handle the take-back of electronic products).

The strategy will depend upon your target market (eg the general public or business-to-business transactions), your mission and your product.

Conclusion

Marketing and public relations people have critical skills to support a sustainability initiative. They can use their understanding of their marketplace and stakeholders to frame their organization's messages effectively. Marketing people are key to creating increasing demand for more sustainable products. Public relations people can help an organization use sustainability to enhance its image. Learn all you can about sustainability and then help your organization understand how best to communicate their commitment to it.

SCORE MARKETING AND PUBLIC RELATIONS

See page 31 for how to complete this assessment and page 33 for how to interpret your score.

MARKETING				
Practice	Pilot *1 point*	Initiative *3 points*	Systemic *9 points*	Points
Marketing strategy: Have a strategy in place that encourages all your customers to choose the more sustainable options.	Assess market segments for their understanding and opinions about sustainability to identify messages that will resonate with each segment.	Develop a message that will resonate with each market segment such that it encourages them to make the sustainable choice (eg take-back opportunities as a marketing strategy).	Develop an aggressive customer education campaign around sustainability to build demand for sustainable products and services.	
Product positioning: Make all products more sustainable	Assess all your major product lines for their sustainability impacts.	Eliminate or redesign lines with the worst sustainability performance.	Seek credible eco-labelling or certification for your products.	
Internal marketing: Educate all employees about the organization's sustainability efforts.	Incorporate sustainability into employee communications on an ad hoc basis.	Communicate at least quarterly via at least two types of media.	All employees are fully aware of sustainable activities.	
Marketing materials and give-aways: Make sustainable choices about materials to use.	When printing, use high-recycled content paper and soya-based inks. Reduce the use of give-aways and choose products that exemplify sustainability. Make it easy for customers to eliminate duplicate mailings or get off your mailing list. Honour do-not-call lists for telemarketing.	Minimize the use of print marketing materials through the use of technology where life cycle assessment indicates this would be preferred.	Promote the concepts of sustainability in your marketing materials to educate your customers.	
			Total	
			Average	

PUBLIC RELATIONS				
Practice	Pilot *1 point*	Initiative *3 points*	Leader *9 points*	Points
Public relations outreach strategy: Educate stakeholders about your sustainability efforts.	Assess your stakeholders' opinions of sustainability.	After the organization has shown significant internal progress on sustainability, promote sustainability as part of your image to those stakeholders or markets that will care.	Produce a publicly available formal annual sustainability report that honestly portrays your progress as well as your areas for improvement.	
Stakeholder engagement: Provide mechanisms for stakeholders to express their expectations, priorities and concerns.	Identify your major stakeholders and actively assess their trust, perception and ideas for improvement.	Conduct formal stakeholder audits and involve key stakeholders in major and sensitive decisions.	Partner with key stakeholders on projects to shift the sustainability performance of your industry (eg aggregating purchasing power, setting standards, creating political pressure for change, etc.)	
Incident/ emergency response and media communications: Ensure everyone has the best information.	Provide timely, accurate and complete information to authorities and the public when a crisis does occur. Give higher priority to protecting public health and the environment than protecting your short-term financial interests and image.	Provide ready access for the media and public about incidents and responses (eg via website).	Operate with transparency, avoiding the temptation to spin bad news in your favour. Take full responsibility for your actions and move quickly to solutions.	
			Total Score	
			Average	

12

Accounting and Finance: How to Account for Environmental and Social Impacts

Most people are familiar with the old maxim 'what gets measured gets done'; finance and accounting departments are primarily responsible for what gets measured and so have a powerful influence on organizational strategy and decisions.

One problem, however, is that traditionally these fields have only tried to measure one 'leg' of the three-legged stool of sustainability: economic impacts. As Ralph Estes, author of *Tyranny of the Bottom Line: Why Corporations Make Good People Do Bad Things*, eloquently explains, our accounting system is a vestige of the early corporations' focus on trading. When this became our only measure of success, it led to a host of predictable problems: short-term thinking, employee and public safety problems, and even corporate fraud. Estes and many others contend that the solution is to begin measuring performance against other stakeholder expectations as well.

In this chapter we focus on issues pertinent to accounting and finance inside organizations. Related issues for economists are also equally important but space does not allow us to go into those issues as well. For readers interested in sustainable economics, we suggest beginning with works by Herman Daly, Geoffrey Heal and Gretchen Daily.

WHAT YOU SHOULD KNOW ABOUT SUSTAINABILITY

Increasingly, accounting and financial analysts are being expected to develop metrics and decision frameworks for social and environmental performance. There is also a significant rise in the number of companies publishing sustainability or corporate social responsibility reports. As already mentioned, the 2003 PricewaterhouseCoopers survey of 1300 CEOs from 43 different countries discovered that 66 per cent included sustainability in their annual reports while 37 per cent created a separate sustainability report. This trend toward a more complete sustainability report is growing as an additional 16 per cent plan to include one in the near future. (The entire report can be downloaded from www.pwc.com/pl/eng/ins-sol/publ/2003/ceo_jan2003.html.)[1]

This then raises the question of how an organization should measure non-financial performance? While financial accounting has been standardizing for over a century, there are as yet no generally accepted practices for evaluating social and environmental performance. The Global Reporting Initiative issued by the Coalition for Environmentally Responsible Economies (CERES) has attempted to provide guidelines for such reports. The usefulness of the frameworks is still in question, however, and until appropriate standardization occurs finance and accounting professionals must resolve a number of thorny issues.

Many of the negative impacts of organizational operations are externalities. Externalities are costs that are borne by someone other than the ones that caused them. These are usually caused by organizational boundaries (ie the limits on what we consider the organization to be responsible for) and subsidies (tax breaks and the like). When a timber company chops down trees and sends silt into the rivers, they do not pay for replacing or cleaning the water treatment centre's filters or for compensating the fisherman for his poor catch. Car companies do not have to pay for building and maintaining roads. A governmental agency does not pay for the business impacts of its regulations. Too often, these conventions reinforce unsustainable practices in organizations.

Government has a particularly useful role in this situation. If an individual business internalizes some of the costs that are traditionally externalized, they may be at a competitive disadvantage, so often business needs government to create a level playing field. Currently, it is popular to use market forces, for example cap-and-trade systems, rather than prescriptive regulations. One example of a market solution is the European programme of carbon trading to offset climate impacts associated with burning fossil fuels.

As Robert Kennedy, Jr. writes in *Crimes Against Nature*:

> *You show me a polluter and I'll show you a subsidy. I'll show you a fat cat using political clout to escape the discipline of the free market and load his production costs onto the backs of the public.*
>
> *The fact is, free-market capitalism is the best thing that could happen to the environment, our economy, our country. Simply put, true free-market capitalism, in which businesses pay all the costs of bringing their products to market, is the most efficient and democratic way of distributing the goods of the land – and the surest way to eliminate pollution. Free markets, when allowed to function, properly value raw materials and encourage producers to eliminate waste – pollution – by reducing, reusing and recycling.*
>
> *As Jim Hightower likes to say, 'The free market is a great thing – we should try it some time.*[2]

We believe that Kennedy is overstating the situation here in that there is no such thing as a completely free market. However, his basic point is valid: if organizations bore the costs of the impacts they caused, they would make more sustainable decisions. Applying this concept to our complex, global economy will be no easy task, but the paradigm is ripe for consideration.

There are no accepted ways to measure social and environmental performance. There are a number of people and groups working on ways to measure social and environmental performance. However, it's likely to be decades until any standardization occurs; in the meantime, financial analysts will have to blaze their own trails. There are some places to look for guidance, however, much of the work being done in Europe:

- CERES has been working on the Global Reporting Initiative (GRI), which is intended to provide standardization. Over 180 organizations have used this framework but not all are finding it as useful for internal use, www.gri.org.
- The European Academy of Business in Society, www.eabis.org, and Forum for the Future, www.forumforthefuture.org, are also working on these issues, especially vis-à-vis social impacts. Similarly, the European Federation of Accountants (FEE) has a Sustainable Working Party working on these issues, www.fee.be.
- SA8000 is a framework for social accounting.
- AccountAbility 1000 (also known as AA 1000) is an assurance standard emphasizing stakeholder involvement.
- Global Citizenship 360 (GC360) is an assessment process developed by Coca Cola and The Future 500. It produces a 360-degree summary of corporate performance, a report builder for corporate social responsibility reports and a data repository.
- The British Standards organization is working on sustainability management guidelines for corporations called BS 8900, www.BSI-global.com/British_Standards/sustainability/index.xalter.
- Japan's Ministry of the Environment provide its Environmental Accounting Guidelines, www.env.go.jp/en/ssee/index.html.
- Highwater Research, established by Paul Hawken, is raising the standards for the socially responsible investment industry as a whole. The Highwater methodology is structured to focus the investment universe on only those companies that are truly beneficial to society and the environment. The key component of this methodology is an examination of a company's business intention and model. Does the company contribute to social and environmental health? Marketing junk food to children does not qualify; renewable energy does. Making violent video games does not; creating childcare facilities does. Ultimately, Highwater Research will be available to all investors and hopes to become the preferred method for socially responsible investing selection in the future, www.highwaterresearch.com.

- For some elements of sustainable performance, especially where consistency across organizations is critical, reporting protocols have been developed. One example is the Greenhouse Gas Protocol for reporting climate-related impacts, www.ghgprotocol.org.

Traditional accounting methods mishandle natural assets. It seems unbelievable to those outside the field, but economists often value natural assets and natural systems at zero. If humans treat wastewater, there is an economic impact on GDP, but if nature does it, nothing goes on the ledger. Similarly, a fishing fleet counts the cost of the vessel, the fuel, people, rigging and transportation but treats fish, the primary raw material as free. There is no accounting system factoring in the fact that fish stocks have now been depleted. This leads to a 'tragedy of the commons' problem: as fish become scarce, they become more valuable, which only encourages more fishing. Should there not be a debit on the balance sheet? Shouldn't there be a requirement to invest in the natural capital?

Sometimes the trick is getting the denominator right. The Collins Companies, a vertically integrated US forest products company, bases the 'value growth' of a tree on the amount of ground that it occupies rather than the value growth on the tree's existing value. This is uncommon thinking in the forest management world. While mature trees grow more slowly, their girth is larger so adding a little around a large circumference, in their view, can be better than having more small-diameter trees on the same piece of ground. This economic model supports their decision to maintain a diversity of tree ages, including trees over 50 inches in diameter, supporting much greater biodiversity than the standard tree plantation. Owner Terry Collins says, 'You have to look at economics in a more timeless way, for the next generation,' instead of as discounted cash flows.[3]

Current financial decision tools cannot easily account for risk or intangible benefits. Common financial tools, including payback periods, internal rate of return and net present value, only account for direct financial effects; they do not factor in such issues as risk avoidance or intangible benefits except where those can be clearly and definitively estimated. However, sustainability has as much to do with risk management as it does direct payback. What is it worth to eliminate all toxic chemicals from your property? It's more than just the cost of the chemicals and permits. Your insurance risk declines. The liability for employee and community safety problems declines. The potential for catastrophic environmental disasters also goes down. Sustainability often generates multiple unintended benefits, but if you don't account for them, they often count for nothing in management decisions.

Discounting underestimates the needs of future generations and long-term impacts. To deal with the effects of time on the value of money, discount rates are usually factored into financial analyses. However, this makes no sense when it comes to natural assets. Is a forest going to be less valuable in the future? Will water? How do we deal with the inter-generational equity issues associated with sustainability? As Geoffrey Heal points out in his paper 'Interpreting Sustainability':

> *A positive discount rate forces a fundamental asymmetry between the present and future generations, particularly those very far into the future. This asymmetry is troubling when dealing with environmental matters such as climate change, species extinction and disposal of nuclear waste, as many of the consequences of these may be felt only in the very long run indeed, a hundred or more years into the future. At any positive discount rate these consequences will clearly not loom large (or even at all) in project evaluations. If one discounts present world GNP over two hundred years at 5 per cent per annum, it is worth only a few hundred thousand dollars, the price of a good apartment. Discounted at 10 per cent, it is equivalent to a used car.*

Instead, Heal says, we need methods that provide symmetry between current and future generations while also recognizing the intrinsic value of environmental assets.[4]

The accounting system itself results in aberrations. The structure of the accounting system itself causes problems. Sustainable decisions often have multiple positive benefits, but they often occur across different departmental budgets. Eliminate a hazardous substance in your manufacturing process and you may simultaneously reduce environmental permits and paperwork for the EH&S department, protective equipment for plant operations, hazmat training in the training department, and expenses in the human resources benefits plan. Similar problems exist between capital and operations and maintenance budgets. The person managing the capital budget for a building expansion gets hassled if he goes over budget, even if those additional costs would be paid back in two years through energy savings in the facilities budget. How do you create incentives to optimize the whole system? How do you make it easy for someone to take a reduction in their own budget if the savings will show up in someone else's? This is not a problem unique to sustainability, but because sustainable thinking tends to affect many elements across the organization, it is more pronounced.

RESOURCES

Schaltegger, Stefan and Roger Buritt (2000) *Contemporary Environmental Accounting: Issues, Concepts and Practice.* Greenleaf.

Heal, Geoffrey (2000) *Nature and the Marketplace: Capturing the Value of Ecosystem Services.* Washington DC: Island Press.

ACCA, the British accounting body (www.accaglobal.com), has an accounting and sustainability e-newsletter that can help you stay abreast of this emerging field.

STRATEGIES YOU CAN USE

At one level or another, you will need to solve these problems. You'll have to help your organization develop a management framework and metrics so that you can report (internally and/or externally) on your performance in social, economic and environmental areas. We have organized the practices and tools here into three main areas:

1   developing a metrics framework and reporting on results – you need a system in place to gather and report appropriate sustainability performance metrics;
2   determining what is 'better' – you'll need methods to help you understand, from a holistic perspective, which options are more sustainable; and
3   developing decision tools to help you manage the inevitable trade-offs.

Develop a metrics framework and report on results

Whether you work on an internal or external sustainability report to track your organization's progress, you will need a framework to organize your data and to ensure it is complete. At present there is no universally accepted way of doing this, so you will need to choose, modify or invent one. In the chapter for senior managers there is a list of common sustainability frameworks, so we will only provide a couple of examples here so that you can see a range of options. The framework you choose will affect what you measure and how you report your sustainability performance. Here are some general guidelines:

- Choose a framework that can provide a shared mental model inside the organization. Find one that fits the culture and mission.
- Create linking, cascading measures. For example, your external stakeholders may be interested in your progress toward eliminating greenhouse gases but your plant manager may be more interested in energy use per product produced. But the latter can inform the former.
- Focus on measuring the most important elements rather than everything. Develop metrics for your most egregious impacts, not every paperclip. Choose metrics that will be useful, where the data gathering is worth the effort.
- Take advantage of the work of others. It can be better to use a method that is generally accepted or used by others so that you can compare your results with other organizations.
- Be satisfied with imprecise data where it is just not possible or practical to get accurate data, as long as you are confident the trend lines will represent what is happening on the ground.

- Report both normative data (eg energy use per product) and gross totals. Management will care about the ratios but nature only cares about absolute values.
- Show the data in relation to other trends as appropriate (eg economic growth, sales increases, new plant start-ups or population growth).
- As you would do for any financial measures, put into place effective systems for gathering, tracking, reporting, evaluating and improving on metrics.
- In addition to the traditional web and hardcopy reports, consider creative ways to get people to focus on the data. When Tri-Met, a transit authority in Portland, Oregon, posted their electricity bill in the elevator, the employees were so horrified to see what the organization was paying that usage decreased by 20 per cent the following month! Use the data to encourage behavioural change.

Below we describe several different frameworks that are commonly used in organizations. See if one fits your situation. If not, look at the other frameworks described in Appendix A or invent your own.

The Natural Step

The Natural Step is based on the physical sciences and does a good job of describing environmental sustainability, with only a quick nod to the socio-economic realm. Its four principles, or 'system conditions', can provide a useful way to organize your activities and they also imply end-state targets for your metrics. Because the framework was created by scientists, the language of the system conditions is sometimes hard for the average person to understand, even though the wording is precise and meaningful. To avoid going into a long-winded explanation here, we provide in Table 12.1 a simpler version of the principles and suggested metrics. The system conditions describe what we should not do to have a sustainable world. You can see how these metrics can cascade, providing different data for different groups.

Depending on your line of work, it can be just as important to create metrics for those outside your organization as for those within. ShoreBank Pacific, based in Ilwaco, Washington, used The Natural Step as the basis for evaluating their loan applications. The bank has a mission to promote sustainability so it only made sense to evaluate their loans based on it. Over time, Kathleen Sayce, their bank scientist, developed their own system of metrics.

Triple bottom line/Three Es

Many corporations have focused on corporate social responsibility or what is often called the triple bottom line (economic, social and environmental) or the Three Es (Economy, Environment and social Equity). It may be simpler to use this existing framework and then embed something like The Natural Step principles where appropriate.

Table 12.1 *Metrics based on The Natural Step system conditions*

Principle or 'System Condition'	Possible Metrics
Don't **move** substances from the crust into nature faster than they are redeposited. (This relates mostly to fossil fuels and to rare/toxic metals and minerals.)	Energy use per unit of product (eco-efficiency). Proportion of energy from sustainable sources/renewables (energy sources). Carbon-equivalent emissions, including carbon offsets (climate impact).
Don't **make** things that nature can't handle. (This relates mainly to man-made substances, especially those that do not readily biodegrade, but also to excessive quantities of other materials that are produced faster than nature can process them.)	Proportion of solid waste diverted from landfill (ie reused, recycled, upcycled or composted) (zero waste). Proportion of products in chemical inventory that contain chemicals of concern (eg the 'dirty dozen' or grey/black listed chemicals) (toxicity).
Don't **take** from nature faster than it can regenerate. (This refers to natural resources that can be depleted through over-harvesting, development and genetic manipulation.)	Proportion of major purchases that come from sustainable sources (eg organic, certified). Investments in natural capital (eg restoration activities).
Don't **hurt** quality of life and human dignity. (This acknowledges that basic human needs must be met worldwide for the above conditions to be possible.)	Employee satisfaction (internal quality of work life). Community contribution in hours and money (local impacts). Proportion of vendors/suppliers with SA8000 or equivalent commitment to fair labour practices (international impact).

The Oregon Museum of Science and Industry in Portland, Oregon has taken this approach. We helped them identify internal and external performance metrics and are in the process of creating a decision framework to balance the trade-offs between them when faced with a decision.

Sustainability or environmental management system

Many organizations have an environmental management system (EMS), either ISO 14001 certified or not, and this can provide a process for managing sustainability, especially if sustainability becomes embedded into the EMS. (This is covered in more detail in the Environmental Affairs chapter.) Since such a management system provides a mechanism for setting goals, identifying priorities, choosing long-term targets and monitoring results, it can benefit from the involvement of a financial analyst.

Table 12.2 *Metrics based on the triple bottom line*

	Environmental	Social	Financial
Internal	Energy reduction	Employee satisfaction	Net operating dollars
	Waste reduction	Turnover	Net margin percentage
	Proportion of sustainable materials in museum exhibits		Museum attendance
External	CO_2 emissions reduction	Scoring of sustainability content in educational programmes and exhibits	Scholarships

Organization's vision or values

Some organizations discard all available sustainability frameworks and use as their primary organizing structure something core to their operation. Staff at Stonyfield Farms based in New Hampshire, which sells organic dairy products, translated their organization's mission into measures, as outlined in the table below:[5]

Table 12.3 *Metrics based on mission and values*

Mission Statement	What they measure
To serve as a model that environmentally and socially responsible businesses can also be profitable.	Resource use (solid waste, wastewater, packaging)
	Pesticides and toxics
	Energy use and global warming for facility and supply chain
	Acidification
To educate consumers and producers about the value of protecting the environment and of supporting family farmers and sustainable farming methods.	Proportion of organic sales
	Organic acres supported
	Number of small dairy farms supported
	Proportion of milk from small family dairy farms
	Price paid to farmer (milk)
To provide a healthy, productive and enjoyable workplace for all employees, with opportunities to gain new skills and advance personal career goals.	Lost work day illness/injury rate
	Compensation, holidays, vacation, turnover, etc. as compared with national benchmarks
	Internal promotions
	Education and training; tuition reimbursement as compared with national benchmarks
	Employee climate survey

Table 12.3 *Metrics based on mission and values* (cont'd)

Mission Statement	What they measure
To recognize our obligations to shareholders and lenders by providing an excellent return on their investment.	Net sales
	Gross margin
	Share price
	Earnings before interest and taxes
	Net income
	Overheads
	Market share
	Earnings before interest, taxes, depreciation and amortization
To produce the very highest quality all natural and certified organic products that taste incredible	Quality checks (over 900 each day)
	Consumer complaints
	Shelf-life studies
	Chill cell compliance
	Sanitation

RESOURCES

The Global Reporting Initiative is developing standards for sustainability reporting, www.gri.org.

The Carbon Disclosure Project is a coalition of institutional investors responsible for over US$21 trillion in assets. They have created a database of information on the business implications associated with climate change.

The Center for Sustainable Management in Lüneburg, Germany has a sustainable balanced scorecard. See Figge, F., Hahn, T., Schaltegger, S. and Wagner, M. (2001) *Sustainability Balanced Scorecard. Wertorientiertes Nachhaltigkeitsmanagement mit der Balanced Scorecard.* Lüneburg: Center for Sustainability Management.

The accounting firm KPMG published the International Survey of Corporate Sustainable Reporting in 2002.

For a registry of corporate reports, go to www.accaglobal.com.

The Corporate Register provides an online directory of non-financial corporate reports, www.corporateregister.com.

The State and Territorial Air Pollution Program Administrators and the Association of Local Air Pollution Control Officials have produced software for communities to track their greenhouse gas emissions.

Beckett, R. and J. Jonker (2002) 'AccountAbility 1000: A New Social Standard for Building Sustainability,' *Managerial Auditing Journal*, Vol 17, Nos 1–2, January, pp36–42.

Determine what is 'better'

In addition to helping their organizations develop valid and useful sustainability metrics and reports, financial analysts must also help their organizations make better, more sustainable decisions. To date, there are three main accounting and financial decision-making methods that can overcome some of the problems associated with traditional financial analyses covered at the beginning of this chapter. Table 12.4 below ranks these from minor change to major shift in traditional practice.

Activity-based costing (ABC)
Activity-based costing is a good place to begin as it collects all or most of the costs associated with products or services. As we have already noted, sustainable thinking tends to create multiple benefits that may show up in different parts of the organization. Activity-based costing helps you get a handle on the true costs, regardless of how the organization and budgets are structured. The basic process is to:

- analyse the activities associated with a product or service;
- gather the costs associated with these activities;
- establish output measures; and
- analyse the costs as compared with other options.

On one occasion, talking to managers from a department store chain about sustainability, we raised the issue of all the pesticides they carried in their garden section. The company's policy was to dispose of any broken bottles or spills as if they were a hazardous waste generator, even though their small volumes did not put them in a regulated category requiring these more-expensive steps. We asked if they had ever analysed all the costs they incurred associated with carrying these products (hazmat training, spill response, disposal fees, legal liability, etc.) against the profits they earned from them. There was a stunned silence. It had never occurred to them to ask.

Table 12.4 *Comparison of ABC, LCC and LCA*

Activity-based costing	Life cycle costing	Life cycle assessment
Assigns costs that are typically hidden in overheads or other departments to products or other relevant units.	Considers longevity, taking into account the useful expected life of certain products or financial decisions.	Assesses the full impacts of decisions along the entire life cycle, from resource extraction, transportation and manufacture to use and end-of-life disposal.

Minor change → Major change toward sustainability

RESOURCES

A global portal for activity-based costing is www.offtech.com/au/abc/Home.asp.
   Shank, John K. and Vijay Govidarajan (2003) *Strategic Cost Management*. New York: The Free Press.

Life cycle costing (LCC)

The next step is to take into account the longevity of decisions you make. All too often, the cheapest first cost is not the cheapest in the long term. For example, vinyl flooring costs much less than many other floors in terms of initial outlay, but if you take into account the cost of replacing it two to three times more frequently than other flooring options, it may in fact be the more expensive choice. An LCC analysis may reveal that it would save time and money to go with the alternatives.

   The financial department can help organizations make more sustainable decisions by doing LCC studies. As we noted in the chapter for facilities, the California Department of Finance commissioned a study by the Capital E group and Lawrence Berkeley Laboratory to determine whether green building practices paid off. Often building a 'green building' carries a much as a 10 per cent premium in construction costs. Is it worth it, they wondered? After studying 100 buildings across the country and other studies, they concluded that financial benefits of green design are between $50 and $70 per square foot in a LEED-certified building, over ten times the additional cost associated with building green.

RESOURCES

Life Cycle Cost Analysis Handbook, www.eed.state.ak.us/facilities/publications/LCCAHandbook1999.pdf.
   Life Cycle Costing, www.ogc.gov.uk/sdtoolkit/deliveryteam/briefings/businesschange/PDFs/lifecyclecosting.pdf.

Life cycle assessment (LCA)

Unlike the two tools discussed above, LCA emphasizes impacts more than costs. If your goal is to produce more sustainable products and services, you should take into account the full life-cycle impacts of your decisions. This helps to answer the many 'paper or plastic' dilemmas. Are cloth nappies better than disposables? Is it better to use certified wood that has been transported thousands of miles or local uncertified timber?

For manufacturers, LCA can help you determine what is most important to improve. For example, when Electrolux wanted to redesign their washing machines, they discovered that the biggest impacts of their products had less to do with what they were made of or how far they were transported than with the amount of water and energy their customers used in operating their washers. This led them to develop the now common front-loading machines that use a fraction of the amount of water and energy of traditional models.

Stonyfield Farms in New Hampshire conducted an LCA on their yogurt product delivery system. In part, they wanted to compare different options for containers. They found that the size of the container and the distance to retailer were actually more important. If all of their yogurt were sold in 32-ounce containers, they could save the equivalent of 11,250 barrels of oil per year. And transportation to the retailer represented about a third of the energy impact. The LCA also indicated that thermoformed cups would be preferable as a container.[6]

LCAs can be conducted at two levels. Initially you might carry out a cursory LCA for internal use to guide your decisions. However, if you want to make public claims about your product, a full LCA study, most likely by a disinterested third party, will be needed. Refer to ISO 14040 for guidance on how LCAs should be done.

The maxim 'the devil is in the details' was never more true than for LCAs. Your assumptions can make all the difference, so it's important to 'ground-truth' your assumptions and make sure your comparisons are based on a function or service of the products studied. For example, Ecobalance in Bethesda, Maryland conducted an LCA for the Textile Rental Services Association. They wanted to compare the impacts of reusable, washable incontinence pads versus single use disposables. The research behind the LCA discovered that when disposable pads were being used, the thinner composition gave rise to the perception of their being less sanitary and less effective at keeping the patient and bed dry. As a result, nurses would use two to three disposable pads. On the other hand, only one thicker, seemingly more absorbent reusable pad would be used. Thus the true comparison was not one disposable versus one reusable but two disposable to one reusable. While a sensitivity analysis was performed on the number of disposable pads (from 1 to 4 pads), the modelling assumption of using one versus more than one pad really skewed the results.

In practice, LCAs can often be frustrating and unsatisfying. They are hard to do, the results are often not easily transferable and they seldom provide unequivocal results. For example, in the hospital linen example above, one of the main factors determining which product was more sustainable was whether the hospital washed its own linen on site or sent it out.

Nevertheless, there are efforts under way to make LCAs somewhat easier. For example, BEES (Building for Environmental and Economic Sustainability) software helps architects select environmentally preferable building materials. Some use embodied energy as a proxy for environmental impacts. The Okala Ecological Design Course includes useful tables of data too.

RESOURCES

LCA for Mere Mortals by Rita Schenck, published by the Institute for Environmental Research and Education, www.iere.org/mortals.html.

Okala Ecological Design Course Guide, www.idsa.org/whatsnew/sections/ecosection/IDSA_okala_guide_web.pdf.

Industrial Designers Society of America, www.idsa.org.

BEES (Building for Environmental and Economic Sustainability) is a software tool to help you select environmentally preferable building products, www.epa.gov/oppt/epp/tools/bees.htm

DG Employment has published a guide, *ABC of CSR Instruments*, which covers socially responsible management, socially responsible consumption and socially responsible investment, www.europa.eu.int/comm/employment_social/soc-dial/csr/abc.htm.

The Investor Responsibility Resource Center is a good place to start for information on socially responsible and sustainable management practices and investing, www.irrc.org.

For one example of an LCA, see Brachfeld, D. et al (2001) 'Life Cycle Assessment of the Stonyfield Product Delivery System', Ann Arbor, Michigan: University of Michigan, 5 April 2001.

Decision tools to balance trade-offs

Regardless of whether your organization uses the three formal tools described above, you will need a way to balance trade-offs and enhance sustainability performance. We have identified three distinct decision-making methods that are in use at this time; these are described below in order of least to most sophisticated.

Brainstorm how to add more value

Probably the simplest way to enhance the sustainability performance of any activity you do now or are planning is to ask the question, 'How could we change how we do this to get more social and/or environmental benefits?' This often leads to innovative ideas that don't add costs. For example, the Oregon Department of Corrections routinely sends a bus-load of newly convicted criminals a couple of hundred miles to the rurally located prison. For years, the bus came back empty, until department employees wondered if there was something else that could be done with the empty bus. Now they work with local farmers, who donate their surplus produce (instead of ploughing it under), enlist the prisoners to sort and bag it, and transport the bagged produce back to the city in the empty buses for the Oregon Food Bank to distribute to the needy. Everyone wins. The farmers get a tax deduction, the prisoners get something meaningful to do, the prison improves its image in the community and the hungry get more fresh produce.

Table 12.5 *Weighted criteria chart*

Criterion	Weight	Option 1	Option 2	Option 3
Financial	10	5	10	3
		50	100	30
Social	5	10	1	3
		50	5	15
Environmental	5	10	3	1
		50	15	5
TOTAL		150	120	50

Weighted criteria charts

Whichever method you use to analyse your impacts and costs, eventually you will find yourself in the position of having to make trade-off decisions. A weighted criteria chart lets you evaluate multiple options against multiple criteria and to assign different degrees of importance to certain criteria. Using this method, you can balance the social, environmental, and economic benefits and costs of your options. The simple weighted criteria chart above (Table 12.5) gives equal weight to financial and social/environmental performance. (For another example of such a chart, see Table 9.3, page 183.)

For those unfamiliar with these decision tools, here is an explanation of how to use them. For any particular decision, identify the relevant criteria on which the choice is based. In the example, we use the three elements of sustainability, but you could just as easily use other frameworks or add other criteria such as ease of adoption, opportunity to enhance corporate image, or ability to educate employees.

Assuming the importance of the criteria varies, you then assign a weight to each, usually from 1–10 with 10 being the most important. Your alternatives are listed along the top of the remaining columns. For example, if you are comparing different copy papers, the different brands would be listed. Then you look at each option against each criterion, assigning a score from 1–10; this score is recorded in the box. Then multiply the score by the weight to get a weighted score. When all options have been scored against all criteria, add up the weighted scores. Note that in the example above, option two was the best financially but option one came out with the highest score, balancing the trade-offs between cost and social/environmental benefit.

Compare a sustainability rating with cost

Scott Dethloff and Paul Burnet from the large international engineering firm CH2M Hill developed a software product called SD Solutions (Sustainable Development Solutions).

This tool is basically a large weighted criteria chart in spreadsheet form which evaluates sustainability performance separately from cost. In the weighted criteria example above, 'financial' was interpreted as simply reflecting cost. SD Solutions provides a model for how to evaluate economic benefit to the community separate from cost.

This tool can help groups make complex decisions. First, for each of the three sustainability elements (social, economic and environmental) the team identifies specific factors they consider important and relevant for their project. For example, under 'social' they may determine that providing educational opportunities for young people is key. If desired, the team can then determine benchmark standards for each factor, ie what would earn a ten, five or one.

In a similar way to the weighted criteria example in the previous section, the team then evaluates each of its options against all the factors they have identified. This then produces a sustainability score for each option. Sensitivity analysis can also be carried out to determine if changes to certain scores (perhaps advocated by a vocal minority) would make any difference to which option received the highest sustainability score.

The final step is to map the sustainability score against cost for each option. This yields a scatter diagram similar to the one shown below. Projects or options that have both a high sustainability score and a low cost are no-brainers, things to approve without more discussion. Projects with low sustainability benefits, regardless of cost, can be eliminated unless there are other compelling reasons to do them. The team can then focus on discussing the relative merits of options with high sustainability benefits but also high costs.

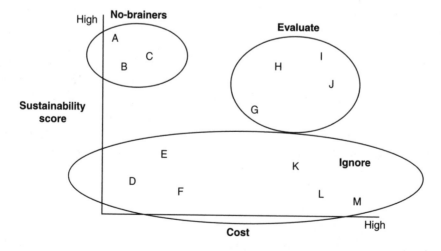

Figure 12.1 *SD Solutions results*

Conclusion

Of all the different functional areas, the fields of finance and accounting are perhaps the least developed in terms of incorporating sustainability into their practice. By at least identifying the problems with traditional practices, we hope to have stimulated the creative thinking that will be required to solve them. There are helpful tools being developed to measure, track and report sustainability performance, but the field is still in its infancy. When you select metrics, be sure to include a fully sustainable target. This clarifies what the abstract concept of sustainability really means to your organization and can spur out-of-the-box thinking. Be sure also to link these metrics and reports to some form of sustainability management system so that the results can be evaluated and acted upon. For more information on sustainability management systems see the chapters for Senior Management and Environmental Affairs.

SCORE FINANCE AND ACCOUNTING

See page 31 for how to complete this assessment and page 33 for how to interpret your score.

FINANCE				
Practice	Pilot *1 point*	Initiative *3 points*	Systemic *9 points*	Points
Financial analysis: Use tools to provide a more complete assessment of options which take into account sustainability.	In addition to traditional financial methods for determining a return on investment, include an assessment of risks and intangible benefits when assessing options.	Use total cost of ownership (not first cost) and identify externalities related to the life cycle of the product or capital investment.	Make life cycle analysis available and take responsibility for all identifiable externalities when making major decisions; avoid discount rates that unfairly impact on future generations.	
Sustainability reporting: Make available and use qualitative and quantitative data on your progress towards sustainability.	Produce an internal report highlighting accomplishments and areas for improvement.	Include sustainability reporting as part of existing public reports.	Publish a separate, detailed and audited sustainability report.	

FINANCE				
Practice	Pilot *1 point*	Initiative *3 points*	Systemic *9 points*	Points
Investments: Factor in sustainability when making investment decisions (eg pension plans, stock purchases, bonds).	Employ negative screens for such criteria as tobacco, arms, child labour, etc. Shun investments that contribute to human misery, war, and environmental destruction.	Give preference to investments that demonstrate a commitment to sustainability practices.	Only invest in sustainability-related investments. .	
			Total Score	
			Average	

ACCOUNTING				
Practice	Pilot *1 point*	Initiative *3 points*	Systemic *9 points*	Points
Budgets: Modify your systems so that people are encouraged to optimize the sustainability performance of the entire organization rather than their own budgets.	Provide a method of accounting for benefits that accrue to different budgets (eg capital versus O&M; operations versus customer service department).	Include sustainability as one of the criteria that should be assessed before money is spent.	Where significant systemic barriers exist, provide a way to return some of the savings to the departments that created them.	
Metrics: Develop a set of sustainability metrics.	Develop a set of metrics to assess the benefits and costs of pursuing sustainability.	Develop a complete set of sustainability metrics for the organization and report on them at least annually.	Regularly conduct sustainability best-practices studies with other organizations to uncover opportunities for improvement.	
			Total Score	
			Average	

Appendix A
Sustainability Frameworks and Tools

There are a plethora of sustainability-related frameworks and tools. This has led to a lot of 'my framework is better than yours' arguments. It's important to understand how they fit into a hierarchy and which frameworks are more useful in certain situations. In this appendix, we hope to untangle the different terms so that you can choose the frameworks and tools that will be most appropriate in your situation.

To be sustainable, we must be able to operate in accordance with natural laws. We don't get to change the laws of thermodynamics or gravity. So any sustainability must take these natural laws into account. The only framework that translates these natural laws into rules for human society is The Natural Step framework. Some organizations use The

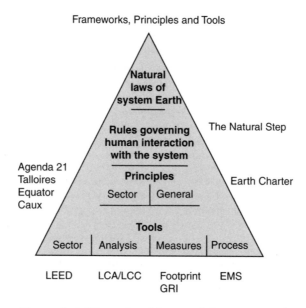

Figure A.1 *Hierarchy of Sustainability Frameworks*

Source: Adapted from the Five System Levels used by The Natural Step

Natural Step as their organizing structure while others have struggled with The Natural Step and prefer to use another framing. However, in our view, The Natural Step system conditions must be embedded in your sustainability framework in some fashion. Otherwise, you are still only working on being, as McDonough would say, 'less bad', ignoring the undeniable limits of nature.

Many of the existing frameworks for sustainability fall into the category of principles; guidelines for how to become more sustainable. These include a number that have evolved out of the United Nations Earth Summits, such as Agenda 21 and the Caux Roundtable principles for business and government. Others are sector-specific, such as the Tailloires Declaration for universities and the Equator Principles for financial institutions. While these are useful, they often sound like motherhood-and-apple-pie platitudes and are generally toothless if they are not married to The Natural Step in some way. They provide more specific guidance about the areas to address but suffer from a lack of clear sustainable end-points.

Then there are a host of different tools. Some, like LEED, are specific to an industry sector. Some provide methods of analysis, such as life cycle costing and life cycle analysis. Others are primarily useful for measurement; we put here the Ecological Footprint as well as the Bellagio Principles. Finally, some provide a process for pursuing sustainability, usually based on environmental management systems and ISO 14001.

Figure A.1 shows these different levels with a sampling of specific frameworks and tools listed to the side. In some cases, the level we have assigned to a specific term was arbitrary. For example, LEED could be considered a sector-specific set of principles, a measurement system, or a sector-specific set of tools. Below, we provide an analysis of a larger set of these frameworks and tools that are in common use.

Overarching principles

Framework/Tool	Comments
The Three Es: This is based on the United Nations' work regarding what is needed for sustainable development. The Three Es are usually referred to as Economy, Environment and social Equity.	This framework gives no guidance about what to do but can help you organize your thinking. Social equity is really only a part of the social aspect of sustainability; compare this with the Triple Bottom Line, which has a broader interpretation of the social element.
The Triple Bottom Line: Sometimes used interchangeably with the Three Es but different in subtle ways. Basically the same framework as corporate social responsibility: often framed as Social, Economic and Environment or as People, Planet and Profits.	This framing of the social component allows for the inclusion of other social issues such as human health, governance, etc. Business for Social Responsibility is probably one of the best sources for this approach.

Overarching principles

Framework/Tool	Comments
The Natural Step Framework: This provides a planning framework in the form of four 'system conditions' or principles based on science that guide decision-makers of an organization or governmental body systematically toward sustainability. For society to be sustainable nature must not be subject to increasing concentrations of substances from the Earth's crust; it must not be subject to increasing concentrations of human-made substances; its functions and diversity must not be impoverished (displacement, over-harvesting, etc.), and resources must be used fairly and efficiently in order to meet basic human needs globally. (See The Natural Step, www.naturalstep.org, and the Oregon Natural Step Network, www.ortns.org.)	Because the framework is derived from fundamental scientific principles, it has more face validity than some of the other frameworks. This framework does an excellent job of describing for a lay audience the environmental aspect of sustainability but it is often criticized for not adequately addressing the other two 'legs' of sustainability, ie social and economic elements. It can be used as an overarching framework or the system conditions can be nested inside another framework. The 'backcasting' process provides a process for using the framework, but this process can be strengthened if it is embedded into an environmental management system.
CERES Principles: Created in response to the Exxon Valdez disaster, CERES offers a code of conduct and a credo for organizations to adopt. The principles address issues such as energy conservation, waste reduction and disposal, and management commitment, www.ceres.org/.	CERES, and other sets of principles like it, are arguably not sustainability frameworks because they don't overtly recognize the limits of nature.
Conservation Economy: Ecotrust has put together a website that documents best practices for social, economic and environmental practices. They have identified 'patterns' (eg certification, labelling) that have application in many situations, www.conservationeconomy.net.	Based on the three legs of sustainability. The web tool may be useful but it is not clear whether Ecotrust is continuing to support this framework after its creator left the organization.
Natural Capitalism: A book of the same title (by Hawken, Lovins and Lovins) lays out a set of principles for a sustainable economic system. The main principles involve dramatically improving the productivity of natural resources, redesigning production around biological models (biomimicry), rethinking business as a service and reinvesting in natural capital. (See the website for the book which identifies the principles in detail, www.naturalcapitalism.org/.)	An awkward blend of an overarching set of principles and a set of tools.

Overarching principles

Framework/Tool	Comments
Six Es: Trades unions in Europe are developing a working model that will support companies and organizations that wish to change their operations on the basis of the goals set for Agenda 21. This model is called 6E, which stands for ecology, emissions, energy, ergonomics, efficiency and economics. (For more information, see www.tco-info.com/.)	This includes more quality of work life issues than other frameworks but suffers from the lack of clear end-points.

Industry-specific frameworks

Framework/Tool	Comments
Agenda 21: Created at the Rio Earth Summit through the UN, this lays out actions needed at a national and international level to reach sustainability.	Talks about what needs to happen but provides no accountability to make it happen.
UN Global Compact: Created by the UN to foster corporate citizenship, www.unglobalcompact.org.	Puts forth ten principles for business in three areas – labour standards, environment and anti-corruption – in support of the Agenda 21 goals.
Talloires Declaration: A set of principles for colleges and universities. Provides ten principles. Signed by universities from all over the world. Created by the University Leaders for a Sustainable Future.	Like CERES, provides no clear targets.
Equator Principles: Similar to Talloires but for financial institutions.	Like CERES, provides no clear targets.
Leadership for Energy and Environmental Design (LEED): Provides a scoring system for evaluating the sustainability of buildings. Certification is possible. See the World Green Building Council (www.worldgbc.org) or the US Green Building Council (www.usgbc.org).	Used in the US and a number of other countries, LEED does not define a fully sustainable building but it is the intent of the US Green Building Council to slowly raise the bar as practices and technologies improve.
Environmental Management System/ISO 14001: International guidelines for environmental management systems and their certification. Most often used by manufacturing and, to a lesser extent, government.	Can provide a process for managing your sustainability effort but by itself does not provide sustainability targets. Can easily be dovetailed with other frameworks.

Industry-specific frameworks

Framework/Tool	Comments
Smart Growth/New Urbanism: Provides guidelines for land use planning.	Provides important guidance for the development of liveable communities.
Hannover Principles: Developed by William McDonough Architects for EXPO 2000, held in Hannover, Germany. (For a complete listing of the principles, see www.virginia.edu/~arch/pub/hannover_list.html.)	The nine principles focus on the design of 'green' buildings, or the 'built environment' and stress the interdependent relationship human society has with nature.
Biomimicry: Using nature as inspiration for human designs. (See the book by the same title by Janine Benyus.) Most useful for research and development.	Co-opted by Natural Capitalism as one of their principles, this is also a practice unto itself.
Zero Waste: One approach to sustainability is to eliminate all forms of waste, turning our linear economy into a cyclical one, like nature's, where waste from one process becomes input to another. The Zero Waste Alliance has assessments and services to help you implement this approach. (See www.zerowaste.org or the Grassroots Recycling Network at www.grrn.org.)	Can seem more tangible than some of the other frameworks but people often interpret it as only dealing with solid waste.
Industrial ecology: Designing manufacturing systems so that the waste of one process is input to another.	In Europe the focus has been on co-locating facilities (sometimes called eco-industrial parks). This has been less successful in the US. This concept pre-dates but is related to Product Stewardship.
Green chemistry: Designing chemical processes to eliminate hazardous by-products and improve the efficiency of the processes themselves.	An emerging practice with a lot of promise for product development.
Product stewardship, Extended producer responsibility, Extended product responsibility (EPR): These three terms are roughly synonymous with subtle distinctions about who should bear responsibility. Preferred terms vary by country. The concept is to make manufacturers responsible for their products for their entire life cycle, including end of life.	While many efforts here are end-of-life (ie taking back products at the end of their useful life), they necessarily deal with the entire life cycle.

Measurement-related tools

Frameworks/Tools	Comments
Global Reporting Initiative: standards for sustainability reports, www.gri.org.	Created by CERES. It is intended to provide consistency across organizations but to date some organizations using it are finding it difficult to implement.
Bellagio Principles: Provides criteria or guidelines for the selection of metrics.	Useful when creating metrics.
Genuine Progress Indicator: Gross National Product adjusted so that spending on 'bad things' like prisons and environmental clean-up are deducted.	Useful for economists.
Greenhouse Gas Protocol: A standardized method of reporting climate impacts.	Important to follow if you plan to trade carbon credits or make public claims about reductions in greenhouse gases.
Life cycle assessment: A method of examining the impacts of a product or decision over its entire life cycle (from raw materials and manufacture to transportation, use and disposal).	Can be overwhelming to do a thorough job.
Life cycle costing: A method of examining the costs of financial decisions (eg construction of buildings) over their lifetime (versus first cost).	This is a smart financial practice that may already be standard practice in your organization.
Ecological Footprint: If you put a bubble over your city, it would quickly die because there would be no place to get raw materials or dispose of wastes. So the ecological footprint of our cities is much bigger than the area within the city limits. The Ecological Footprint approach shows you how to estimate the land needed to sustain your way of life. For example, the average American needs 30 acres, the average Italian less than half that. (For more information, see Wackernagel, Mathis and William Rees (1996) *Our Ecological Footprint: Reducing Human Impact on the Earth.* BC, Canada: New Society Publishers or go to www.rprogress.org/progsum/nip/ef/ef_main.html. To calculate your household footprint, go to www.rprogress.org/progsum/nip/ef/ef_household_calculator.html.)	Interesting concept but can be overwhelming to try to compute.

Certification Schemes

Agriculture: Food and Drug Administration (US, National Organic Program, www.ams.usda.gov/nop/); Food Alliance (US, www.thefoodalliance.org/); Indocert (India, and international, indocert.org); Naturland (Germany); Skal EKO-label (international). As part of its NutriClean® programme, Scientific Certification Systems evaluates and certifies fresh produce as being 'pesticide residue free' based on laboratory limits of detection as determined by government-accepted limit-of-detection protocols.

Buildings: LEED (Leadership in Energy and Environmental Design; programmes in many countries including the US, Canada, Taiwan, Mexico, India and Brazil. See www.worldgbc.org, www.usgbc.org.); BREEAM (BRE Environmental Assessment Method) in the UK.

Consumer products: Green Seal (US, www.greenseal.org); Environmental Choice (Canada); Nordic Swan (northern Europe); Ecolabel (Europe); Eco Mark (Japan); Blue Angel (Germany); Energy Star (US, www.energystar.gov/).

Fair trade: Transfair (US and Canada).

Fish: Marine Stewardship Council (international, www.msc.org/).

Hotels: Green Seal (US, www.greenseal.org).

Pest management: Mothers and Others (US); Scientific Certification Systems (Nutriclean, international); Nature Conservancy (international); Rainforest Alliance (international).

Manufacturing and management systems: ISO 9000 (quality); ISO 14001 (environmental management systems (international, www.iso.org); Scientific Certification Systems (international, www.scscertified.com).

Wood products: Forest Stewardship Council (international, www.fsc.org); Sustainable Forest Initiative (US, www.aboutsfi.org); Smart Wood and Eco-OK programmes of the Rainforest Alliance (international).

Eco-labels: For information about eco-labels used in the United States, go to www.ecolabels.com.

Notes

Chapter 1 – Sustainability as a strategic issue

1 Hammond, A. and Prahalad, C. K. (2004) 'Selling to the Poor', *Foreign Policy*, May/June, http://pubs.wri.org/sellingtopoor-pub-3990.html, accessed December 2005.
2 AtKisson, A. (1999) *Believing Cassandra: An Optimist Looks at a Pessimist's World*, White River Junction, VT: Chelsea Green Publishing, p24.
3 'The Millennium Poll on Corporate Social Responsibility', executive briefing by Environics International and Prince of Wales Business Leaders Forum and the Conference Board (1999), www.environicsinternational.com/news_archives/MPExecBrief.pdf, accessed 2005.
4 Friedman, T. (2002) *Longitudes and Attitudes: Exploring the World After September 11*, New York: Farrar Straus Giroux.
5 Auster, B. B. (1998) 'Enviro-Intelligence: The CIA Goes Green', *U.S. News & World Report*, Vol 124, No 10, March 16, p34.
6 For more on this topic, see Heinberg, R. (2003) *The Party's Over*, New Society Publishers; Appenzeller, T. (2004) 'The End of Cheap Oil', *National Geographic*, June, magma .nationalgeographic.com/ngm/0406/feature5/ or Google 'Hubbert's Curve'.
7 DesignTex data from the BuildingGreen website, www.buildinggreen.com/auth/article .cfm?fileName=040607a.xml, accessed November 2005.
8 Carey, J. (2004) 'Global Warming: Why Business is Taking it so Seriously', *BusinessWeek*, August 16, p62.
9 Nattrass, B. and Altomare, M. (1999) *The Natural Step for Business*, Gabriola Island, BC: New Society Publishers, pp87–88.
10 www.mtn.org/iasa/tgmaxneef.html, accessed October 2005.

Chapter 3 – Services

1 Crowther, Y. (2004) 'Coffee Talk: Supplier Guidelines at Starbucks', *Sustainability RADAR*, April/May, www.greenbiz.com/news/reviews_third.cfm?NewsID=26691, accessed December 2005.
2 Ashforth Pacific Case Study from the Oregon Natural Step Network Tool Kit, p2.
3 Norm Thompson – An Oregon Natural Step Network Case Study, www.ortns.org.
4 Mellon, M. and Fondriest S. (2001) 'Hogging It!', *Nucleus*, Spring, 1 March, pp1–3, www.ucsusa.org/food/0antibiotic.html.
5 Norm Thompson – An Oregon Natural Step Network Case Study, www.ortns.org.

6 Hart, S. L. and Milstein, M. B. (1999) 'Global Sustainability and Creative Destruction of Industries', *MIT Sloan Management Review*, Fall, Vol 41, No 1, pp23–33.

7 Desmarais, M. (2001) 'Prahalad says India can Lead by Marketing to the Poor', *IndUS Business Journal* Saturday, December 1, www.indusbusinessjournal.com/news/2001/12/01/Community/ Prahalad.Says.India.Can.Lead.By.Marketing.To.The.Poor-166748.shtml.

Chapter 4 – Sustainability in manufacturing

1 Paine, L. S. (2003) *Value Shift: Why Companies Must Merge Social and Financial Imperatives to Achieve Superior Performance*, New York: McGraw-Hill, p21.

2 www.greenbiz.com/news/news_third.cfm?NewsID=26607, accessed December 2005.

3 Nicholls, M. (November, 2002) 'Executives Could Lose Climate Change Insurance Coverage', www.tufts.edu/as/wright_center/iecws/news/environmental_finance.pdf, accessed December 2005.

4 Asmus, P. (2005) 'Protecting Brand Value: How (and Why) the World's Most Valuable Brand is Building a Corporate Citizenship Pyramid', *Green at Work Magazine*, July/August, p12.

5 Bonda, P. and Sosnowchik, K. (2004) 'Sustainability from Within', *Green at Work Magazine*, March/April, p24.

6 McDonough, W. (April 1999) 'The Next Industrial Revolution', www.consciouschoice.com/ 1999/cc1204/nextindustrialrev.html, accessed December 2005; McDonough, W. and Braungart, M. (2001) 'The Next Industrial Revolution' (video), Stevenson, Maryland: Earthome Productions.

7 TRI reports are available from the EPA website; the address for the 2001 report is www.epa.gov/tri/tridata/tri01/index.htm, accessed December 2005.

8 US EPA, '1997 Alternative Synthetic Pathways Award', www.epa.gov/greenchemistry/aspa97 .html, accessed December 2005.

9 Romm, J. J. (1999) *Cool Companies: How the Best Businesses Boost Profits and Productivity by Cutting Greenhouse Gas Emissions*, Washington DC: Island Press, p164.

10 Oregon Natural Step Case Study, www.ortns.org.

11 Kopczak, L. R. and Johnson, M. E. (2003) 'The Supply-Chain Management Effect', *MIT Sloan Management Review*, Spring, Vol 44, No 3, pp27–34.

12 'Suppliers' Perspectives on Greening the Supply Chain', Business for Social Responsibility, www.bsr.org.

13 Clifford, M., Tashiro, H. and Natarajan, A. (2003) 'The Race to Save a Rainforest', *BusinessWeek*, 24 November, pp125–6.

14 Oregon Natural Step Network case study under Resources, www.ortns.org.

15 Ayres, R. U. (1989) 'Industrial Metabolism: Technology and Environment', in Ausubel, J. and Sladovich, H. (eds.) *Technology and Environment*, Washington DC: National Academy Press.

16 This and other case studies are available at www.zerowaste.org/publications.htm.

17 Wilson, D. (2001) *Fateful Harvest: The True Story of a Small Town, a Global Industry, and a Toxic Secret*, New York: Harper Collins.

18 Hitchcock, D. and Chalfan, L. (2002) *Approaching Zero Waste*, Portland, OR: AXIS Performance Advisors, p26.

19 www.nec.co.jp/eco/en/annual2005/02/2-3.html, accessed December 2005.

Chapter 5 – Sustainability in government

1 Kay, J. (1998) *Asphalt Nation: How the Automobile Took Over America and How We Can Take It Back*, University of California Press. For a review, go to www.walkbikenashville.org/Documents/jnreview.pdf, accessed December 2005.

2 Myers, N. and Kent, J. (2001) *Perverse Subsidies: How Tax Dollars Can Undercut the Environment and the Economy*, Washington: Island Press.

3 GreenBiz.com (2003) 'Green Building Investments Yield High Returns, says Study', 28 October, www.greenbiz.com/news/news_third.cfm?NewsID=25830&CFID=1079143&CFTOKEN=50038365.

4 Whittington, J. (2004) 'China Facing Environmental Crisis', BBC Beijing, 23 September.

5 www.sustainable.doe.gov/freshstart/case/soldiers.htm, accessed December 2005.

6 Brown, L. (2001) *Eco-Economy: Building an Economy for the Earth*, WW Norton Company, p195.

7 Daily, G. (ed.) (1997) *Nature's Services: Societal Dependence on Natural Ecosystems,* Washington DC: Island Press.

8 Daily, G. and Ellison, K (2002) *The New Economy of Nature: The Quest to Make Conservation Profitable*, Washington DC: Island Press, p1.

9 Special Report (2003) 'Asia's Future', *Business Week*, 27 October, p58.

10 Heal, G. (2000*) Nature and the Marketplace: Capturing the Value of Ecosystem Services*, Washington DC: Island Press, pp156–7.

11 'Economic Incentives and P2', Pollution Prevention Northwest, Seattle, WA: The Pollution Prevention Resource Center, Fall 2004, www.pprc.org/pubs/newsletter/index.cfm.

12 Peet, J. (2003) 'Priceless: A Survey of Water', *The Economist*, 19 July, www.economist.com/surveys/showsurvey.cfm?issue=20030719, accessed December 2005.

13 Heal, G. (2000) *Nature and the Marketplace: Capturing the Value of Ecosystem Service*, Washington DC: Island Press.

14 Daly, H. E. (1996) *Beyond Growth: The Economics of Sustainable Development*, Boston: Beacon Press.

15 Heal, G. (2000) *Nature and the Marketplace: Capturing the Value of Ecosystem Services*, Washington DC: Island Press, p188.

16 George, C (interviewer) (2005) 'Civic Engagement – With Robert Putnam and Steven Johnson', Oregon Public Broadcasting – Oregon Territory, 30 September.

17 Eisenberg, E (1998) *The Ecology of Eden*, New York: Alfred A. Knopf, p356.

18 Meyer, A. (2004) 'Local Responses to a Global Problem', *Catalyst*, Spring, p20.

19 Alliance for Global Sustainability, www.esc.u-tokyo.ac.jp/ags/outline-e.htm, accessed December 2005.

20 Gates, J. (1998) *The Ownership Solution: Toward a Shared Capitalism for the 21st Century*, Reading, MA: Addison-Wesley.
21 http://216.239.53.104/custom?q=cache:cog7q_IhqZoJ:www.calpers-governance.org/principles/global/globalvoting.pdf+public+employee+retirement+social+responsibility&hl=en&ie=UTF-8, accessed December 2005.

Chapter 6 – Senior management

1 'Leadership, Responsibility and Growth in Uncertain Times', PricewaterhouseCoopers, www.pwcglobal.com/gx/eng/ins-sol/survey-rep/ceo6/pwc_6_ceo_survey.pdf, accessed November 2005.
2 Guenster, N., Derwall, J., Bauer R. and Koedijk, K. (2005) 'The Economic Value of Corporate Eco-efficiency', 25 July 2005, paper presented to the Academy of Management Conference, reprint available at http://papers.ssrn.com/sol3/papers.cfm?abstract_id=657628.
3 Collins, J. and Porras, J. (1994) *Built to Last: Successful Habits of Visionary Companies*, New York: Harper Business.
4 Magretta, J. (1997) 'Growth Through Global Sustainability: An Interview with Monsanto's CEO Robert B. Shapiro', *Harvard Business Review*, January, p79, reprint #97110.
5 Hall, J. and Vrendenburg, H. (2003) 'The Challenges of Innovating for Sustainable Development', *MIT Sloan Management Review*, Fall, Vol 45, No 1, pp61–8.
6 Grow, B., Hamm, S. and Lee L. (2005), 'The Debate Over Doing Good', *BusinessWeek*, 15 August 2005, p76.
7 Barbaro, M. and Barringer, F. (2005) 'Wal-Mart to Seek Savings in Energy', *New York Times*, 25 October, www.nytimes.com/2005/10/25/business/25walmart.html.
8 'Wal-Mart to Toughen Overseas Standards', *Forbes*, 20 Oct 2005, www.forbes.com/associatedpress/feeds/ap/2005/10/20/ap2290130.html, accessed December 2005.
9 Hitchcock, D. (2001) 'Greening the Supply Chain', *Sustainability Series™*, Portland, Oregon: AXIS Performance Advisors, p15, www.axisperformance.com/publications.html.
10 Estes, R. (1996) *Tyranny of the Bottom Line: Why Corporations Make Good People Do Bad Things*, San Francisco: Berrett-Koehler Publishers, Inc.

Chapter 7 – Facilities

1 Kats, G. (2004) 'Are Green Buildings Cost-Effective?' *Green at Work Magazine*, May/June, www.greenatworkmag.com/gwsubaccess/04mayjun/ss_green.html.
2 Garris, L. (2004) 'The Deliberation on Daylighting: What You Really Need to Know to Make an Informed Decision', *Buildings*, April, www.buildings.com/Articles/detail.asp?ArticleID=1827.
3 Van der Ryn, S. and Cowan, S. (1996) *Ecological Design*, Washington DC: Island Press.
4 'Building Commissioning' (brochure), Oregon Office of Energy, November 1998.

Chapter 8 – Human resources

1 Schein, E. (2004) *Leadership and Organizational Culture: A Dynamic View*, San Francisco: Jossey Bass.
2 Diamond, J. (2005) *Collapse: How Societies Choose to Fail or Succeed*, New York: Viking, p450.
3 Romm, J. J. (1999) *Cool Companies: How the Best Businesses Boost Profits and Productivity by Cutting Greenhouse Gases*, Washington DC: Island Press, pp164–5.

Chapter 9 – Purchasing

1 Ayres, R. U. (1989) 'Industrial Metabolism: Technology and Environment' in Ausubel, J. and Sladovich, H. (eds.) *Technology and Environment*, Washington DC: National Academy Press.
2 Christopher, M. and Peck, H. (February 2004) 'Supply Chains are becoming More Vulnerable to External Disruptions', *Logistics Europe*, www.rmcs.cranfield.ac.uk/ddmsa/resilience/LogisticsEurope.pdf, accessed December 2005.
3 US EPA (2002) 'State and Local Government Pioneers', www.epa.gov/oppt/epp.
4 *San Francisco Chronicle*, 18 June 2005, http://sfgate.com/cgi-bin/article.cgi?file=/c/a/2005/06/18/BAGAFDAM801.DTL, accessed December 2005.
5 Adapted from Hitchcock, D. (2001) 'Greening the Supply Chain', *Sustainability Series™*, Portland, Oregon: AXIS Performance Advisors, www.axisperformance.com/publications.html.
6 Hitchcock, D. (2001) 'Greening the Supply Chain', *Sustainability Series™*, Portland, Oregon: AXIS Performance Advisors, www.axisperformance.com/publications.html.
7 US EPA (2002) 'State and Local Government Pioneers', www.epa.gov/oppt/epp.
8 NEEA (1998) 'New Washer Propels Past Market Barriers', December, www.neea.org.
9 Laughlin, J. and Fleming, R. (2003) 'Opportunity Grows for Organic Cotton Market', *LOHAS Journal*, October, www.organicconsumers.org/clothes/cotton101503.cfm.
10 Hitchcock, D. (2001) 'Greening the Supply Chain', *Sustainability Series™*, Portland, Oregon: AXIS Performance Advisors, www.axisperformance.com/publications.html.

Chapter 10 – Environmental affairs

1 Speth, J. G. (2004) *Red Sky at Morning: America and the Crisis on the Global Environment*, New Haven, CT: Yale University Press, p190.
2 US EPA '1997 Alternative Synthetic Pathways Award', www.epa.gov/greenchemistry/aspa97.html, accessed December 2005.

Chapter 11 – Marketing

1 Asmus, P. (2005) 'Protecting Brand Value: How (and Why) the World's Most Valuable Brand is Building a Corporate Citizenship Pyramid', *Green at Work Magazine*, July/August, p16.
2 Hitchcock, D. (January, 2004) 'Gerding/Edlen Development, LLC: A Natural Step Case Study', www.ortns.org/resources_grn.htm, accessed December 2005.

3 Speer, T. L. (1997) 'Growing in the Green Market – Marketing Environmentally Friendly Products', *American Demographics*, August 1997, www.findarticles.com/p/articles/mi_m4021/is_n8_v19/ai_19657797.

4 'IKEA: A Natural Step Case Study', www.naturalstep.org/learn/docs/cs/case_ikea.pdf, accessed December, 2005.

5 'Green Marketing', www.greenmarketing.com/Green_Marketing_Book/Chapter02.html, accessed December 2005.

6 Willard, B. (2005) 'Five Signs that Sustainability's Tipping Point is Close', *Green at Work Magazine*, July/August, p32.

7 Rubin, H. (2001) 'The Perfect vision of Dr V', *FastCompany*, February, p146.

8 Hollender, J. (2004) *What Matters Most: How a Small Group of Pioneers is Teaching Social Responsibility to Big Business, and Why Big Business is Listening*, New York: Basic Books.

9 Artz, N. and Cooke, P. (2005), 'Coming Full Circle: Internal Marketers Learn Commitment Techniques from Social Marketers', *Competition Forum*, Vol 3, No 2, pp414–18.

10 'Leadership, Responsibility and Growth in Uncertain Times', PricewaterhouseCoopers, www.pwcglobal.com/gx/eng/ins-sol/survey-rep/ceo6/pwc_6_ceo_survey.pdf, accessed November 2005.

Chapter 12 – Finance and Accounting

1 'Leadership, Responsibility and Growth in Uncertain Times', PricewaterhouseCoopers, www.pwcglobal.com/gx/eng/ins-sol/survey-rep/ceo6/pwc_6_ceo_survey.pdf.

2 Kennedy, R. F., Jr (2004) *Crimes against Nature*, New York: Harper Collins, p190.

3 Hitchcock, D. (2005) 'The Collins Companies: Having Your Forests and Cutting Them Too', an unpublished case study written for Oregon Economic and Community Development Department, 2005.

4 Heal, G. M. (1996) 'Interpreting Sustainability', *Columbia Business School*, pp7–8.

5 Greiner, T. (2001) 'Indicators of Sustainable Production: A Case Study on Measuring Sustainability at Stonyfield Farms', Ann Arbor, MI: Lowell Center for Sustainable Production, Spring.

6 Brachfeld, D. et al (2001) 'Life Cycle Assessment of the Stonyfield Product Delivery System', Ann Arbor, MI: University of Michigan, 5 April.

Index

ABC *see* activity-based costing
accounting   213–230
activity-based costing (ABC)   223
air conditioning   145–146
audits   137, 148, 179–180
authority   26–30
awards   29, 107, 162

backcasting   125–126
behaviour   103, 157, 164
biomimicry   64–65
black lists   61–62
break rooms   43–44
bridging terms   127
bubble diagrams   18–19
buildings
    contracts   173
    design   130, 192
    energy and waste   141
    green   45, 85, 120, 129, 142–146
burn-out   24
business systems alignment   133–134
by-products   62–63

cannibalization   8
capital, social   104–105
carbon dioxide   46–47, 65–66
cause-related marketing   207–208
certification schemes   29, 68–70, 170, 208
    see also labelling
change management   157, 159
chemicals   61–63, 149, 192–195
civic involvement   104–105
cleaning services   149–150, 164, 173,
    193–194
colleges   10–11
commons   79, 81, 90–96, 216
community-based social marketing   206–207

competition   4, 53–54
compliance   62, 66, 189–197
construction waste   146
contests   162
contracts   63–64, 85, 172–174
cooperatives   44–45
corporate social responsibility (CSR)   12, 120, 134,
    213
    see also responsibility; Three E's; triple bottom line
costs
    accounting   223–224
    externalities   214–215
    facilities   85, 141–142, 144, 147, 151, 192
    government agencies   97–98
    insurance   5
    life cycle   59–60, 178–179, 223–224, 232
    manufacturing industry   66
    marketing   204
    product design   57, 59
    public goods   94
    purchasing   172, 182
    ratings   227–228
    senior management   120
    waste   3–4, 71
credibility   25, 30, 185, 206
CSR *see* corporate social responsibility

daylighting   143–144
decision tools   216, 226–228
demographic level   202–204
demonstrative actions   132–133
design   57–59, 88–90, 143
disadvantaged business   177–178
discussion groups   27

eco-efficiencies   189–197
ecological footprints   92
economic level   8–9, 16, 47–48, 97–98, 177–178

education   93, 103, 108–109
efficiency   88–89, 147, 189–197
EH&S *see* employee health and safety
electronic waste   99
employee commitment   4–5, 16, 121, 155–167, 201
employee health and safety (EH&S)   189–190, 195
energy
    efficiency   54, 57, 65–67, 83–84
    facilities   40–41, 141–153
    organizational sustainability   10–11
    supply threats   14
    sustainable operations   18
    technology   41–42
environmental level
    accounting   213–230
    compliance   189–197
    health factors   13–14, 17–18
    management systems   191–192, 220–221
    preferable purchasing   171–172
    product design   57–59
    scoring systems   176–177
    supply chain management   174–176
EPR *see* extended producer responsibility
equal opportunities   109–110
Europe   96
executives *see* senior management
expectations   8, 12, 156–157
extended producer responsibility (EPR)   71, 72
externalities   44, 91–92, 97, 99, 214–215

facilities   141–153
feel-good activities   190
financial level   213–230
first mover advantage   200
food industry   10–11
funding   66–67, 86, 105–106

GDP *see* gross domestic product
genetically modified organisms   121–122
global level   13
government level   10–11, 79–115, 181, 214
green buildings   142–146
green chemistry   62–63, 194–195
green taxes   93, 97
green teams   27–28
greenhouse gases   65–67
greenwashing   7–8, 200, 202
grey lists   61–62
gross domestic product   (GDP) 79, 97–98

hazardous materials   54, 71
health factors   13–14, 16–18, 142
heating, ventilating and air-conditioning (HVAC)
        systems   145–146
high-performance buildings   142–146
housing   101–102
human resources   155–167
hunger   101–102
HVAC systems *see* heating, ventilating and
        air-conditioning systems

image   5, 7, 38–39, 55, 170, 199
        see also public relations; reputation
incentives   92–93, 105–106, 111, 176–177, 181, 210
infrastructure   80–81, 87–90
innovation   4, 53–54, 200, 204, 226
insurance   5, 38, 46, 56, 216
integrated approaches   108–109
inventories   149–150, 193
investment   44, 111, 163

JAG *see* Job Alike Groups
Job Alike Groups (JAG)   161
job descriptions   160

labelling   108, 203, 208
        see also certification schemes
landscaping services   149–150, 173
lawsuits   56
LCA *see* life cycle assessment
LCC *see* life cycle costing
leadership   23
legal level   5, 7, 46, 171, 200
level playing fields   81, 96–100, 214
liability   6
life cycle assessment (LCA)   59–60, 178–179, 182,
        224–225
life cycle costing (LCC)   59–60, 178–179,
        223–224, 232
lighting   143–145
liveability   90
location   144–145
long-term aspects   216–217, 224

management
    change   157, 159
    energy   147
    environmental systems   191–192, 220–221
    respect   24

supply chain 174–176
sustainability systems 29–30
waste 148–149
manufacturing industry 10–11, 53–76, 95, 99, 169–187
marketing 199–212
markets
 government agencies 103–104, 111
 incentives 92–93
 manufacturing industry 55
 new 4, 7, 47
 segments 203–205
 targeted products 181–182
 transformation 209–210
mechanical systems 145–146
message framing 205–206
metrics frameworks 218–223
missions 221–222

natural assets 13, 98, 216
The Natural Step framework 17–20, 126, 219, 220
needy people 81, 100–102
NGOs see non-governmental organizations
non-governmental organizations (NGOs) 55, 69–70, 135–136, 175, 185
non-profit organizations 178

online systems 172
ownership 96–97, 100, 109–110, 191

paper products 42–43, 45, 136
participation 26–30
partnerships 79, 135–136, 175, 185, 207–208
pension funds 111, 120
performance measures 215–216
perverse subsidies 98–100
planning 121–122, 124, 133
policy level 93, 106–107, 171
pollution 6, 189–190, 195
precautionary principle 95
preserves 94–95
privatization 96–97
productivity 141–153
products 19, 54, 57–65, 71–74, 95, 130, 199–200
project teams 28–29
promotion 202–203
protected areas 94–95
public goods 94

public relations 199–212
 see also image; reputation
purchasing 103–104, 161, 169–187, 192–193

quality of life 5, 90

ratings 227–228
red tape 85
regulations 4, 55–56, 72, 96
reliability of products 54
reporting systems 135, 209, 213, 218–223
reputation 200–201
 see also image; public relations
requests for proposals (RFPs) 103–104, 172–173
research 105–106, 182–185
resources 81, 84, 90–97, 155–167
respect 24, 30
responsibility 44–45, 71–74, 99, 170
 see also corporate social responsibility
retirement funds 163
revenue 80, 83–87
reviews 161
rewards 161–162
RFPs see requests for proposals
ripple effects 37–38, 44–45
risk 5–7, 54–56, 62, 120, 149, 216

scenario planning 124
scepticism 25
scoring systems 129, 143, 161, 176–177
SD solutions 227–228
security 80–81, 87–90
senior management 119–139, 157–159
service industry 10–11, 37–51, 63–64, 91–92, 173–174
sick building syndrome 142
site selection 144–145
social level
 accounting 213–230
 capital 104–105
 environmental focus 191
 expectations 8, 12
 government agencies 81
 health factors 17
 instability 14
 investment 111
 marketing 201, 206–208
 purchasing 177–178
 service organizations 39–40

stakeholders   125, 134–137, 208–209
standards   200, 208
standing teams   131–132
steering committees   28, 131, 159
stewardship   71–74
subsidies   98–100
substitution   193–194
supply chains   6–7, 55, 61–62, 67–68, 169–187
support   24–30, 129–133
survival economy   47–48

take-back systems   56, 72–74
targets   192, 229
task forces   28–29, 131, 159
taxes   80, 83–87, 93, 97
technical jargon   190
technology   41–42
terms   126–128
third-party certification *see* certification
Three E's   219–220
    see also corporate social responsibility;
        triple bottom line
trade-offs   226–228
trading systems   93
tragedy of the commons   81, 216
training   156, 160
transformation of markets   209–210
transparency   134–137

transportation   45, 80, 88–90, 150–151, 162–163
triage   101
triple bottom line   8–9, 219–220, 221
    see also corporate social responsibility;
        Three E's; triple bottom line

universities   10–11
urban spaces   88–89
vision   192, 221–222
voices of doom   190

wages   161
waste
    audits   179–180
    costs   3–4, 71
    facilities   141–153
    image   38–39
    manufacturing industry   53–54, 70–71, 72–73
    perverse subsidies   99
    pollution liability   6
    product design   19, 57
    purchasing   169
    zero   3, 70–71, 120, 148
water   94, 141–153
weighted criteria charts   182–184,
        227

zero waste   3, 70–71, 120, 148